TEA AND TASTE

THE GLASGOW TEA ROOMS 1875-1975

TEA AND TASTE

THE GLASGOW TEA ROOMS 1875-1975

PERILLA KINCHIN

White
Cockade

Published by

White Cockade Publishing
Wendlebury House, Church Lane
Wendlebury, Oxon ox6 8PN

British Library Cataloguing-in-Publication Data

A catalogue record for this book is available from the British
Library

ISBN 0 9513124 2 1 Hardback

Jacket design by Cinamon and Kitzinger
Typeset in 10 on 12½ point Photina at the Oxford University
Computing Service
Printed in Great Britain by The Bath Press

For Orlando and Benedick
with all my love

Contents

Preface

'Altogether the up-to-date Glasgow tea-room is an interesting institution', wrote a journalist in 1895. 'Future historians might do worse than give it a paragraph.' In justification of an entire book I can only say that the gentleman was commenting on the first decade or so of the tea rooms, and that they were just about to become even more interesting as Miss Cranston hit her stride and began to employ Charles Rennie Mackintosh to design for her. Long after she left the scene they continued to be very interesting. And they were dearly loved throughout.

It is harder to justify why I, a southerner, who never knew the tea rooms, should take it upon myself to write this account. I can only plead the spell which Glasgow has cast over many an outsider, and which has made me as chauvinistic an admirer of the city as any true-born Glaswegian, though of course a lot more ignorant. I came to the subject through writing with my sister, who does live in Glasgow, an account of the Great Exhibitions from 1888 through to 1988. The exhibitions all had tea rooms, and I slowly realised how they related to the city-centre tea rooms, and that these were something special.

Such a subject is a bottomless pit for a researcher, and I am only too well aware of much more I could have done with time. I look forward to receiving letters with more information, and, I don't doubt, corrections.

I have divided the century of the tea rooms into a beginning, two main periods, and an end. There is a central chapter concentrating on Miss Cranston and the artistic tea room, but there is more material on her in the other chapters. It was partly to set Miss Cranston and Mackintosh in context that the book grew to such proportions. It is admittedly rather a hybrid, written both for outsiders and natives: but I hope that for people who approach from an interest in design history this exploration of the Glasgow context will be illuminating; that those generally interested in social history will find useful material here on a significant part of the way people lived; while those reading it for the history of their city will feel that these dimensions enhance the specialness of the tea rooms.

A fuller version of the directory has been deposited in the Glasgow Room of the Mitchell Library, which has been my main resource.

The Mitchell Library is a wonderful example of what a public library should be, and I am deeply grateful for the generous help I have had with this project at all levels. I also thank particularly Pamela Robertson at the Hunterian Art Gallery, University of Glasgow, who has been so liberal with access to the University's magnificent Mackintosh collection, and so efficient and helpful in all our dealings. I have also been greatly assisted by Lesley Richmond and Michael Moss at the University of Glasgow Archives, the staff of Strathclyde Regional Archive, Elspeth King at the People's Palace, and Douglas Annan of T. & R. Annan & Sons. I thank them all very much.

I am extremely grateful to all those private individuals whose willingness to help has been truly invaluable. Dr John Mackinlay, David and Eileen Rombach, Mysie and Harry Ross, Peter Stewart and Andy Stuart have most generously lent material. They and many others have spent time talking and corresponding with me, and will recognise snippets of their information buried in the text: I thank here Jim Adams, Rose McAslan, Flo Briscoe, James Bryce, Mrs M. J. Faris, George Gilfillan, Mairi Howie, Jolyon Hudson, Stanley Hunter, Helen Lillie, James and Ann Macaulay, Alastair Macdonald, Angus MacDougall, Liz Mackinlay, Charles Oakley, Philip Rodney, George Smith, and Sir Reo Stakis. I also profited from talking to the late Jack House. I owe special thankyous to Jerry Cinamon, Mark O'Neill, Susan Scott, and above all my long-suffering husband, Ewen Bowie, for practical help of various essential kinds.

Finally this book would have been impossible without the inspiration and support of my dear sister Juliet, whose idea it was, and I offer it as a tribute to someone of whom I am very proud.

Perilla Kinchin

Illustration Acknowledgements

For access to illustrations and permission to reproduce them we gratefully acknowledge the following: T. & R. Annan & Sons 11, 49, 51, 52, 53, 72; Sir Hugh Casson 73; Christie's Scotland 14; C. R. Mackintosh Society 71; The Glasgow School of Art 80; Guthrie & Wells Ltd, now part of the Cosmos Decorators Group (photographs Strathclyde Regional Archive) 81, 84, 90; Harper Collins Publishers Ltd 21; The Highton Collection, University of Glasgow Archives 87; The Hunterian Art Gallery, University of Glasgow, 1, 31, 33, 47, 55, 56, 57, 58, 59, 60, 64, 65, 66, 67, 68, 69, 70, 75, 76, 78, 79; Jolyon Hudson 104, 105, 110, 111, 112; The Mitchell Library, Glasgow 2, 3, 4, 5, 6, 8, 9, 10, 12, 16, 17, 18, 20, 22, 23, 24, 26, 28, 29, 32, 37, 38, 39, 40, 41, 42, 43, 48, 54, 61, 63, 86, 88, 91, 92, 93, 94, 99, 109, 113, 115, 118, 119, 123, 126; The People's Palace, Glasgow 46, 74; David and Eileen Rombach 35, 77; Mysie Ross 34; *Scottish Field* 114; Strathclyde Regional Archive 95, 96, 122; Peter Stewart 19, 62, 102, 106; Andrew Stuart 25, 44, 45, 82, 83, 98, 101, 103, 117, 121, 124; The Estate of Edward Walton 50.

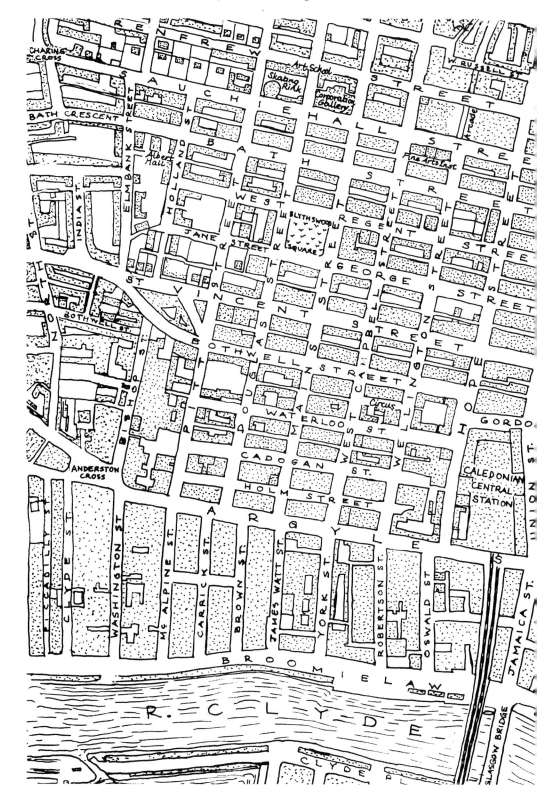

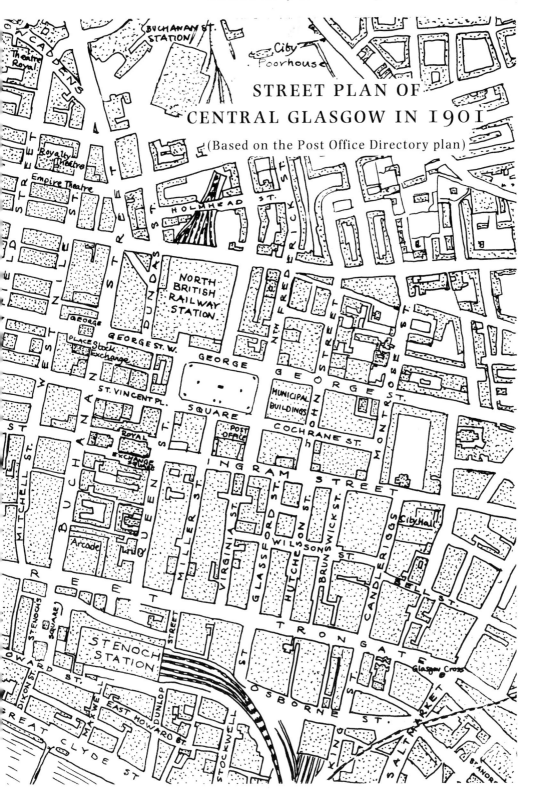

STREET PLAN OF
CENTRAL GLASGOW IN 1901
(Based on the Post Office Directory plan)

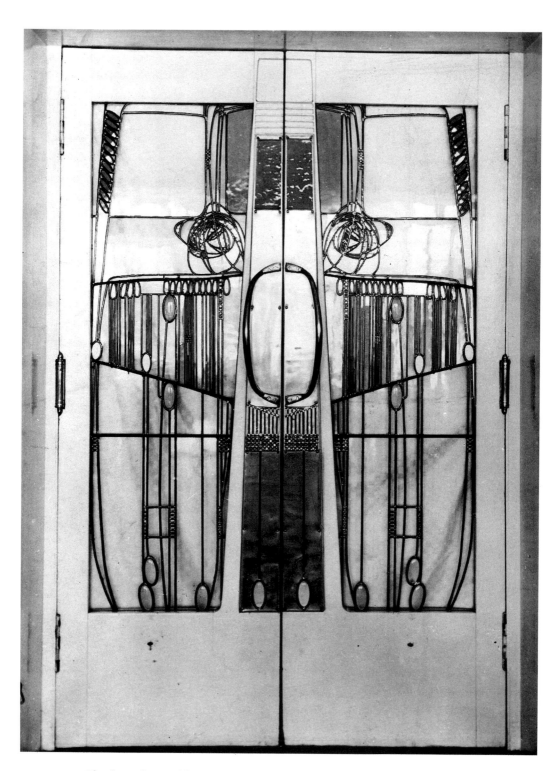

1. The doors designed by Charles Rennie Mackintosh in 1903 for the Room de Luxe in Miss Cranston's Willow Tea Rooms.

Introduction

Tea rooms began in Glasgow. Just why, and what was so special about them, is the subject of this book. From their beginning in 1875 they grew and multiplied so that at the start of the new century Glasgow was described as 'a very Tokio for tea rooms. Nowhere can one have so much for so little, and nowhere are such places more popular or frequented.'[1] Other cities might have tea rooms, but nowhere had them like Glasgow: the best comparison is with the coffee houses of Vienna.

The story of the tea rooms illustrates perfectly the special qualities of Glasgow as a city. They were produced by its entrepreneurial 'mindset'. They were nothing to do with amateurish faded gentlewomen but a direct expression of the city's prosperous, gregarious, effective urban life; and they were championed with a compelling Glasgow chauvinism. This was after all a creation of global significance: 'What happened in Glasgow was rather tardily copied in London; other large cities following suit, and the movement spread over the length and breadth of the land, and was taken up on the Continent, and spread to every civilised spot on earth.'[2] It was indeed almost twenty years after Stuart Cranston opened the first tea room in 1875 that Jo Lyons, who had picked up a few ideas in Glasgow, established his famous chain in London.

The climate of openness to new ideas which produced the tea rooms alongside so much mercantile and industrial innovation in the last quarter of the nineteenth century also produced Glasgow's distinctive flowering in art and design. Business and art were triumphantly united in Glasgow's most famous tea rooms, those of Miss Cranston. In her time this formidable but humane lady, who established her separate empire shortly after her brother's, was one of the city's best-known figures: her name is still repeated with affection, though she withdrew from business at the close of the First World War. She was remarkable on any assessment, but most of all for her committed patronage of what is now called the 'Glasgow Style'. Miss Cranston introduced generations of ordinary Glaswegians to a direct experience of Charles Rennie Mackintosh's work, putting bottoms on chairs that now fetch thousands of pounds. They accepted her tea rooms as one of the special things about their city, weird but wonderful, their avant garde design supported by top quality catering and service. So synonymous was Miss Cranston's with the Glasgow tea room that interiors which featured in German art magazines were also the automatic setting for venerable jokes like 'Jeannie, will you hae a cookie or a meringue?' 'Naw Jock, you're right, I'll hae a cookie.'

But one object of this book is to set Miss Cranston in context, for there were countless other tea rooms in Glasgow. In the first half of this century tea rooms, or tea shops as they were generally called in the south, became part of common experience in the towns and cities of Britian. Edinburgh had some fine examples. But in Glasgow they remained something special, distinguished by high standards of catering and decor, and very dear to the middle classes, so that Glasgow outstripped all rivals for many decades in the overall quality of its eating places. After the First World War the tea rooms took on a new lease of life in the hands of Glasgow's big family baking firms. They marked a precious continuity with the prosperous past, right on through the grim years of depression, which bore harder on Glasgow than most places. From little rooms above or behind or beneath baker's shops to the great flagship tea rooms built in the thirties, they comforted their patrons with clean tablecloths and tons of the scones, tea breads and cakes in which Scottish baking excelled.

The Second World War however brought about changes in public tastes which the tea rooms could not withstand. Their slow decline and collapse was a symptom of nationwide social upheaval, and more locally of deep difficulties in Glasgow's economy. Together with their cheap and cheerful relations, the Italian cafés — another special feature of Glasgow life — the tea rooms had once kept at bay all colonisation by such as Lyons and the A.B.C. But from the mid fifties onwards, when tastes were increasingly assimilated to national norms, the city was wide open to Indian and Chinese restaurants, steak houses, Wimpys, Macdonald's, Pizzalands and the rest.

Like Glasgow's vanished steamers and trams, ice cream parlours, milk bars, cinemas, and dance halls, the tea rooms evoke the simple pleasures of a lost past and the memories are affectionate. But the sad part of the story can wait until the end. Let us return now to the origins of the tea room phenomenon, in the years of Glasgow's growing prosperity and self-confidence.

The Beginnings,
1875–1888

A Glaswegian would not be surprised to learn, if he or she didn't know it already, that Glasgow invented the tea room: Glasgow after all can claim many innovations which have improved the human condition. It is outsiders, who are always surprised by Glasgow, who might need convincing. It was in 1875 that Stuart Cranston, a tea dealer, first arranged accommodation for sixteen customers 'elbow to elbow' and announced: 'A sample cup of 4/- Kaisow, with sugar and cream, for 2d. — bread and cakes extra; served in the sample room, No. 2 Queen Street'. Nothing comes from nothing of course, as we shall see in exploring the background from which the tea rooms emerged, but the city was credited — and certainly credited itself — with originating an identifiable 'movement'.

The tea rooms filled a 'felt need', as their proliferation at the end of the nineteenth century shows. They were called into being by various things: by the strength of the Temperance movement in the West of Scotland; by a native tradition of fine sweet baking; by the Scottish 'high tea'; but most of all by the practical demands of a busy mercantile city. With their smoking and billiard rooms they catered particularly for men, in days when the business man's morning coffee, a notable Glasgow habit, was believed to be a powerful tool of wealth creation. This may come as another surprise to people who associate tea rooms with ladies in hats. But it was really the deftness with which the tea rooms met the separate social needs of both men and women that wove them so inextricably into the fabric of middle-class life.

While it was as a tea dealer that Stuart Cranston (1848-1921) took the momentous step of opening the first tea room, his family background in hoteliering perhaps prepared him for this diversification. His father's cousin Robert was the pioneer of the Temperance Hotel, as we shall see, while his father George, after being in business as a baker and pastry maker, became from 1849 the proprietor of a succession of hotels, all in George Square: the Edinburgh and Glasgow Railway Chop House and Commercial Lodgings, which metamorphosed into the Royal Horse Hotel and then Cranston's Hotel; then from 1857 the Crow; and finally the Crown.[1] A regular lodger was the gentlemanly old representative of Twining & Co. of London, and it was he who induced the young Stuart into the wholesale tea trade, where he began as a lowly invoice clerk with Wright Napier and Co. in about 1862. He soon managed to slip from the chilly warehouse into the warmth of the tasting room, however, and tea became a passion with him. With a determination which was evidently characteristic of his family, he set himself to conquer this business, training his palate to excellence while he worked as a sub-agent for another familiar London firm, Joseph Tetley and Co.[2]

It was symptomatic of an entrepreneurial instinct for dealing with the public that when he set up by himself in 1871, as 'Stuart Cranston and Co., trained tea taster', at 44 St Enoch Square, it was in the retail, not wholesale, trade. He was however a major buyer in the market, making quality his absolute rule as he strove to make Cranston's teas 'a household word'. Indeed it was his almost fanatical wish to educate his customers into taking tea seriously that prompted him to keep a kettle at hand to offer sample cups. When he moved to slightly more central premises at 76 Argyle St/2 Queen St in 1875 he set aside tables for his customers, supplied some bakery and started to charge them for their tasting. And so the tea room was born. Dry tea retailing however remained a cornerstone of the business while Cranston was alive. Tales of his prowess in tasting and sangfroid in dealing abounded — with his assistance, for he was always a great self-advertiser — and enhanced the reputation of his tea rooms. He later trained himself in coffee-tasting too — and invented a patent coffee-roaster.

It is perhaps not surprising that this should have happened in Glasgow, where tea had long had an honoured place in the economy. After the collapse of the tobacco trade on which Glasgow's first fortunes were built, tea and sugar became its major imports, establishing strong trading links with the Far East and India. Tea and coffee merchants flourished from the 1830s on and Glasgow became a clear rival to London as a blending centre. Approximately one hundred and sixty tea dealers were listed in the directory for 1871; by 1890 there were three hundred and forty.

Stuart Cranston's move also reflected the enormous development in retailing at this period, another area in which Glasgow can lay claim to leadership. 1871 also saw another expert tea dealer, Thomas Bishop (1846-1922), begin trading on the assertion that Scottish water was unsuitable for tea blends marketed by London firms. His new business of Cooper & Co., named after an aunt who put up the money, grew from its beginning in Howard Street into the Pure Foods grocery empire of Cooper's, which soon made its own contribution to the tea room story. Like Cranston, his close contemporary, Bishop loved to be in the forefront of progress. He rigged up a field telegraph between his Howard St, Great Western Rd and Sauchiehall St shops, and the last was one of the first British shops to be lit by electric light — which caused a sensation. Later he was among the first to install a cash railway, and later again to use motor vans for deliveries. By 1895 there were thirty-one branches throughout Scotland and the North of England, the biggest in Liverpool, and two important shops in London.

1871 was indeed an *annus mirabilis* for this branch of retailing: this was also the year in which Thomas Lipton (1850-1931), the son of an Ulster immigrant butter-and-egg shop keeper, returned from a spell in New York with his head full of new ideas and opened his own shop at 101 Stobcross St.

2. and 3. Rival claims from Glasgow grocery giants Cooper's and Lipton's in 1897. Lipton's advertising characteristically emphasises his policy of direct supply.

This non-smoking, non-drinking and very single-minded young man then set about building a business which soon overtook Cooper's to become by the First World War a country-wide empire of around five hundred stores, revolutionising the grocery business in the process. He did not move seriously into the tea with which his name is still firmly associated until, already a millionaire, he purchased an estate in Ceylon in 1890. After this he swept all before him by applying his well-tried techniques of brilliant advertising and price control through exclusion of middlemen ('direct from the tea garden to the tea pot' was his boast), and seizing upon the potential of packeted tea for the mass market.[3] Tea rapidly made him a multi-millionaire: by 1894 he was already able ostentatiously to hand over a cheque for £35,000 in payment of import duties, a well-publicised indicator of his success in this field. In the same year he moved his headquarters to London, and through his friendship with Edward VII and his public generosity became a national figure. But he never forgot Glasgow, and left his estate to the poor of the city.

Stuart Cranston did not expand beyond Glasgow, but stayed there fighting a spirited but ultimately hopeless rearguard action, emphasising to the discerning the quality of his loose teas and continuing to champion China tea, which was being ousted from public favour by Indian and Ceylon blends at the end of the century. Perhaps scenting the way things were going, he began to concentrate on expanding the tea room side of his business.

All these dealers were profiting from and promoting a steadily increasing consumption of tea in Britain at large. In the early part of the eighteenth century tea was the preserve of the well-off, the precious leaves doled out from locked caddies by the mistress of the house. Tea gardens became fashionable places of resort. Glasgow had them too, in the suburbs: the attractions they offered were plants and flowers, menageries (a bear in one, an eagle at another), tea, whisky and ale.[4] Later, as tea became a popular taste, they slid into disrepute and were soon vanished and forgotten. By the mid nineteenth century tea was a luxury that even the poor tried to afford, drying out the leaves — often sold to them adulterated — for repeated use. But it was the reduction of heavy duty from the mid 1840s that turned tea into a staple of the popular diet: from 1s 10d per pound weight in 1853, it had fallen to 6d by 1865 and down again to 4d in 1890.[5] Gladstone, a serious tea addict, proved a powerful ally for the consumer. Consumption rose strongly from the mid nineteenth century and went on climbing until the Second World War and the advent of powdered coffee.[6]

There was a boom too from the 1880s, when food in general was becoming cheaper and more plentiful, in the consumption of biscuits, confectionery and jam, where production was becoming increasingly mechanised. Before the First World War Scottish consumption of sweet things was about three times the English average, and contributed more than was healthy to the enormous per capita consumption of sugar in which Britain at this period easily outstripped the rest of the world.[7] The notoriously sweet

Scottish tooth and a particularly well established tradition in baking and confectionery had their own part to play in the rapid development of tea rooms.

'The cup which cheers but not inebriates' also had virtue on its side. As Gladstone urged in his budget speech of 1882, 'the domestic use of tea is a powerful champion able to encounter alcoholic drink in a fair field and throw it in a fair fight.' In Scotland where tea was pitched against whisky rather than beer the battle was especially hard. But for those who aimed to make society more temperate, in one of the largest social movements in British history, tea was an important ally. The background to this significant influence on the rise of the tea rooms is worth sketching.

The misery of alcohol abuse went hand in hand with the enormous social dislocation of the industrial revolution, and just as Glasgow could claim to be the Workshop of the World in the second part of the nineteenth century, so also it had a long reputation as Britain's most drink-sodden city. It is not surprising that the temperance movement in Europe could trace its roots to the West of Scotland: in 1829 John Dunlop established societies in Maryhill and Greenock, and his work was immediately supported by the Glasgow publisher William Collins. These first societies aimed to loosen the stranglehold of spirits on society, for in Scotland the glass of whisky was fused into the routines of daily life. They did not demand total abjuration of alcohol and appealed chiefly to the middle classes.

The more radical total abstinence movement swept in from England in the 1830s and proved more popular from the start with the working classes, with its evangelical overtones of conversion and redemption, a new life in a new brotherhood. This was one reason why the Churches, whose ministers were themselves notoriously fond of their wee drams, put up such shameful resistance to the new movement in its early days, regarding it as dangerously subversive. Here for instance is the fulmination of the Bishop of Edinburgh in 1844: 'Under the general name of the temperance societies, they are, or may be, spouting and debating societies, political societies, speculating societies, tea and coffee-drinking and dancing societies; in short, anything and everything but what their appellation exclusively implies, *viz.* sober societies'.[8]

Temperance propaganda was directed chiefly at the working classes. Their betters were adept at hiding drunkenness behind closed doors and denying the problem, but the vehement teetotalism of many middle-class women and their prominence in the temperance movement often reflected private experience of alcoholic fathers and husbands. When a crowd of ladies turned out to demonstrate against an application for a licence in 1887 *The Bailie* magazine (Glasgow's influential *Punch*) warned of '"the monstrous regiment of women" interfering with, and over-riding us at every turn'. As guardians of that precious middle-class property, respectability, women did exert a strong influence at this period on public habits. Licensed businesses could well feel threatened by feminine tastes and the spread of recreational tea drinking. Their trade magazine seized with alacrity in 1895 on Dr Sophia Jex-Blake's statement, to a conference of Women Workers at Glasgow, that tea drinking could be carried to excess. 'The learned lady stated that though comparatively few women injured their constitutions by drinking too much alcohol, a great number came into doctors' hands by drinking too much tea.' Stewed tea in particular should be avoided: 'That way danger (and insanity) lies.'[9]

Temperance societies, unions and leagues proliferated in Scotland but the movement was weakened from the start by internal warring. Broadly speaking the early split between total abstainers and moderationists was replaced by a conflict between abolitionists and moral suasionists over the right way to tackle the problem. On the one hand were those who took the hard line, believing that lack of moral fibre was the root of the trouble, and that removal of temptation would be sufficent cure: they wanted parliamentary legislation for the power of local veto or abolition. On the other side were the more humane, who, while supporting legal restrictions on the sale of drink, concentrated on propaganda and alternatives, recognising that drink was a symptom rather than a cause of social problems, rooted in the appalling living conditions of the poor in cities like Glasgow.[10] Parks, art galleries, mechanics' institutes and libraries indeed multiplied during the second half of the nineteenth century, but the efforts of philanthropy tended to concentrate on education rather than recreation, and did not meet the need for mindless relaxation after a day of exhausting labour.

For the menfolk of the high proportion of families living in one- and two-room houses pubs served as extra living space, though legislation in Glasgow made them less comfortable than their English counterparts. In 1901 'J. H. Muir', observing 'the horrible side of humble life in Glasgow', described its pubs as 'purely shops for perpendicular drinking ... crowded, garish, inhuman, unmerry places'. Driven out by the fatigue of standing a man wandered on from one to another. 'A natural instinct for comradeship and brightness has driven him from a squalid home into illuminated streets, and from these the weather drives him for shelter to the public-house. 'Tis his only refuge from discomfort and weariness, and if he goes home drunk, he never meant to, and you cannot blame him.'[11] The sympathetic Muir sided with radicals like the Bishop of Chester, no less, who called in 1892 for the conversion of pubs into 'club-houses' for the poor, in public control, offering newspapers, games, food and the like: his idea was that alcohol would be recognised but 'deposed from supremacy' by the promotion of attractive, cheap temperance drinks.

Most campaigners thought this was going too far towards countenancing alcohol, and stuck rather to the doctrine of 'counter-attractions'. Countless clubs and social activities for the 'operative classes' were promoted by the temperance organisations, contributing greatly, as Elspeth King has shown, to the vitality of popular culture in Glasgow.[12] Among the most successful were the City Hall Saturday concerts run by the Glasgow Abstainers' Union, known as 'bursts' from the enthusiastic popping of the paper pokes in which eatables were given out to accompany the tea which was a welcome part of the proceedings. The demand for such entertainments was almost insatiable. The Corporation contributed by running Halls throughout the city which were available for 'bursts', lantern slide shows and so on. The Mission Halls established in the wave of evangelical revivalism from the mid 1870s offered similar attractions. Attempts were also made to clean up the favourite Glasgow family recreation of a trip 'doon the watter', with the commissioning in 1880 of the Ivanhoe, a temperance boat. Steamers were so strongly associated with alcoholic binges that 'steamboats' and 'steaming' are still among the many Glasgow expressions for drunkenness.

Temperance refreshment rooms flourished, some philanthropically run, others commercially — for there was good money to be made here. The cocoa rooms begun by Robert Lockhart in about 1879 are a good example: they soon expanded from Glasgow into the north of England and by 1888 their success was 'almost phenomenal in character.' They served 'Tea, coffee, cocoa, eatables in great variety, aerated drinks etc.' at low prices in a chain of small, clean, shops. When Lockhart's became a limited company in 1895, it had allegedly been showing returns of £14,000-£18,000 over the previous four years, 'proof of the large profits to be made out of catering for the poorer classes.'[14] Cocoa was at this period bidding hard against tea for public favour: firms like Fry's advertised heavily, with medical testimonies to its dietetic value, and consumption boomed.

Britain had once of course been a nation of addicted coffee-drinkers. In coffee's heyday in the seventeenth, eighteenth and early nineteenth centuries, coffee houses were most famously a feature of political and literary life in London, but the phenomenon was as notable in Glasgow as in other British cities. They were informal merchants' clubs serving coffee, food and ale, where men routinely gathered to await the mail, read the newspapers — too expensive to be taken privately before duty was removed in 1861 — and discuss current affairs. They functioned as business addresses for their regulars and often as lodgings for commercial travellers. In the nineteenth century however these traditional coffee houses had faded away before the spread of taverns and public houses on the one hand, and hotels, clubs and restaurants on the other.[15]

Coffee rooms in Glasgow had by the later part of the nineteenth century been brought clearly into the domain of the temperance movement. Most of them were attached to temperance hotels, the appearance of which as a distinctive feature of the Scottish scene, paving the way for the tea rooms, is itself an interesting story, and dominated again by the name of Cranston. The steps which brought Robert and Elizabeth Cranston to found their renowned Waverley Temperance Hotels illustrate exactly how the coffee house evolved from its traditional role as a focus of political discussion into an outpost of temperance ideals.

Robert Cranston (1815-1892) was born to parents who kept the Bay Horse Inn at East Calder, before they moved into Edinburgh.[15] Robert was apprenticed at the University Printing Office, but after he lost his left leg, aged sixteen, in an act of youthful bravado that misfired — the story insists that it was sawn off on his mother's kitchen table without an anaesthetic — he was apprenticed instead to a tailor. This sedentary employment proved a liberal education, for he was often chosen to read aloud while his fellows worked, and there was of course a lot of talking. It was after heated discussions about the new temperance societies that Robert Cranston and two friends embarked upon a trial dry period of three months. Deciding at the end of it that they were better off without drink, they took the pledge, and Cranston abstained firmly for the rest of his days.

Applying an open-minded intelligence to other social and political issues, Robert developed markedly progressive views. Like his friend John Aitken, he abandoned tailoring and opened a Temperance Coffee House and Lodgings in 1843. This was liberally supplied with newspapers, and soon became a popular meeting place for Chartists: Robert was actively involved in this movement for political reform and was in fact twice briefly arrested. A great part of the success of the Coffee House was due to the managerial skills of his wife, Elizabeth Dalgleish (1813-1873), and her famously excellent pies, and the business was very much a joint enterprise. Only five years later, in 1848, they took the bold step of opening the Waverley Hotel on Edinburgh's famous Prince's Street. Many thought them mad to open a temperance house in such a prime site, but they had shrewdly detected a gap in the market. While disregard of the hotel's temperance rule was not tolerated, they aimed from the start to make it a first class hotel and invested in quality fittings. It was an immediate success and its roll of notable visitors lengthened through more than a century of family ownership.

4. Advertisement of 1874 for Robert Cranston's Waverley Temperance Hotels.

Expansion was prompt: a Waverley opened in Cheapside, London in 1851 to fill a niche in the capital and offer a reassuring home-from-home to Scottish visitors to the Great Exhibition. The next expansion was into Glasgow in 1860, followed by the New Waverley in Edinburgh, in 1866, while what became known as the Old Waverley was later enlarged and then reconstructed in 1884. The hotels were run on clear principles, the scale of charges the same in each. Robert Cranston became a wealthy man, a long-serving Bailie and progressive town councillor. The esteem in which he was held was measured by the length of his funeral cortège in 1892.

Few of his imitators achieved such social prominence or built on such a grand scale, though the 1880s and 1890s saw the development of large temperance 'hydropathics' in Scottish tourist resorts. Most urban temperance hotels were modest establishments, aimed mainly to begin with at commercial travellers. Glasgow's earliest was John Whyte's Temperance Hotel at 132 Trongate from 1844. Like the tea rooms later, they proliferated once begun, often in the proprietorship of married women, and by 1875 nearly half the hotels listed in the Glasgow directory had 'Temperance' in their name. They were respectable enough to accommodate both women and men, generally providing a 'family room' as well as a gents' coffee room.

All but four of the nineteen coffee houses listed in the *Glasgow Post Office Directory* for 1875 were part of temperance hotels. Of the remaining four, two at least were conducted 'on strictly temperance principles' although they were not labelled as such: Matthew Waddell's long-lived City Commercial Restaurant and Coffee Saloon at 60 Union St (Waddell catered for vegetarians and was later connected with the Christian Institute); and William Logan's Mercantile Dining Rooms. Their names reflect their provision for business men in the old tradition of coffee houses. Logan had in fact dropped some of his early city missionary work to establish his new

5. Advertisement of 1874 for William Logan's temperance dining rooms.

WM. LOGAN'S MERCANTILE DINING ROOMS,

21-23 MAXWELL STREET, GLASGOW.

HOT JOINTS, SOUPS, &c.

From Twelve till Five o'clock.

TEA, COFFEE, &c.

From Eight a.m. till Seven p.m.

THE "TIMES," "DAILY NEWS," "HERALD," "MAIL," "SCOTSMAN," "GOOD WORDS," "PUNCH," AND OTHER JOURNALS TAKEN IN.

CONDUCTED ON STRICTLY TEMPERANCE PRINCIPLES.

enterprise for the common good. In the directory for 1875, the year in which Stuart Cranston opened the first tea room, Logan announced the removal of his business to larger premises at 34 Argyle St after nineteen successful years in Maxwell St. As his advertisement shows, the service provided — for men — was very much what the fully developed tea rooms later offered.

The temperance campaigners kept up such an unremitting pressure against alcohol that in 1880 Glasgow's Wine Spirit and Beer Trade Association added 'Defence' before the last word in its name. Although it seemed statistically that the campaigners had done little more than keep abreast of the problem in Scotland — it took the First World War and serious price increases to make a real reduction — towards the end of the century there had been a marked change in the public behaviour of the respectable classes. The tea rooms were the most recent class of establishment catering for a new inclination to sobriety, but were particularly successful in doing so. When *The Bailie* gave Stuart Cranston the honour of its 'Men You Know' profile slot in 1889, it summed up: 'A practical, although not a professed teetotaller, Mr Cranston has done more, probably, to advance the cause of temperance, than all the Permissive Bill agitators put together' (the Permissive Bill agitators, vocal in Scotland, were those who wanted legislation for local veto).

The attitudes expressed in this article perhaps give a clue to why the tea rooms took off so noticeably at this period. Together with its rivals *The Quiz* and *St Mungo*, and reflecting a common view, *The Bailie* put up some spirited editorial resistance to the temperance movement,[16] but pronounced itself in favour of the recently evolved tea rooms. 'Not so long ago there was nowhere, for those who desired refreshment, beyond the bar of the public house and the parlour of the restaurant. Now, public houses and restaurants, while excellent, and even necessary institutions in their way, are not, admittedly, to the liking of everybody. Certain of the straiter-laced eschew them altogether, and every one of us is willing, at times, that is, to seek for a milder species of beverage than any of those which form the staple commodities in which they deal.'

While *The Bailie* ignores in the interests of journalistic clarity places like Logan's and the temperance hotels, it shows where the tea rooms scored. Despite his impressive temperance connections, Cranston approached the business from a new angle, from his passionate dedication to quality in tea. His sister Kate established her first tea room, in 1878, in the bottom of a temperance hotel, but made her name from the beginning by quality of service, catering and decor. Between them they created something new enough to catch the spirit of the times, attractive to a clientele repelled by the hard-line respectability or missionary atmosphere of many avowedly temperance establishments. Though a large number of tea room proprietors were, like both Cranstons, abstainers, whether paid-up or not, temperance was not an issue in the running of the businesses. The smoking rooms which were standard and the billiard rooms provided by the larger tea rooms were not temperance 'counter-attractions' but an entrepreneurial response to the needs of the commercial classes of the city. By 1900 the daylight drinking exploits of Glasgow clerks before the 1880s survived only as office legends. Recalling their hard-drinking youth some indeed maintained with wry disgruntlement that the tea rooms were a snare for the unwary: 'lured in and seduced by the innocence of the liquid purveyed', young men issued out as 'tea-sodden wretches that are worse than drunkards. Moreover, they inhale the smoke of cheap cigarettes.'[17] But it was really quite hard to see the tea rooms as dens of vice. They catered for sobriety and in doing so certainly promoted it.

So while the tea rooms had moral superiority on their side, they flourished on the far more reliable and businesslike footing of servicing a need economically, conveniently, and attractively. This demand came in the first place from men. Like the other distinguishing characteristics of Glasgow, all its fineness and ugliness, the tea rooms arose directly from its nature as a manufacturing and mercantile city. This was understood by the author of 'The Story of the Tea Rooms' in *Glasgow To-day* 1909, who, seeking the origin of the phenomenon, opined: 'the Western Metropolis is ideally adapted, both physically and temperamentally, for this particular type of refreshment place ... A city of business men recognises the value of a light refection and the saving of time in the busiest hours of the day, and the Tea-Room has proved the solution of the situation.'

Through the eighteenth and nineteenth centuries the hour of dining, or the day's main meal, had in fashionable circles been pushed slowly back from the middle of the day through the afternoon to the evening time now common. Queen Victoria had established an hour around 7.30 p.m. for the aristocracy, while the middle classes settled somewhere around 6 o'clock. This necessitated the invention of luncheon, although it remained for a long time a ladies' meal, curiously resisted by men. While plenty stuck to the old habit of eating well at midday, often going home, many men living in the fashionable new residential areas began to work through an inexorably lengthening business day with no more than a snack from a coffee house or pastry baker to keep them going.

It is characteristic of Glasgow's practical outlook that it was ahead of other cities in adapting to this growing need. Before it invented the tea room, Glasgow invented the self-service quick-lunch bar (and before that, it less reliably claimed, the Scottish Twopenny Pie, popularly attributed to one 'Granny Black', whose sixpenny teas were famous). Whatever Glasgow's shortcomings, wrote *The Quiz* in 1881, 'at least we possess the champion luncheon rooms of the country ... we have always the satisfaction of introducing the stranger within our gates to Lang's, with the pleasing feeling that here we can show something unequalled from Land's-end to John o'Groats.' Well meriting its label 'unique', Lang's deserves some space.

No. 1.—LANG'S AT LUNCH TIME.

6. Lang's in 1881 (*Quiz* 'Sights of the City' no. 1). Throughout its long life men always stood and kept their hats on, to support the impression that they were not really stopping, not really having lunch.

William Lang opened a small eating house at 73 Queen St in the middle of the nineteenth century, specialising from the first in pies, buns and sandwiches. By the 1860s his business was distinctive enough to be hymned by a visiting Englishman in *Punch*. 'You turn into Lang's of a forenoon, and lo! you are in the midst of a Rabelaisian collection of creature comforts. On your left is a counter, behind which three or four ladies stand at the receipt of custom, but you turn to the right and please yourself. For in a handsome apartment you find, on slabs and tables round the place, and others in the centre, such varied arrangements for supplying your wants as I have seen nowhere else. Mr. Lang is the Napoleon of sandwiches, and announces, I am told, that he has a hundred kinds of Lord S.'s invention. Among the ordinary show I observed sandwiches of the usual meats, of frizzled bacon, of lobster, salmon, grouse, blackcock, herring, partridge, pheasant, and shrimp, and others of all the potted meats that Crosse & Blackwell could supply. Then there were oysters, taken from their shells, and placed, with their liquor, in delicate little glass vases, a silver fork by each; there was coffee made in the Napier invention so popular in the north; claret in neat casks; milk, which was drunk by bearded men, and did not, I daresay, do them any harm; beer and porter; spirits of the primest quality.'

This mouth-watering description was quoted by *The Bailie* in 1880 as still holding true, except insofar as the institution was now 'much more so': the variety of sandwiches was well over two hundred (later still allegedly as many as the days of the year), and the premises had been extended and included adjoining smoke and coffee rooms. 'Local, colonial and foreign papers lie plentifully about the tables, and the rooms are decorated with admirable taste and effect.' Lang's at midday became one of the sights of Glasgow, 'packed with prominent citizens from the Royal Exchange and its purlieus, all standing, balancing glasses of malt or milk, and browsing on assorted sandwiches'. The 'slight discomfort' of lunching like this seemed only to increase its attraction to devotees. Its fame spread well beyond the city, carried by business men, actors and musicians. The sandwich bars opened literally 'to fill an aching void' in London by Kenelm Foss when he retired from the theatre were confessedly inspired by his familiarity with Lang's around 1910.[18]

Not much imitated outside Glasgow however was Lang's 'payment on honour' system. As *Quiz* says, 'Everybody knows the principles of faith and charity on which the place is conducted … you simply eat and drink anything you like, do a sum in mental arithmetic, and pay the result as you leave.' This pleasant reliance on the customer's honesty in making up his own bill was a feature universally adopted by the tea rooms. Mr Lang, opined *The Bailie*, taught two lessons: 'that it's the best possible policy to give your customer the proper return for his money, and … that when you depend on the honour and good faith of your neighbour, you are never, in the long run, disappointed.' The system was still working perfectly when Lang's was described for outsiders by the 1933 Glasgow Guide: 'so jealous are the habitués of the confidence and trust reposed in them that dishonesty would instantly be detected and reported' (donations to charity were exacted from transgressors). It continued throughout the restaurant's long life until, like many traditions, it was terminated by the Second World War. But nothing is sacrosanct: Jack House recalled the horror of the day before the War when a defiant woman first entered and helped herself to the good things at the bar. This induced general apoplexy, and must have seemed the beginning of the end.

Altogether Glasgow's restaurant business adapted itself very effectively to changing patterns of eating, so that by the time Kirkwood's *Dictionary of Glasgow* appeared in 1884, it could fairly be said that 'in Glasgow one may eat what he pleases, when he pleases, and where he pleases. Luncheon means with some a glass of milk or beer and a sandwich, and with others a sumptuous repast; and at most restaurants there are luncheon-bars and also dining saloons, where those of either class will find their wants supplied.' Luncheon rooms, imitating aspects of Lang's, were generally areas between the entrance and the dining room where customers helped themselves and were trusted to pay the correct sum on leaving. There were still several old-fashioned taverns too, serving slices of silverside and flagons of ale. Other famous establishments offering 'perpendicular lunches' to the snacking business man included 'Pie Smith's', on the corner of Maxwell and

Argyle St; and Forrester's in Gordon St, whose twopenny London buns lubricated with wine or porter sustained more than one generation of business man. John Forrester who had returned in 1863 from adventures in various parts of the Empire to expand the business run by his mother for thirty-three years, was credited with being the first Glasgow baker and confectioner to introduce the architectural wedding cake, and to export shortbread to the Empire for Christmas and the New Year. (These premises were later absorbed by James Craig's Gordon: at the time of writing they are, tellingly, a Pizzaland). Many confectioners and pastry bakers like Forrester evolved at this period into 'restaurants'.[19]

'Restaurants', as their name indicates, were a foreign importation, and hardly existed before the middle of the century, when like grand hotels they slowly began to displace the plain native chop-houses, dining-rooms, taverns and inns in general esteem. The 1860s in Glasgow saw the establishment of some notable restaurants, and the next decade brought considerable expansion as Glasgow's economy boomed and the commercial centre expanded: indeed Glasgow took to restaurants well before Edinburgh and London.[20] Prosser's Queen's Restaurant was typical: established in 1863 it moved to grander premises in Dunlop St in 1873, where it accommodated one hundred and fifty gentlemen in the magnificent dining hall behind its 'artistically arranged bar', and advertised Breakfasts, Luncheons, Dinners, Teas, Suppers, and Wines. Above were 'elegantly fitted private rooms' for ladies or gentlemen, lavatories and a large comfortable smoking room. Similarly typical, offering both lunches and dinners, were Andrew Stark's smoking rooms and restaurant in Queen St (the forerunner of the Bank Restaurant of recent years), and John Scott's. Numerous Billiard Rooms, generally offering light refreshments, were also well established. All these places were safe from feminine intrusion. In the days before telephones it was easy to justify going out to do business over coffee or lunch or a smoke, and this tendency was enhanced by the gregariousness and social mobility of Glasgow's entrepreneurial society. Thus business men's needs combined with pressure from the temperance movement to prime the ground for the tea rooms.

Women were the new and the crucial element in the flowering of the tea rooms. The development of afternoon tea as a female social meal was, like most changes in middle-class eating habits, led by the aristocracy. Its spread from the 1840s on was aided by the dainty ostentation of its ritual, which demanded special cups, silver teapots and so on. It gave a focus for the empty hours between morning activities and dinner in polite circles which had shifted their main meal to the evening. But before the tea rooms afternoon tea was a domestic occasion, where women whose social status forced leisure upon them presided at the centre of their natural setting.

However with the loosening of the early Victorian home obsession in the closing decades of the nineteenth century there was a freedom and a desire among females to go out and about more. This was perhaps particularly marked in Glasgow where the city centre was easily accessible and middle-class life was less bound by convention than in a more static, hierarchical society like Edinburgh's. Shopping was obviously the main possibility for the woman with money and time on her hands, and this brought the burgeoning from the 1880s of palatial department stores, together with a clear need for places to rest from such exertions. Tea rooms, with their decor often appealing to ladies, and their essential 'conveniences', offered an attractive way to fit socialising into an afternoon about town, and women took to them gladly. They were useful for lunch as well as tea: as Kirkwood notes in his discussion of places suitable for ladies in 1884, 'very fair lunches can be had in several tea-rooms, which when first opened were ostensibly for the purpose of sampling teas, but have now become regular luncheon rooms'.

Eating out without a male escort had earlier been virtually impossible. The provision before the 1880s was almost exclusively for men: even temperance coffee and dining rooms were geared to men and out of the question for unaccompanied women. The licensed restaurants did not generally expect ladies, though they could usually be accommodated out of sight if they arrived with men. Increasingly in the 1880s eating places adapted to the demand by adding separate ladies' rooms when they upgraded. Even the Athenaeum Club opened a 'conversation room' for ladies in 1886. Kirkwood in 1884 lists as places which ladies could enter Waddell's in Union St, F. & F.'s (Ferguson & Forrester's, 'the Delmonico's of Glasgow') and the Queen's in Buchanan St, Thornton's and Forrester's in Gordon St, and the ladies' luncheon-room *par excellence*, Assafrey's.

CORN EXCHANGE RESTAURANT,
82 GORDON STREET, GLASGOW.
ROBERT M'LEISH, Proprietor.
BREAKFASTS, LUNCHEONS, DINNERS, TEAS, &c.
TEA HOURS, from FIVE till EIGHT o'clock P.M.   *LADIES' ROOM.*

F. & F.'s,
36 BUCHANAN STREET.
THE LADIES' RESTAURANT.
THE FASHIONABLE RESTAURANT.
THE POPULAR RESTAURANT.

---

7. Advertisement of 1874 for the Corn Exchange, a long-lived restaurant, drawing attention to its tea hours and ladies' room.

8. Advertisement of 1897 for Ferguson & Forrester's, for many decades Glasgow's leading quality restaurant, and an early provider for women.

A. T. Assafrey had established himself as 'chocolatier et confiseur' at 171 Sauchiehall St in about 1871, an early representative of foreign sophistication in the city. By 1888 it could be claimed that 'The name Assafrey in relation to bon-bons is a synonym for excellence throughout Great Britain. His house is most particularly renowned for these ever-popular sweetmeats, many of which are of his own invention, and he is recognised as the practical introducer of these goods in this country.' His ices were also famed, and he had become a major manufacturer of cocoa powder for the Scottish market. At the rear of the main shop in Sauchiehall St and a branch at 78 St Vincent St, which opened in time for the Exhibition in 1888, there were 'luxuriantly' appointed refreshment saloons, serving tea, coffee, cocoa and any number of the firm's gorgeous confections and fancy dishes. Assafrey's was a fashionable haunt aiming from the beginning at women. It had much to do with shaping feminine habits at the top end of the market, and thus had an influence on the growing tea rooms.

Stuart Cranston's recognition of the leisured female as an important customer for his tea rooms grew naturally from his dry tea business, where most of his customers were women. When he expanded his new venture he took special care to cater for them, as his advertisement shows. Stuart was one of those who stuck to the pre-eminence of tea: he did not cater beyond cakes and sandwiches until he opened Fruitarian lunch rooms next century. But when Kate opened her Crown Tea Rooms in 1878, she listed herself as a 'restaurateur' and catered on a much more serious basis, offering lunches and high as well as afternoon teas. She can therefore be seen as the originator of the essential Glasgow tea room,[21] and she indubitably promoted the feminine 'artistic' atmosphere which became one of its distinguishing features. The influence of this more intimate 'tea room style' was soon noticeable: when Paxton's Restaurant and Luncheon Bar at 199 Argyle St (the forerunner of the Queen Anne Restaurant) was remodelled in 1887, for instance, its luncheon room was fitted up in the 'most modern style' with small tables for four, and settles round the sides of the room. This contrasted with the refectory-style arrangement of long tables currently standard in restaurants and hotels (*cf.* fig. 19).

So while many restaurants were offering comparable facilities from the 1880s, the new tea rooms had the edge on respectability in their patent denial of alcohol, and they flourished. Even the smallest premises arranged segregated areas so that both sexes could use them freely without social embarrassment or interference.

But if the origins of the tea rooms lay in Glasgow's adaptation to social change, many of their characteristics can be traced back to the Cranstons, and to Kate in particular. This was a period when the type of gifted, energetic person Glasgow is particularly proud of did make pioneering changes to the way things were done. The Cranstons set standards and inspired many others, and the result was that Glasgow never fell to the

9. A page from *Quiz*, 1889: Stuart Cranston was quick to capitalise on the demand from women — whose new freedom to go out and about evidently brought M. F. Thompson good business too.

English chain tea shops but continued in a tradition of something better, affecting other Scottish cities in a similar way. Some further background biography is called for.

That Stuart Cranston was full of ideas and keen to make his mark in his own field is clear from what has already been said.[22] *The Bailie* speaks of his 'eager, fervid nature' and certain things, as we shall see later, suggest a slightly obsessive character. But despite his large business and lavish advertising he was later eclipsed by his younger sister and we know less of him than of her.

Strength of will was very clearly a Cranston trait. When Kate (27 May 1849 – 18 April 1934) decided to take up an independent career she was flying in the face of convention, which imposed leisure, or philanthropic work only, on ladies wishing to belong to the upper echelons of the middle class. The family tradition is that once her mind was made up 'she paid p.p.c. calls on all her friends because she said she knew that they would not want to know her when she had become a business woman'.[23] The extent to which she broke through social restrictions, blazing a trail down which many other women eagerly followed her, is one of the most impressive things about her story.

She is remembered in the family biography as 'a most attractive young girl with many admirers', but she was evidently not convinced that any of them was what she wanted. In her late twenties she was still unmarried and needing an outlet for her creative and managerial talents. The reaction of her own father is not clear, and it seems that she got most encouragement from her cousins, the 'Waverley' Cranstons: it was apparently Bailie Robert Cranston who financed her start-up. An early supporter of women's suffrage, his own family had taught him to recognise the capacities of women — his paternal grandmother, Rachel Elliot, known as 'the wise woman of Langholm'; his well-educated mother; and especially his wife. Elizabeth Dalgliesh was 'a large-hearted woman, remarkably able and phenomenally rapid and accurate with figures'. As her elder son Robert wrote, the success of the hotels 'was principally due to my mother. There never was a better mother and a more loyal woman. From morning to midnight she was at her post, whilst my father, although managing the general affairs, was given more to politics and the people than to his business. Undoubtedly the foundation of the hotels was due to my father, but the superstructure, the education, the training and the welfare of the family, let it be said and truly said, was due to the devotion of my beloved mother.'

The Bailie spent freely on the education of his two daughters and recognised the elder, Mary (1846-1932), as a natural inheritor of his business instincts. When she married the Glasgow photographic dealer George Mason in 1872, her father's wedding present was nothing less than a new hotel, the Washington Temperance Hotel in Sauchiehall Street, on an excellent site opposite the department store Copland and Lye (now occupied by Marks and Spencer). She renamed it the Waverley Temperance Hotel after

10. Stuart Cranston *c.* 1908, a portrait which captures his 'eager fervid nature'.

the original Cranston Waverley in Buchanan St was sold in 1885, and it ran successfully for many years. Like other Cranstons she was a kindly person who would yet 'stand no nonsense'. On her father's death in 1892 she took up active management of the Waverley empire together with her brother Robert,[24] and after her husband's death in 1901 entered public life as a member of the Glasgow School Board, which unlike the Town Council was open to women. Her Sunday tea parties were well remembered for their gathering of distinguished friends and lively relations,[25] including of course her second cousin Kate, for the two were firm friends.

So Kate Cranston had powerful role models in her own family. Though Elizabeth Cranston died in 1873 she had managed the Glasgow Waverley from the start, and must have been a profound influence on Kate; and there is no doubt that Mary, established in her own business, egged her on. Family connections also secured the eminently respectable location for her new Crown Tea Rooms, named after the now vanished family hotel, below John Aitken's Temperance Hotel at 114 Argyle St.

Of course in Glasgow as elsewhere women had long been active in the catering business, but generally in titular subordination to husbands. On the whole it was only when men died that women emerged into the directory listings, carrying on under their own names businesses which they were evidently well used to managing.[26] There were exceptions: a Miss Hudson and Jane Reid were listed *c.* 1870 at 59 Ingram St as 'restaurateurs and pastry cooks'. This enterprise was probably very similar to later tea rooms. More prominently Mrs Semple had taken over by 1870 from Mrs Jane Gray at 117 Virginia St, where she built up a successful restaurant which later passed through many hands. And just before Kate Cranston began the redoubtable Jane Murdoch took over William Brownlie's business as 'family baker, restaurateur and wine merchant' at 345-9 Sauchiehall St: this she ran from 1877 to 1898 as 'The University', mentioned in 1888 as one of the the the city's 'fashionable' restaurants, and the first to list a telephone number, in 1889.

So Kate Cranston was not unprecedented or alone, but her panache set an inspiring example. While Mrs Semple and Jane Murdoch ran licensed restaurants, the temperance credentials of the tea rooms helped to open this field to middle-class women as an exciting opportunity to make real money. And like dressmaking and teaching, the other traditional standbys, catering could be seen as an acceptable extension of traditionally feminine occupations. This was the period when the 'woman question' was beginning to become serious, as society acknowledged that many unmarried middle-class women had to earn their living. The catering business at large, of course, depended on a large class of capable manageresses, whose names are generally lost to history.

Kate Cranston first appeared as plain 'C. Cranston' in directory listings, which was probably a deliberate decision to disguise her sex for business purposes, if only to outmanoeuvre the convention, enshrining social

11. Kate Cranston *c.* 1900, in the eccentrically unfashionable style of dress she wore to the end of her life.

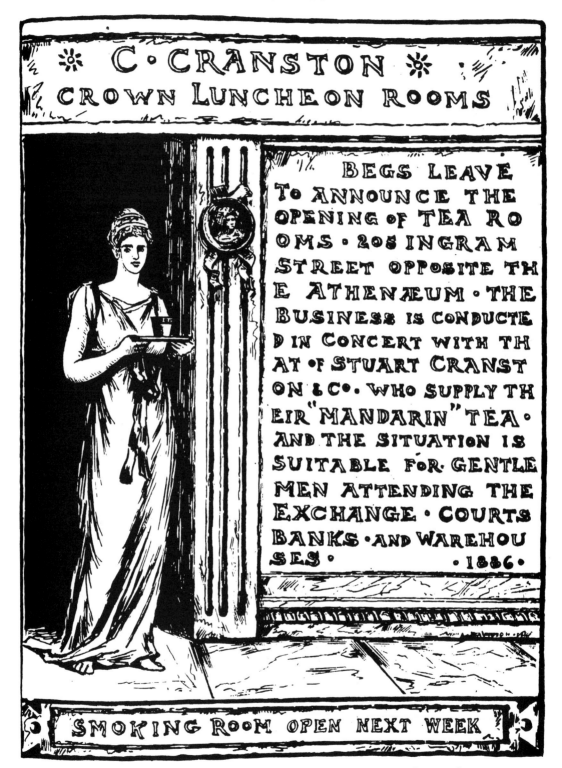

12. Artistic advertisement for Miss Cranston's new tea rooms at Ingram St .

pecking order, of listing all males of the same surname alphabetically by initial, then all married women, and lastly spinsters. Cranston, unlike most Scottish surnames, was uncommon; nevertheless this did get her in above her brother Stuart, her cousin Robert, and later a John Cranston who was a restaurateur and Scotch haggis maker from 1885 to 1895.[27] Ironically it was not until after her marriage in 1892, which made her Mrs Cochrane, that she really flowered in business as 'Miss Cranston'. Her attachment to her name reflects a proud sense of her independent self and what she owed to her family. Marriage, which conventionally terminated a woman's independent career, for her only began, as we shall see, a new period of expansion. She inaugurated something of a tradition of capable 'Misses' in the tea rooms, Miss Buick and Miss Rombach being the best known. Both these like Miss Cranston married late and were childless.[28]

Kate's relationship with her brother is tantalising. Clearly she owed him a great deal and she never contested his insistence that he was the originator of the tea rooms. In the family tradition they were 'great friends'. The popular story that they hated each other is doubtless an extrapolation of what clearly became a keen business rivalry as they vied in the expansion of their separate fiefdoms. One sympathises with Stuart's struggle to keep abreast of his sister's effortlessly magnetic reputation, for she soon turned her sex from a business liability into a flamboyant advantage.

Miss Cranston's small and exceedingly dignified figure became one of the best known in Glasgow. It often put people in mind of Queen Victoria, an impression enhanced by her eccentric retention of the ruffled clothes of her mid-Victorian youth, topped off with unusual hats. Like her cousins, Kate was generous, sociable, fond of music, and gifted with a lively sense of humour, but could be quite formidable and did not like to be crossed. She was a real business woman, insistent on perfection, and from this stemmed the excellence of the Glasgow tea room tradition. The outstanding sign of her singularity, and the thing which brought the tea rooms fame beyond Glasgow, was of course her marked and practical taste for progressive interior design, which deserves a chapter to itself.

But this is to look ahead. Kate in her early days was operating closely with her brother. They shared a house at 91 Sauchiehall St and moved together to a house listed in Kate's name at 425 Sauchiehall St by 1881, before Stuart moved out to Bearsden on his marriage. Kate's first expansion, into the ground floor of a commercial building at 205 Ingram St, began as a joint venture, and was presumably the occasion for financial help from Stuart mentioned in the family account. This new tea room, opened on 16th September 1886 in the heart of Glasgow's business centre, was designed chiefly for men. The Bailie commented on its comfort and artistic charm: 'There is a large commodious room for gentlemen, and a neat little apartment — I should almost say arbour — for ladies.' A smoking room was opened a little later. The street directory shows this as 'Cranston's Tea Rooms', and oddly they continued to be labelled in that confusing way long after they were securely part of Kate's domain.[29] Confusion was inevitable from the beginning, but Stuart's business was properly known as Cranston's Tea Rooms Ltd, Kate's as Miss Cranston's Tea Rooms from 1889.

Miss Cranston opened up in a bad year for Glasgow, for the crash of the City of Glasgow Bank in 1878 caused widespread economic devastation. Developments were doubtless checked by this, but recovery was phenomenally rapid and only ten years later Glasgow mounted its first International Exhibition, a tangible expression of the city's growing self-confidence and prosperity. The city's caterers prepared themselves for the year from which we can date the first great age of the tea rooms.

Various special exhibition publications illustrate the point reached in 1888: claims abound for the large number, excellent range, modern management and moderate tariffs of Glasgow restaurants, 'second to none in the United Kingdom'. Baddeley's *Guide to Glasgow and its Environs*, divides them into the 'fashionable', the 'commercial' and the 'special', the last category occupied solely by Stuart Cranston at 2 & 46 Queen St *and* 205 Ingram St, and Lang's, and a reference to supper and oyster bars round the theatres of Sauchiehall St. Noting that the restaurants in his 'fashionable' category are as a rule connected with the confectionery business and open to 7 or 8 p.m., Baddeley includes here Assafrey's, the Panorama, and Jane Murdoch's 'University' on Sauchiehall St; the Alexandra Café, the Queen's Restaurant and F. & F.'s on Buchanan St; and Daniel Brown's on Queen St. Far larger is the list of 'commercial' restaurants.[30] *Glasgow of To-day* picks out James Arbuckle's Caledonian Restaurant on Jamaica St as typical of the response to a great demand in recent years for 'a first class meal without exorbitant prices': he provided for the vegetarian as well as the carnivore, in premises divided into general and ladies' dining rooms. Recent provision of rooms where ladies might eat is everywhere reflected: so for instance Gillespie's St Enoch Restaurant announced 'Just Added Comfortable Ladies' Room and Smoking Room'. Luncheon is almost universally advertised alongside dinners and teas.

The 1880s had seen an enormous growth in the number of restaurants, and 'confectioner & purveyor' businesses. Tea rooms were on the move but not yet identified as something distinctive: the next decade would change that.

The First Age of the Tea Rooms, 1888–1918

The years from 1888 to the First World War were a golden age for Glasgow, in which a sense of sophistication and well-being pervaded the city — and the tea rooms grew and multiplied. In the year of Glasgow's first Great Exhibition, as we have seen, recognition of the tea rooms as a phenomenon was just dawning. By the time of its successor in 1901 Glasgow was, to repeat a memorable phrase, 'a very Tokio for tea rooms'. There followed the gay Edwardian decade, consolidating the tradition. Towards the end, at the time of the 1911 Exhibition, appeared a new generation of tea room proprietors who would rise to prominence after the First World War. But meanwhile it was the Cranstons who held centre stage.

The first Exhibition itself gave a tremendous boost to the idea of tea-drinking and snack-eating for pleasure. Indeed for a population — the middle classes of it at least — with a Protestant distrust of enjoyment and entertainment, it was a thoroughly intoxicating experience, with its fountains and fairy lights, switchback and gondola rides. After this of course Glasgow never looked back, and later became one of the great cinema-going and dancing cities of Europe, but in 1888 pleasure had all the attractions of novelty. While the substance of the exhibition lay in its spectacular displays of manufactures and machinery for educational and commercial benefit, it was predictably the colourful ambience that made most impression.[1]

The Exhibition was soon nick-named 'Bagdad by the Kelvin' from the vaguely 'eastern' style of its enormous main building and the various restaurants and kiosks dotted picturesquely around Kelvingrove Park. Tea with its oriental associations seemed to fit the scene perfectly. Visitors could play at the imperial way of life during an unusually fine summer by taking tea on the verandah of the Royal Bungalow Restaurant, with service by an assortment of fascinating 'real live natives'; or in the Indian or Ceylon Tea Rooms. These reflected not only Glasgow's strong trading links with this part of the Empire, but also the rapidly increasing popularity of their tea: China had previously held complete domination.[2]

Strenuous efforts by temperance campaigners to have alcohol banned at the Exhibition had been unsuccessful. George Mackenzie, proprietor of the Royal Restaurant in West Nile St, was the Exhibition's sole licensed contractor, and his three bars were 'embarrassingly popular', though tea was also served in his other establishments — the exclusive Royal Bungalow, the 'popular' Clan Dining Rooms in the main building, and the Bachelor's Café by the shooting range for men who preferred a female-free environment. But the middle-class ethos of the exhibition meant that there was plenty of provision for the sober at all levels of catering, especially those designed for the lower classes.

Unglamorously sited next to the dynamo shed off the Machinery Court, were Jenkins' Temperance Refreshment Rooms, or 'Working-men's Dining Rooms'. As manager of the Great Western Dining Rooms, an early catering chain with by now around thirty houses feeding 10,000 regular customers daily, Thomas Jenkins was well equipped for his task of 'catering for the masses'. For less basic requirements there was the large Bishop's Palace Temperance Café, which took its name from the neighbouring reconstruction of one of Glasgow's long-demolished medieval buildings. The waitresses, fetchingly dressed in Mary Queen of Scots costume to maintain this theme,

13. A waitress at Jo. Lyons' Bishop's Palace Temperance Café at Glasgow's 1888 Exhibition.

were soon dubbed 'Lyons' Widows' — for this fat contract had been won, on the strength of his effectiveness at the Newcastle Exhibition the previous year, by one J. Lyons. He left Glasgow with the cash and the inspiration for the establishment of his famous chain of tea shops in London, the first of which appeared in 1893.

At the top 'ladies' end of the market, there was the large oriental 'kiosk' run by the fashionable confectioner Assafrey's (p. 32). Ladies could rest their feet in the elegant tea room on the first floor. A matching smoking kiosk run by Mr Howell catered for men: here they could take their coffee and cigarettes sprawled on oriental divans. Women had another haven in the Glasgow School of Cookery Tea Room in the Women's Art and Industries section, an important part of the exhibition, addressing the increasingly

14. One of several oil sketches made by John Lavery at the 1888 Exhibition: a footsore lady in the tea room of Assafrey's confectionery pavilion (detail).

pressing question of how middle-class women might respectably earn their own livings. Its craftwork exhibits accelerated the explosion in Glasgow of women's work in this field in the 1890s; and perhaps it also helped implant the idea of running a tasteful tea room as a possibility. This was certainly something that a number of women took up in the next decade.

Cocoa rooms as we have seen were currently widespread and popular, and at the Exhibition chocolate put up some stiff resistance to tea. Van Houten's brought over from Holland a complete sixteenth-century style Dutch cocoa house. Scrupulously managed, decorated with genuine Delft tiles and antiques, and staffed by boys and waitresses in national dress, it was predictably well-patronised. However tea was definitely the drink of the Exhibition, from the day of its royal opening, when *Quiz* magazine's ladies' gossip column, 'Afternoon Tea', noted with satisfaction: 'we, who commit what some people call the barbarism of taking cream in our "afternoon tea," will be pleased to know that the Princess of Wales does the same.'

The Bailie meanwhile indignantly took up the cudgels against inflated prices, which applied to tea but not alcohol. 'Why should the teetotal contractors in the Exhibition increase their ordinary prices by 50 and 100 per cent.? ... In the Indian tea rooms, the Bishop's Palace Café, and the tea rooms of the School of Cookery, the price for a cup of tea is 3d and 4d. What would be thought of the licensed houses if 3d and 4d were charged for a glass of beer, and 4d and 6d for a glass of the hard stuff? There is one satisfaction for the T.T.s — a cup of delicious Van Houten can be got in any of the refreshment rooms for 2d. In view of this how ridiculous to charge 4d for a medium sized cup of tea. One might fancy that tea was still rated at 5s and 6s per lb.'

The magazine returned to the attack the following week. Tariffs had apparently been imposed by the Exhibition management, resulting in a 300 to 400 per cent increase in prices and few customers in the working mens' dining rooms. 'No more three course fivepenny dinners for the horny-handed one and his belongings; no more penny rolls, bath bricks, or penny cups of tea, coffee or cocoa ... Now that the prices have doubled or trebled, I think the working man entitled to a table-cloth instead of the forbidding waxcloth.' Protest was effective, and by the end of May, with freedom to fix his own prices restored, Mr Jenkins had filled his rooms to overflowing. The tariff for the Bachelor's Café — tea, coffee, cocoa 2d; bread and cheese 2d; whisky 2d-3d; soda, lemonade 2d — shows tea competing fairly with its rivals, but one understands better why alcoholism was widespread at this period.

With thousands of visitors descending on Glasgow (attendance figures reached 5.75 million), the Exhibition gave a general boost to the city's catering trade at all levels. John Picken's business on Paisley Road was typical of those which took off during exhibition year, when he reckoned to have provided no fewer than 100,000 with 'substantial victuals and temp-erance drinks'. His large premises, 'very elegantly appointed', were arranged in three divisions: bakery, dining saloons and confectionery, and offered dinners, teas, etc, 'deftly served by neat and civil attendants'. He catered for all sorts of functions too.[3] However he did later go bankrupt.

Several simple tea rooms opened in the city centre aiming at the middle classes, among them 'The Bungalow' Tea Room set up at 17 Howard Street, advertising weekly in *Quiz*: 'A cup of Pure Indian Tea, 2d; served instantly. Ladies' Room. Lavatories.' Others included Burn's, Dene's and Kirkland's Tea Rooms.[4] Miss Cranston herself opened new luncheon rooms at 209 Ingram St as an extension to her tea rooms there in September, while

15 and 16. Two city-centre tea rooms opened in 1888.

Walter Wilson's Colosseum became the first of Glasgow's growing department stores to open 'two large saloons' and a ladies-only room for temperance refreshments. Serving café au lait and french pastries, and 'fitted up most sumptuously' with Japanese drapes, they aimed for artistic refinement in the most sophisticated contemporary manner.[5]

An indicator of the Exhibition's generally cosmopolitanising effect on Glasgow life is the sudden increase in the number of foreigners in the restaurant business at this time. Foreigners had always set the pace in catering for the fashionable end of the British market: aristocratic soldiers who had eaten well in Paris brought French chefs home with them after

Waterloo, and it was foreigners who towards the middle of the nineteenth century began to establish their 'restaurants'. Glasgow however had seemed perhaps too remote and barbarian to attract many, and developed its own home-grown tradition. A. T. Assafrey has already been noted as an exception, successfully targetting the Scottish sweet tooth from around 1871. After operating at the Exhibition he expanded the tea and luncheon room side of his business in the 1890s, and opened a branch in Edinburgh. Another important representative of the French tradition was Jules Boullet, who came to Glasgow as a chef at 'F. & F.s', then at the Grand Hotel, before following the trend and setting up a tea room and light refreshment business in partnership with M. Meng. In 1894 he decided to go it alone and fitted up 'at a cost of several thousand pounds' tea rooms in J. J. Burnet's new Charing Cross Mansions. 'It is without exception one of the best appointed in Scotland, and in point of artistic design stands almost alone', maintained *The Scottish Advertiser*. With 'lady waiters' and 'ices and pastries on purely Parisian lines', he was attempting to emulate Assafrey's success. However there were risks in up-market entrepreneurialism and Jules Boullet went bankrupt twice, in 1908 and again when after discharge in 1911 he established a tea room at 294 Sauchiehall St as Jules Boullet & Bros.

The Exhibition however had attracted a noticeable number of the Germans and Austrians often found as more or less itinerant managers of high-class hotels and restaurants at this period. Perhaps the romance of the Highlands, so beloved of Prince Albert, appealed to their Germanic souls. Among the most colourful was Albert Thiem. Drawn to Glasgow by the possibilities of the Exhibition, he branched out from the hotel business and built a striking circular domed building at 326 Sauchiehall St to house the Bannockburn Panorama. Panoramas were undergoing a renewal of popularity at this period — Thiem built a similar thing in Manchester showing 'The Battle of Trafalgar', which then came to Glasgow, followed by 'Waterloo' and 'The Battle of Omdurman'. This became the main entertainment outside the Exhibition, and helped fill the void after it was gone. A major part of its success lay in the glamorous Restaurant and Ladies' Café it incorporated. 'They are fitted with every convenience in the most approved and finished style, even to the walls and ceiling, which are decorated in a most artistic manner. Lighted by incandescent electric lamps, these rooms are unique for their imposing appearance at night, and it is certain that they will become the most popular of the kind in the city'.[6] When the novelty wore off the building became briefly a Real Ice Skating Rink, then the home for several years of Hengler's Circus (then the Waldorf Dance Hall, and then the Regal cinema). Several other chefs of Germanic extraction appeared in or soon after 1888: they took over well-established existing businesses, often upgrading them with modern ideas, but most did not apparently settle for very long.[7] The Italians however arrived and stayed, as remarkably successful colonisers of the British catering scene. For some interesting reason they found Glasgow particularly congenial, and had a

17. The Panorama opened at 326 Sauchiehall St in 1888, with its fashionable continental restaurant and ladies' café. The core of this building still survives as a cinema.

pronounced effect on popular catering at levels below the tea room stratum: their ice-cream parlours added colour and vitality to working-class life in the 1890s and they secured a virtual monopoly of fish and chip shops. In the more up-market restaurant lists the first Italian name was G. Godenzi, 'French pastry cook and confectioner', on Sauchiehall St from 1887: he then took into partnership the first of the clan of Swiss-Italian Ferraris which now took firm root in Glasgow.[8] They made a deep impression on restaurant life with late hours and continental cooking. Another 'foreigner' attracted by the atmosphere in Glasgow who became a well-known fixture was Walter Coombes from Worcestershire, who came first on his holidays and returned to work at, then buy, the Pope's Eye Tavern on Argyle St.

The 1888 Exhibition, then, left Glasgow with an upbeat economy, new social tastes, and tea rooms poised for expansion. For would-be employers there was no shortage of trained waitresses: Lyons for example had employed 170 staff, Mackenzie close on 400. Lured from domestic service for a season's work, gruelling but lively, at the Exhibition, most were understandably reluctant to return to house-bound servitude. Though hours were long and wages low, and at this period not augmented by tips as was customary in licensed premises (see further p. 134), there were the compensations of being addressed as 'Miss', of companionship and free evenings. The difficulties in getting good domestic servants already noted by Kirkwood in 1884 were greatly exacerbated by the Exhibition and the growth of new openings for women workers, so that complaints from the employing classes became increasingly petulant. In Kirkwood's opinion, however, some of the problem stemmed from the nouveaux riches not knowing how to treat domestics humanely.

Stuart Cranston was more than ready to gamble on the surge in the popularity of tea rooms and seized the opportunity of a lease in Glasgow's quality street. On 2 October 1889 he opened a large new suite of tea rooms, together with a dry tea retailing shop, at 26 Buchanan St, on the southern side of the Buchanan St arm of the Argyll Arcade. 'This is, out of all sight, the biggest set of tea rooms, not only in Glasgow, or in Scotland, but in Britain, or, indeed, anywhere', proclaimed *The Bailie*, as it wrote up Cranston (see p. 26). Clearly the tea room had arrived: *The Bailie* itself said as much.

Stuart's full page announcement in the same issue included a characteristically keen exposition of his air-conditioning system: 'The fresh-air, before being admitted to the salons, is cleaned, deprived of all dust and smoke, heated in the winter by hot pipes, and cooled in Summer by blocks of Ice; and all the air of the rooms is expelled and replaced every twenty minutes by continuous and imperceptible movement.' At a time when ventilation was a public fetish this was guaranteed to get people to come along and see if they could tell the difference, and it struck the note of progressiveness in the air after the Exhibition. However the furnishing and decor, pronounced by *The Bailie* to be 'in admirable taste' — hall-like rooms with long tables and banquettes — followed the traditional style of contemporary restaurants and hotels.

Building his growth carefully Stuart Cranston added a tea room at 43 Argyll Arcade in 1892, and two years later bought the whole Arcade block, in which he was the largest tenant, from what he insisted on spelling 'Argyll' Street to Buchanan St. (His obstinate but completely useless struggle for the orthography of 'Argyll' against the 'Argyle' commonly established for the street's name is indicative of the touch of monomania in his character.) This paved the way for the floating of his company, Cranston's Tea Rooms Ltd, in 1896: though tea and coffee retailing remained an important part of his business, the tea rooms were now central. By this time he had built round them confectionery and oriental nick-nackery departments at

A MARVEL OF PURITY,

Strength, Flavour, and Price, is

STUART CRANSTON & CO,'S

TEA at 1/6 per pound.

Ladies who pay 2/ and 2/6 per pound, under the belief that they are being supplied at "Wholesale Rates," should try this Tea at 1/6, and they will be convinced of the fact that

"THERE IS NO TEA LIKE CRANSTON'S."

This laconic phrase is not of our invention, but has become "a household word" throughout the West of Scotland, by the spontaneous expression of our Customers.

☞ IMPORTANT NOTICE. ☜

New Tea Shop, Tea Rooms, Ladies' Reading Room, and Smoking Room, will be opened in June at

26 and 28 BUCHANAN STREET

(Corner of Arcade next R. WYLIE HILL & CO.'s),

unequalled in extent and beauty, and replete with every comfort which science and experience can suggest. Buchanan Street will be made our headquarters; and the same quality and value which created our unique business will be maintained at

76 ARGYLE STREET, corner of Queen Street.

46 QUEEN STREET, opposite National Bank.

26 and 28 BUCHANAN STREET, corner of Arcade.

STUART CRANSTON & CO.,

TRAINED TEA-TASTERS OF 25 YEARS' EXPERIENCE.

18. Advertisement of 26 April 1889 for Cranston's tea, announcing new tea rooms on Buchanan St, eventually opened on 2 October 1889.

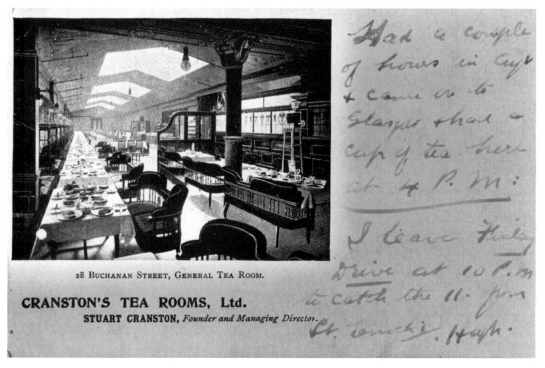

28 BUCHANAN STREET, GENERAL TEA ROOM.

CRANSTON'S TEA ROOMS, Ltd.
STUART CRANSTON, *Founder and Managing Director.*

19. Postcard showing Stuart Cranston's capacious tea room at Buchanan St, opened in 1889, furnished in contemporary restaurant style.

42-43 Argyll Arcade, a cigar and tobacco department at 28 Buchanan St, and a smoking room at 5 Morrison's Court (= 108 Argyle St). He splashed into the restaurant listing in that essential tool of city life, the *Post Office Directory*, at these and his two Queen St locations, taking up an inordinate amount of space by paying for separate line listings and prefacing each address with the preamble 'Cranston's Tea Rooms Ltd (Stuart Cranston, founder and managing director)'. In the same volume he induced the editors to open up a new 'Tea Rooms' listing which he occupied in lonely prominence.[9] This is typical of the way Stuart Cranston pioneered the high profile which the tea rooms achieved in the mid 1890s.

In the following year however his sister took Glasgow by storm when she made her own entry into Buchanan Street at nos 91-3. She had rebuilt the premises entirely on the site of the earlier Alexandra Café, and opened on 5 May 1897. On five floors, with kitchens in the basement, smoking and billiards rooms on the top floor, assorted tea and luncheon rooms on the other floors, and the exciting modernity of a passenger elevator, the tea rooms were remarkable inside for the work of the young designers George Walton and Charles Rennie Mackintosh. The artistic importance of Miss Cranston's tea rooms will be examined in the next chapter, but meanwhile a letter from the young architect Edwin Lutyens to his wife gives a revealing

20. Miss Cranston's new building at 91 Buchanan St, opened in 1897, devoted entirely to tea and lunch rooms (now the Clydesdale Bank).

21. Thumbnail sketch of the sparky
Miss Cranston by her admirer Edwin
Lutyens.

glimpse of a very singular business and its proprietrix. He had fallen for Miss
Cranston and her willow-pattern tableware when he first visited Buchanan
St just after its opening, and passing through Glasgow the following year he
went straight from the train to 'these queer funny rooms and had a most
excellent breakfast — tea, butter, jam, toasts, baps and buns — 2 sausages,
2 eggs — speak it not in Gath — all for 1/1d! so clean. Most beautiful
peonies on the breakfast table and the china the same as ours — in fact this
is where, through the courtesy of Miss Cranston, I got those breakfast
things. Miss C. is now Mrs Cochrane, a dark, busy, fat, wee body with black
sparky luminous eyes, wears a bonnet garnished with roses, and has made a
fortune by supplying cheap clean foods in surroundings prompted by the
New Art Glasgow School.'[10] (For more enthusiasm from Lutyens see below
p. 90.)

Miss Cranston had married John Cochrane, the prosperous owner of
Grahamston Engineering Works and later Provost of Barrhead, in 1892.
Her prominence under her maiden name in business — though she was just
as adamantly Mrs Cochrane at home — should not obscure the extent to
which she was helped by her husband. He was eight years younger than
she, a pleasant man of artistic disposition. Very able in financial matters, he
was clearly invaluable in bringing to pass Kate's ambitious schemes, acting
as the selfless prop, in an unusual reversal of roles, to a spouse whose name
soon eclipsed his own.

That he understood and accepted Kate's priorities was aptly indicated by
his wedding present to her: the lease for the whole of the building which
housed her first small tea rooms at 114 Argyle Street. It became briefly the
The Crown Temperance Hotel before she redeveloped the whole thing as
another major suite of tea rooms, opened after Buchanan St in 1897. John
Cochrane's resources were lavishly channelled into the tea rooms, and there
were rumours that the family engineering business suffered as a result: it
certainly declined rapidly after the early years of the century, but there were
underlying problems in the economy which might better explain this. However with money behind them Kate's artistic inclinations found full expression. One recalls a story told of Bailie Cranston: seeing over the first Cranston
hotel his friend John Aitken reacted with surprise, '"I did not know you had
such good taste." "I'm afraid, John," was the reply, "you have confounded
lack of means with lack of taste."'[11]

Stuart was knocked slightly sideways. There is a note of frenzy in his announcement three weeks after Kate's great opening at 91 Buchanan Street of the re-opening of the enlarged and improved ladies' room at his Buchanan St / Argyll Arcade premises. He advertises its dimensions (54 ft long, 38 ft broad, 13 ft 6 in. high) to support his assertion that it forms 'the largest, airiest, most comfortable, and best ventilated Ladies' Tea Room in Glasgow . . . As now extended and completed this suite of tea rooms in Argyll Arcade is *Unequalled in the Kingdom*'. 'Mattie', author of *The Bailie's* 'Chiffons' column, was a valuable friend and ally: she wrote him up later in 1897. 'Undoubtedly the best ladies' *rendezvous* in town is Stuart Cranston's tea room in Buchanan St . . .' She describes the ladies' apartments with their comfortable lounges, blazing fires and writing tables. 'Nowhere in the city — nor, I believe, in any other — does one find such a generous supply of literature. Then in the enlarged, well-ventilated tea-rooms, delicious tea is served by trim and happy-looking waitresses. Mr Cranston, who was the originator of the tea-room in its modern form, has had many imitators, but no equal, and if I were Queen, I should like to make him 'Sir Stuart,' in recognition of the benefits he has conferred on his townspeople.'[12] (But it was Thomas Lipton who was knighted at the New Year.) Stuart was now vying seriously with his sibling for popular attention.

Cranston also began in 1897 a new tea room at 13 Renfield St, next to Forsyth's, which was opened in September 1898. Here again he quite soon acquired the whole building. It was this shrewd property investment that gave his tea room company the solid foundation that carried on its business until after the Second World War, long after its founder's death. In 1898 he also started up Cranston's Tea and Coffee Pot Company to manufacture Miss Bain's patent Marguerite Tea Pot and other appliances, including his own patent coffee-preparing gadgets. Kate meanwhile was turning her attention to acquiring more space at her Ingram Street premises, extending through from 205-9 to 215 in 1900, where Mackintosh designed the White Lunch Room and a further billiard room (p. 96 ff.).

BY HER MAJESTY'S ROYAL LETTERS PATENT.

"THE MARGUERITE"

Makes beautiful Tea, and separates the spent leaves from the Infusion. Is most economical. Easily cleaned.

Tea Making.   *Tea Infuser & Separator.*   *Separating Spent Leaves after Infusion.*

22. Miss Bain's patent Marguerite Tea Pot, from the share offer of 1898 for Cranston's Tea and Coffee Pot Co. Ltd.

23. Stuart Cranston's building at 13 Renfield St, opened in 1897. In 1916 it was rebuilt to include Cranston's de Luxe Picture House (fig. 83).

The Cranstons' spectacular expansion in the 1890s was mirrored by many successful imitators and competitors. 'A decade ago', wrote *The Evening News* in 1895, 'the tea-rooms of the city could be counted on one's fingers; now their name is legion.' It describes 'a well-defined tea-room area' bounded by Argyle, Hope, Sauchiehall and Queen Streets, and outside this 'sundry more or less chic depots, where Kelvinside and other fashionable ladies sip Souchong and talk dress'. This proliferation reached its height around 1897 when the economy was booming again after one of its cyclical depressions earlier in the 1890s. 'About half the premises in the centre of this Chaste City now undergoing alteration — and there are not a few —

are for cafés. The rest will be restaurants', quipped *Quiz* on 9 September. 'Anyone would judge from the number of tea-rooms sprouting everywhere that these, aesthetic or otherwise, must be profitable concerns', continued *St Mungo* on 26 October. Indeed the tea room boom occupied the magazines in this year almost as much as the female craze for bicycling, together with other upsetting trends like vegetarianism — all these things seeming to threaten the safe old masculine order. In 'The spread of the insidious tea-room' on 17 November *The Bailie* lamented as a sign of the times the displacement of a good healthy 'pint of bitter and a dressed steak' lunch by 'fearful and wonderful pastries, ballasted by buckets of boiling tea'. It accused the tea rooms of creating a new kind of roué, the clerk of artistic temperament, seduced by a potent mixture of tea, tobacco, talk and pretty waitresses.

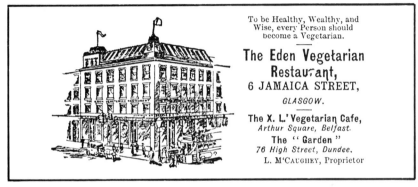

To be Healthy, Wealthy, and Wise, every Person should become a Vegetarian.

The Eden Vegetarian Restaurant,
6 JAMAICA STREET,
GLASGOW.

The X. L.' Vegetarian Cafe,
Arthur Square, Belfast.
The " Garden "
76 High Street, Dundee.
L. M'CAUGHEY, Proprietor

24. The Eden Vegetarian Restaurant, advertising in 1897.

Everywhere there was change and activity, in this last Victorian decade which in retrospect belongs with the Edwardian years. Broadly speaking people had more money to spend and more leisure to spend it. Sport, becoming a 'mania' towards the turn of the century, tended in general towards reducing the drinking of alcohol and promoting tea and non-alcoholic beverages like 'Tonbur' — 'the King of Non-Intoxicants', 'the invalid's delight, the working man's friend and the brain-worker's panacea' — and its competitor 'Zoka'. Other drinks like Vimbos 'fluid beef' and its long-lived rival Bovril also became fashionable on health grounds. The cycling explosion encouraged a sprouting of wayside tea rooms out of town, which were firmly established by the era of motoring for pleasure which followed. The building activity which had begun in Glasgow back in the 1870s became a frenzy in the 1890s, especially towards the end of the decade. New office blocks housed more sober desk workers who escaped joyfully for their coffee, lunch, and smoke. Discount draper's shops expanded into opulent department stores attracting women to browse and meet for lunch and tea. The tea rooms were in their element.

Following Stuart Cranston's lead were other tea and coffee merchants. Flint and Co. opened small 'artistic' premises at 63 St Vincent St around 1895[13] before moving to take over the tea room originally established by

Nisbett & Co., also tea and coffee merchants, at 106 West George St in 1898. William Seaton junior, whose background was likewise in tea dealing (Seaton, Turner & Co.) had ambitions rivalling Cranston's and quickly built up a chain of his Cabin Tea Rooms. With the baker R. A. Peacock as his chairman of directors the company went public in 1897. To tea rooms at 105 St Vincent St, 40 Gordon St, 91 Hope St, and 17 Bothwell St (their names — the Cabin, the Anchor, the Orient, the Mecca — divided between the nautical and the exotic) were added this year the former City Café at 14 Gordon St, and new rooms at 29 West Howard St and 175 St Vincent St. Later expansion included branches in London and a major investment in Aberdeen.[14]

In Miss Cranston's train followed many women, among whom we might pick out Miss Barbara Fergus tucked in next to Robert Adams' 1794 Trades House in Glassford St, where her tea rooms ran quietly for four decades from 1889; Miss Loudon at 42 Sauchiehall St, 1884-95; Margaret Grant at 92

25. William Skinner's advertising in 1894: this had a long history as one of Glasgow's best tea rooms.

26. David Turner's purveying business on the south side occupied premises subsequently run by Wm & R. S. Kerr and A. F. Reid & Sons. 1897.

Tea and Luncheon Rooms.

WILLIAM SKINNER & SON,

477 SAUCHIEHALL ST., CHARING CROSS.

These Rooms will be found commodious and comfortable, and replete with every convenience.

TELEPHONE, WRITING ROOM, &c.

Turner's Tea Rooms and Restaurant,

441 VICTORIA ROAD, CROSSHILL

DAVID TURNER

(Late with FERGUSON & FORRESTER),

Purveyor, Family Baker, Cook, and Confectioner.

WEDDING CAKE MANUFACTURER.

PURVEYING IN ALL BRANCHES CONTRACTED FOR.

ALL TABLE REQUISITES ON HIRE.

REAL CALVESFOOT JELLY FOR INVALIDS.

Suitable Rooms for Private and Public Dinners.

HOT AND COLD DISHES FOR BALL SUPPERS.

Christmas Cakes, Buns, and Shortbread of the finest quality.

MIKADO TEA ROOMS.

21 JAMAICA STREET,

GLASGOW,

Are eminently suited for

CONVERSAZIONES, SMOKING CONCERTS,
PRESENTATIONS,

SUPPER PARTIES, and like GATHERINGS.

TABLE D'HOTE, Three Courses, 1s.

MEAT TEAS AND PLAIN TEAS.

LAVATORIES, &c.

THE FAVOURITE RESORT OF FOOTBALL CLUBS.

———

FRIDAY DINNER A SPECIALTY.

Variety of Fish Soups and Boiled Fish,

THREE COURSES, 1s.

27. William Lee's Mikado Tea Rooms, advertised in 1894, popular with footballers.

Mitchell St, 1888-97; Mrs Wright at the St Vincent Tea Rooms, *c.* 1889-1903; and Mrs Schiller who opened her 'artistic' tea room in West Campbell St in 1896 (p. 99).[15] Specially congenial to ladies as customers were the large number of high-class bakers and confectioners, such as William Skinner's at the Charing Cross end of Sauchiehall St, who opened tea rooms at this period.[16] At the less chic level the United Coop Baking Society also expanded its tea room business in the 1890s.[17]

Many individual businesses found their niche. William Lee, whose advertisement reflects two rather different crazes of the period — for things oriental and football — opened his Mikado Tea Rooms at 21a Jamaica St *c.* 1893, and sold his previous Jamaica St premises to William Whitelaw, a baker and pastry cook who became another stalwart of tea rooms.[18] Among unpretentious but very long-lasting businesses one might pick out here Joseph Wilkinson's 'Govan British Workman Coffee Tavern' at 581 Govan Road, one of the earliest into the new tea room listing in 1897, adapting an old style of business to the new.[19] Alston & Lamb, later Alston's, had Tea & Coffee Rooms at Dundas St and next to Miss Cranston in Ingram St, and later at various downmarket locations on the High St.

RATHIE'S
Luncheon and Tea Rooms,

122 St. Vincent Street, 159 West George Street.

Handsomely Furnished and Fitted with Electric Light.

LUXURIOUS SMOKING LOUNGES.
PRIVATE ROOMS FOR LADIES.

MOST VARIED MENU IN TOWN.

---

28. Advertisement of 1897 for Rathie's. 97 Candleriggs was added later, and the premises became the Hydro Tea Rooms group.

By the time of Glasgow's second great Exhibition in 1901, 'J. H. Muir' could write 'It is not the accent of the people, nor the painted houses, nor yet the absence of Highland policemen that makes the Glasgow man in London feel that he is in a foreign town and far from home. It is a simpler matter. It is the lack of tea shops.' To the Glaswegian's unfailing question 'A say, whit do you folk dae when ye want a good cuppa tea?', the Londoner, he goes on, has no answer: 'Barring gin-palaces and restaurants (where tea is equally tabooed) he knows no middle between, let us say, Fuller's on the one hand and a shop of the Aerated Bread Company on the other. Think of it! Fuller's, the home of all that's expensive and nice in cakes, the place so clean that every lady lets trail her skirt; and an A.B.C. shop, where the very scones must be ordered like cuts from a joint, and tea is set before one already mixed with milk, as at a Sunday school treat ... So the Clyde Scot returns with pleasure to where he may lunch on lighter fare than steak and porter for the sum of fivepence amid surroundings that remind him of a pleasant home.' Muir's delightful *Glasgow in 1901* indeed gives considerable space to the special qualities of the turn-of-the-century Glasgow tea room.

In the first place is noted their particular adaption to the needs of men. 'Edinburgh, it is true, has some pleasant and charming rooms in haberdashers' shops, where most dainty lunches are to be had for a trifle. But the Glasgow man has a delicacy in entering such places which ought, by rights, to be sacred to the other sex; and, if he does so, feels perhaps, that he might be better dressed. In his own town he need have no such qualms. The tea rooms here are meant for him, and it is he who uses them mainly.'

But the strength of the tea rooms was their ability to cater for the broadest spectrum of middle-class society. Between one and two, says Muir, 'the place is full of folks who lunch modestly, whether from necessity or caprice. But at four another kind of person comes — the lady who is shopping, or the smart youth who, two hours ago, had a most useful lunch at "Lang's", standing in the congregation of the upright.' This is not to say that the tea rooms were without class distinctions: *St Mungo* illustrates the bottom line in 1897. 'I hear of a sad incident in a select city tea-room. Five of the waitresses fainted and are only now recovering. On Friday a young man with mud on his boots and a straw in his mouth, accompanied by a rustic maiden in a flowered hat, entered and called loudly for 'A pat o' tea and a big curran' scone and jeely.' Of course country cousins were a standard source of amusement in Glasgow. It is safe to say that the urban middle classes would all find a tea room where they felt comfortable.

The particular attractions of the smoking rooms had been noted in 1895 by *The Evening News*: 'in the bigger and more pretentious tea-rooms of the city, the smoke-room is a capacious apartment, with accommodation for upwards of a hundred'. Here office bosses mingled easily with junior clerks, reflecting the lack of social discrimination notable in masculine Glasgow life. They served as clubs for the clerk of modest means. 'Everything that the heart desires', says Muir, 'from coffee and cigarettes to illustrated papers and draughts and dominoes, is ready to his hand. Even an easy chair, in which, after a night of dancing, he may be visited by sleep. No one, unless he is sitting on the Sketch, will wake him, for the place is Liberty Hall, and free to anyone who has two-pence at disposal for a cup of black coffee.'

The other distinguishing features of the tea room noted by Muir are 'the scheme of their decorations and the location of some of their premises'. Tea rooms had sprung up all over the centre of Glasgow, often in previously unused basements, where rents were low. Smoking rooms in particular were frequently beneath the pavement, safely protected from the traffic of ladies above. As for decor, Muir has chiefly in mind Miss Cranston's advanced interiors, but in general an atmosphere of tasteful, homely excellence was very marked. Contrasting unfavourably the bleak marble of an Edinburgh café or an A.B.C., Muir describes as standard tables pleasantly arranged, made of wood, 'spread with fair white cloths and set with flowers and china'.

A similarly civilised feature was the honour system of payment. Muir continues: 'The scones and cakes, too, are there at hand, to have and to hold. Nor is one overlooked while eating, lest, peradventure, fraud might occur. A printed notice certainly is sometimes there requesting the customer, in the interests of the management, accurately to remember the amount which he has consumed. But this is for the use of country cousins ... One states the amount of one's indebtedness, and receives therefor a check from the attendant maiden. This, with the corresponding coin or coins, one hands in at the pay-desk, and so home. Nothing could be simpler or less irritating. A bas les A.B.C.!' The system regulated itself without any real problems. An icy stare from a waitress was usually sufficient to control dishonesty. Of course, as *The Evening News* reported in 1895, 'Some people eat so much and so absent-mindedly that they lose count and risk a figure (on the safe side as a rule). Men have been known to frequent Glasgow tea-rooms for years and pay a halfpenny for an item figuring on the list at a penny ... On the other hand, it is told ... that not so long ago a tea-room manager in this city, on finding that for over a year a customer had been paying twopence for a penny sandwich magnanimously stood the customer a pint of Pommery Extra Sec, half-a-dozen oysters — (this was before the typhoid days) — and a very fine cigar'.

Only Stuart Cranston and one or two others now ran 'tea shops pure and simple' offering no more than sandwiches and cakes: 'the rest are hybrids, part restaurant, part tea shop; but of course unlicensed'. Their menus were congenial both to the lightly lunching boss, even the plain character who regretted the change of habits that made him 'tak his tea at denner-time, and his denner insteid o' his tea'; and his humble clerk who still called his midday meal his 'denner' and ate a high 'tea' later. Modest prices prevailed, and 'you can lunch in Glasgow more cheaply, and with fewer additional imposts in the way of bread-money or tips than in any other town in Great Britain. For 1s. 4d. you can fill yourself drum-tight in an eating-house much more charmingly decorated than your home.' Competition from this quarter had a salutary effect on the established restaurants, even the most fashionable, which often allocated part of their premises to a tea room: so even in the posh new Grosvenor Restaurant[20] in Gordon Street, 'famous for its waiters and its 3s. table d'hôte dinner, and its band and its circular bars and its long-coated doorkeepers, you find an apartment where a retiring young man may have his "fivepenny wheck"'.

All in all it is easy to see how very attached people became to their favourite haunts. And for some male patrons, as Muir indicates, a further attraction lay in the waitresses. For a shy young man, especially a new-

In a Tea-Room.

STOUT PARTY—Have you a license here?
WAITRESS—Is it on the menu? (carefully studies bill of fare).
No, that's off to-day.

29. Cartoon of 1897 evoking the attractions of the tea-room waitress.

comer to the city, she might be, apart from the landlady, 'the only petti-coated being with whom he can converse without shame'. While adver-tisements for barmaids often stipulated 'Must be pretty', and flirtatious behaviour was part of the job, tea room girls were recruited on a more sober basis, and covered a wider spectrum of age and beauty. However their bewitching qualities became the subject of much journalistic copy. 'She is a product of the age, this sweet votaress of the tea-urn', sighed *The Bailie* in 1897: 'She has a pale and aesthetic appearance'.[21] Good-looking girls often acquired a loyal following of young gents, and some employers clearly deployed their stars carefully, as *St Mungo* noted the same year: 'In one case where several tea-rooms are run by one person a number of girls are frequently changed from shop to shop. Whenever the popularity of a place is on the wane, one of the brightest of the girls is sent to it with the expected result that trade becomes as brisk as possible in that particular corner.'

At the beginning of the new century Glasgow was bursting out all over, and there was considerable enthusiasm for its second International Exhibi-tion in 1901. This itself produced a rash of new tea rooms. The Ceylon Tea Rooms established by Seaton, Turner & Co. in Renfield St proved successful and long-running. Others were a more fleeting response: the exotic 'Madame Bain' — who besides running a tea room was a 'dealer in oriental curios, rare cabinets, pictures etc, and artificial flower manufacturer', disappeared from 184 Sauchiehall St the following year.

The new Kelvingrove Art Galleries and Museum inaugurated at the Exhibition confirmed the cultural status to which Glasgow now aspired. The atmosphere of this Exhibition, considerably bigger than its predecessor, reflected the new sophistication acquired by Glasgow in the last eleven years. While ornate grandeur was still considered the appropriate manner for public buildings, and was admirably supplied by James Miller's 'Eastern Palace' designs, their white-painted finish was in keeping with the spirit of the time, and a more contemporary note was struck by some of the minor structures raised by the caterers.

Some of the same names were back. George Mackenzie took up again the lucrative role of sole licensed contractor, now in partnership with J. & W. McKillop, currently proprietors both of the Royal and the new Grosvenor Restaurant. At the other end of the scale Thos Jenkins & Co. returned to feed the plain man in the Palace Restaurant and Tea Rooms. It is noticeable that the designation 'temperance' has been dropped: 'tea room' is sufficient guarantee. The commanding site that had been occupied by Lyons' Bishop's Palace Temperance Café in 1888 was taken this time by the Prince's Restaurant and Tea Rooms, run by Glasgow's own chain, The Cabin Tea Rooms.

Whether Stuart Cranston had wished for a stake at the Exhibition is not known. His sister however secured an appropriately prime site for her Tea House, right outside the new Art Galleries. 'Tastefully decorated', in the

30. View of the new Kelvingrove Art Galleries opened at the 1901 Exhibition, with Miss Cranston's temporary Tea House slap in front and a special bridge over the Kelvin. On the right is Van Houten's cocoa pavilion.

guide's words, it struck the note of modernity for which she was by now famed. Flint's rival tea rooms adopted a similar up-to-the-minute elegance. For those who preferred ethnic exoticism a cup of 'Government' tea could be taken on the foliage draped verandah of the bungalow-style Ceylon kiosk, and there were tea rooms of a different style in the extraordinary 'Russian Village'.

Van Houten's returned to fight for cocoa against tea, but this time had to resort to price cutting to attract the crowds, offering a 'serviette, biscuit and cocoa in Royal Worcester porcelain' for no more than a penny. Significantly too they dropped national fancy dress in favour of 'tea room style', commissioning leading local firms to design and furnish a pavilion in the modern 'Old English' manner.[22] This is a good indicator of the hold which the tea rooms had gained and of increased attention to the decorator's art during the previous decade. Another index of Glasgow's strides in sophistication is the number of complaints this time around about insufficient provision for amusements and refreshment: citizens now had clearer ideas about how they wished to enjoy themselves.

After the death of the old queen in 1901 Britain entered upon its Edwardian years, and in Glasgow as elsewhere this was a gay and glittering decade for the fortunate. Beneath the surface all was not so well: a 'normal' recession in the early years of the century disguised a deeper rot in Glasgow's economy, too reliant on heavy industry and foreign markets, and now damaged by competition. There were visible signs of change and disturbance in strikes and suffragette activity at the end of this period. But there were also exciting new industrial possibilities in automobiles, in Beardmore's airships and aero-engines, and Lord Kelvin's electrical instruments. For the most part the city continued to feel itself prosperous and secure, enjoying life. These were great days for the music hall, theatre, and later the cinema — and of course for the tea rooms.

Rivals to the Cranstons continued to appear, like Miss Schofield's 'An Old Oak Tea Room', in James Salmon's art nouveau office block at 144 St Vincent St, the spindly 'Hatrack'; or the Regent Tea Rooms in another fine new office block at 51 West Regent Street. The prime sites they occupied show the new prominence of tea rooms, increasingly purpose-built, rather than squeezed into old basements. Both these aspired to 'artistic' status, but Miss Cranston showed that when it came to modern design she left competitors in the dust with her last and most famous new tea rooms opened at the end of 1903. The Willow Tea Rooms, at 215-17 Sauchiehall St, designed inside and out by Charles Rennie Mackintosh, were quite simply inimitable.

Stuart Cranston meanwhile was engaged in destroying a piece of Glasgow's architectural heritage, in a manner characteristic of the progressive age. Having acquired the whole of the Argyll Arcade building in 1894, in 1903 he rebuilt the frontage on Buchanan St, demolishing in the process

31. A watercolour sketch by H. Thomson of Buchanan St in 1902, showing Cranston's premises at the entrance to Argyll Arcade. The following year he demolished the old house and rebuilt the arcade entrance.

BUCHANAN STREET, 1902.

the last remaining representative of the old private houses which had marked the west end of the city in the early nineteenth century.[23] It was replaced by a free 'French Renaissance' block by Colin Menzies, for Stuart did not share his sister's taste for modernity.

However as if determined not to be left behind he soon followed Kate into the increasingly fashionable Sauchiehall St, taking over the Wellesley Lunch and Tea Rooms at no. 145 in 1907. These were typical new 'artistic' rooms, designed by Honeyman, Keppie, Mackintosh, and opened a couple of years previously.[24] In October 1905 Cranston's had issued stock for £250,000. It had gradually bought up the old corner block at 76 Argyle St / 2 Queen St, and slowly consolidated at Renfield St too: these three large blocks in the business centre brought in revenue from approximately a hundred tenants, in addition to the thriving tea rooms and retail outlets.

In 1908 Cranston modified his purist stance on catering to the extent of opening a Fruitarian Lunch and Snack Room at 28 Buchanan St. This was loyally supported by Glasgow's Fruitarians, many of whom appeared daily at their tables, and was allegedly effective in enlisting new supporters for the Movement. The retailing of appropriate specialities followed. Though Glasgow had had its vegetarian restaurants before this (see p. 55), food reform was a newly current issue in the mid Edwardian years. An artistic Food Reform Café, the Arcadian Gallery, had been opened in 1907. This seems to have been a favourite cause of Mrs Cranston, though Stuart also championed it with his habitual energy — on grounds of health, and the

32. The Fruitarian lunch room opened in 1908 at Stuart Cranston's Buchanan St premises, a good example of his preferred decorative style.

33. Publicity card by Jessie M. King
(*c.* 1909) for the artistic Arcadian Food
Reform Café, opened in 1907: see p. 116.

greater employment resulting from the cultivation of fruit, nuts and the like. There was also a temperance factor, and Mrs Cranston lectured several times on 'The benefits of Fruitarian Diet with reference to the Drink Problem'. Further lunch and snack rooms were opened in 1914 beneath the Royal Exchange Buildings.

Cranston was still fighting on against packeted India and Ceylon tea. 'For forty years', he advertised in 1909, 'he has advocated the use of mild China Teas and Darjeelings as against the coarse liquoring Indian and Ceylon Teas, which latter cause indigestion and all its attendant troubles from their excess of tannin ... The public who buy Teas in Packets, whose wrappers are included in the weight, lose one penny per pound by short weight in Tea; and they pay for the paper wrapper three or four times the cost of the paper and the high-falutin' printing thereon'. In general Stuart continued high profile advertising — even persuading the *Post Office Directory* itself to carry embossed advertisements of his tea and his Fruitarian rooms on its spine in

1908 and 1909, an experiment not repeated. He also evidently spoon-fed the author of 'The Story of the Glasgow Tea Rooms', in *Glasgow To-day 1909*, whose lavish account was completed without reference to any other tea rooms. 'It is needless to advert to the comfort and taste that preside like twin goddesses in all the Cranston Tea Rooms'. They are 'the pride of Glasgow men, and the source of admiration from visitors from all ends of the earth'.

But it has to be said that Glaswegians and strangers alike were even more wonderingly impressed by the rival Cranston Tea Rooms, with their more advanced concept of comfort and taste; and it was Kate, not Stuart, who entered *Who's Who in Glasgow, 1909*. This is a significant measure of the extent to which she had broken through social taboos against women in business, and of the esteem in which she was held. Of 461 entries only five were women — the Ladies Chisholm, Overtoun and Primrose, variously engaged in philanthropic work; Miss Paterson, one of the first two women to be appointed factory inspectors in 1893; and Miss Cranston. This was followed by the equally revealing accolade of the 'Men You Know' slot in *The Bailie* in 1911, prompted topically by her prominence as a caterer at the Scottish National Exhibition. 'Everybody knows Miss Cranston. Her name is a household word in Glasgow and the West of Scotland; her renown has spread far and wide; the BAILIE, along with all who know her wonderful business career, is proud of her and her achievements.'

The magazine's eloquent assessment shows how she had effectively usurped her brother's claim to fame. 'Gifted with original ideas, business capacity, and courage, Miss CRANSTON early saw the possibilities of the tea-room if carried out on fresh and original lines, and straightway struck on a new path, along which have trooped, in due course, hosts of followers, not in Glasgow only, but throughout the kingdom. Miss CRANSTON has, of course, been marvellously successful. Everyone knows that. Why? Because of her gifts of organisation, management, taste, originality, hard work, and persev-erance, and her great shrewdness in judging as to what people want. She has created a demand by the supply of just the right thing, in just the right way, and at just the right price. In the domain of lunch and tea rooms she has been a real pioneer, and still holds her place among many excellent rivals. All honour to the distinguished citizen who has introduced a verit-able revolution in catering for our people — a revolution in which temper-ance, comfort, elegance, and economy are allied in a fine progressive form.'

Miss Cranston was a perfectionist, touring her establishments every day to oversee the details of her administration. Her consciousness of a need to excel might be traced to her femininity and even a 'feminist' awareness of her position. At all events she set extremely high standards which had a wide influence on her competitors. Fresh flowers and vegetables, a charac-teristic touch, were sent into Glasgow twice a week from her Barrhead garden in a smart little green donkey-cart, which like the bolt upright figure of Miss Cranston herself, became a well known sight.[25]

34 and 35. Miss Margaret Buick and Miss Rose Rombach, portraits indicative of their characters. Both established long-lasting tea rooms in 1910.

This tradition in tea rooms was carried over into their own businesses by two of Miss Cranston's manageresses, who became her 'excellent rivals' in 1910. Rose Rombach,[26] was a strong-willed and forward-looking woman very much in her employer's mould, who established distinctive artistic tea rooms (p. 116) at 75-9 Hope St in 1910, and soon afterwards took over John Armour's restaurant at no. 176 also. After she eventually succumbed to the long courtship of W. Davidson Hall, an accountant and actuary, she sold the business to her brother David, but it continued throughout its life as 'Miss Rombach's'. Margaret Buick, who opened in West Regent Street in 1910 before moving to 147 West George St in 1912, was a gentler character, loved by all, who operated in a lower key — with armfuls of fresh flowers, and a kettle on a swee in an enormous, unusual fireplace, she created an atmosphere of pleasant comfort. She too married late, aged 38 in 1916, but continued to run her successful business as Miss Buick's. Her younger brother, Alec, joined her after the war, and a second tea room was opened at 19a Renfield St. In 1910 also appeared in the tea room listing another resonant name, James Craig, of whom more later.

Several other tea rooms had made their mark in the Edwardian decade, such as Cooper's, which began to list its café at 30-32 Howard St in 1903, and The Mercantile Tea Rooms opened in West Nile St in 1905. Thomas

White had taken over John Forrester's in Gordon St in 1889: he was subsequently in partnership with John Smith but split from him *c.* 1909 and chose thereafter to list his business under Tea and Lunch Rooms. But Glasgow experienced a severe recession *c.* 1907 and already some significant early competitors had disappeared. The ambitious Cabin chain had folded up about ten years after going public in 1897, and another short-lived attempt at a group of tea rooms, Hydro Tea Rooms Ltd, begun in 1902 as successor to the business established by Walter Rathie in the 1890s, was also largely extinct by 1906. However these tea rooms were commonly taken over as going concerns. The up-and-coming Wm & R. S. Kerr for instance mopped up the ex-Cabin premises at 105½ St Vincent St, which had been briefly operated by the Hydro group, and made them into the Carlton Tea Rooms, and later acquired the Hydro's tea room at 97 Candleriggs. The Hydro's 122 St Vincent St premises became Cameron's Luncheon and Tea Rooms. Flint's tea room was taken over in 1906 by Miss Pauline Barker as 'The Kettledrum'.

The tea rooms clustered in Glasgow's business centre continued to rely to a great extent on male custom. But if Glasgow, which saw itself as a city with no leisured class, made work the norm for men, social convention still prevented their wives from doing anything much useful with their lives, unless in charitable support of a good cause. With domestic servants the rule right down the scale of the middle class before the First World War,

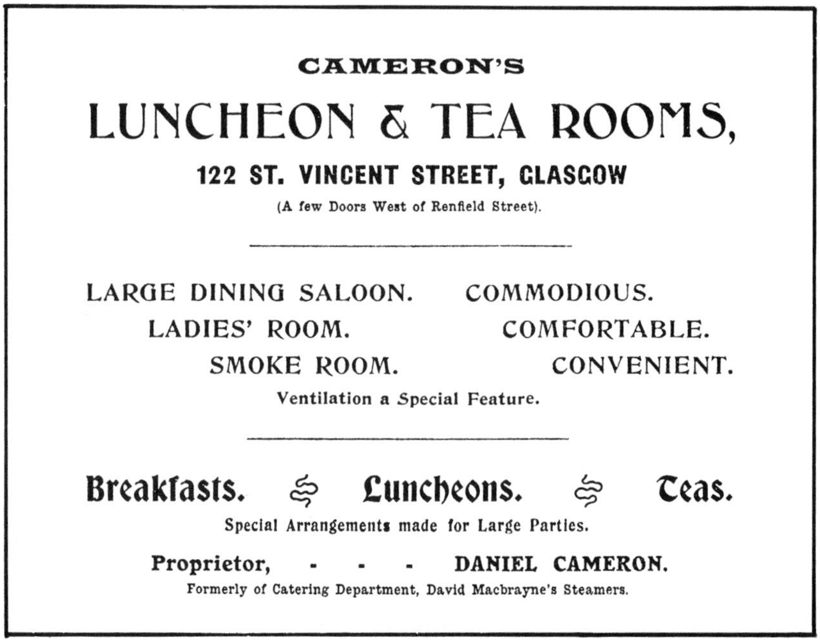

CAMERON'S

LUNCHEON & TEA ROOMS,

122 ST. VINCENT STREET, GLASGOW

(A few Doors West of Renfield Street).

LARGE DINING SALOON.   COMMODIOUS.

LADIES' ROOM.   COMFORTABLE.

SMOKE ROOM.   CONVENIENT.

Ventilation a Special Feature.

Breakfasts. ⸿ **Luncheons.** ⸿ **Teas.**

Special Arrangements made for Large Parties.

Proprietor, -   -   -   DANIEL CAMERON.

Formerly of Catering Department, David Macbrayne's Steamers.

---

36. Daniel Cameron left the steamers to take over Rathie's premises (fig. 28), which he ran to the end of the First World War.

many women had very little to do. George Smith, whose family belonged to the prosperous upper middle class, recalls how his aunt secretly took stenography lessons, only to be forbidden from taking a job by her father. Her frustration could only manifest itself in extreme 'cheekiness' towards the men in her family. It is almost impossible to imagine how women in this predicament managed before the tea rooms: Miss Cranston's was a life-line, as were the other tasteful tea rooms catering particularly for women.

Prominent among these were the tea rooms and restaurants of the great stores which reached new heights of luxuriousness in Edwardian days. The key to their success was the adoption of the 'American system', allowing customers to walk freely through the store without an obligation to buy. Tea rooms and 'resting rooms' were useful magnets. Fiercely competitive, they made shopping into an addictive leisure experience, and because middle class women had real spending power, they burgeoned and flourished.[27]

It was John Anderson, a great and colourful Glasgow figure, who claimed to have introduced in 1845 the idea of 'universal trading'. He had started originally in the Gorbals, then moved to Jamaica St, before bringing his 'Royal Polytechnic' to rest in Argyle Street, where it grew and grew. He had a charming common touch, including a waxworks and 'hall of science' in his store, and entertaining his customers annually on Glasgow Green. The Polytechnic's restaurant and spectacularly capacious Byzantine smoke

37. Advertisement first used in 1916 for the Royal Polytechnic's Restaurant Louis XVI, appealing for the custom of business men.

38. Copland & Lye's spectacular stairwell *c.* 1911, giving splendid views of
other people shopping to those in the spacious tea-room–restaurant. A second
tea-room was opened higher up.

39. All the department stores offered live music at tea-time. This is Copland & Lye's orchestra *c.* 1911.

room (p. 146) were popular with business men at the end of this period. Walter Wilson had similar flair, and his 'Colosseum' on Jamaica St set a hot pace for the competition in the 1880s with advertising gimmicks and innovations like the refreshment rooms already mentioned. However by the 1890s the Colosseum was in the wrong part of town: when Wilson eventually opened his great Tréron & Cie on Sauchiehall St in 1904 his upmarket rivals were there before him.

Copland & Lye had made a shrewd move after outgrowing in five years the premises opened in Cowcaddens in 1873, and were comfortably ensconced when Sauchiehall St took off in the 1890s as the street of fashion and entertainment. More recent was Pettigrew & Stephens, founded in 1888 in premises boasting two front windows and a door on the corner of Sauchiehall and W. Campbell St, at the other end of the block from Copland & Lye. Its phenomenally rapid success was the work of Andrew Pettigrew, who had sole direction after the early death of his partner. He had learnt his business thoroughly, having begun in 1875 at the age of 18 at Daly, Sons and Niven, before moving to Copland & Lye, then the linen department of The Royal Polytechnic, then back to Copland & Lye, and then back to the Polytechnic, before opening as a rival to them all. The first half of the 1890s saw progressive expansion into adjoining property, and the institution of a tea room in 1895 (run at first on a complimentary basis). A major rebuilding created the handsome Manchester House, opened in 1901. There was

Pettigrew & Stephens "Georgian" Restaurant

40. A postcard showing Pettigrew & Stephens' new tea-room–restaurant opened in 1901. The 'Glasgow Style' leaded glass is somewhat at odds with other more traditional decorative features.

further expansion in 1909 when the store absorbed the Royal Glasgow Institute of Fine Art Galleries which lay between it and Copland & Lye, and later consolidation and rebuilding in 1912.

Pettigrew became like Miss Cranston a Glasgow personality, and he too exploited the commercial possibilities of a personal inclination to modern taste. Honeyman & Keppie designed the new building opened in 1901, and Mackintosh's hand was evident in its elegant dome. Mackintosh also designed one of the firm's stands at the 1901 Exhibition. The new tea and luncheon rooms reflected Pettigrew's special interest in decoration and furnishings — they used Pettigrew's 'own-brand' china — and soon became favourite haunts. Here, according to *Glasgow To-day* in 1909, a weary shopper might take tea or 'rest awhile in the lounge so artistically designed, panelled in pale satinwood, upholstered in soft grey and white, so tranquil and agreeable to tired eyes, yet with its brilliant Turkey carpets and cosy green furniture so cheerful and bright a place for a chat.' The restaurant with its 'cool green walls and pleasant furnishings' was also apparently popular among business men.

41. Pettigrew & Stephens: 'A Corner of the Tea Room' in 1909. The Turkey carpets (*cf.* fig. 40) help create the domestic atmosphere sought by artistic tea room decorators. After the First World War the tea room was refurnished in a smart but less distinctive manner.

42. Tréron's, depicted in an advertisement of 1909: 'Luncheon Rooms, Tea Rooms, Resting Rooms, and Writing Rooms are provided for the convenience of patrons, and are also open to the public. The Tuileries Ladies' Orchestra daily.'

On the opposite side of Sauchiehall St Tréron et Cie's 'Les Magasins des Tuileries' (Tréron's for short) was a cunning move by Walter Wilson to play the Parisian sophistication card. This palatial building included a conversion of the the Corporation's McLennan Art Galleries superannuated by the new building at Kelvingrove. At the head of the great staircase was its tea room in white and gold, and next to it the restaurant 'walled in a tasteful harmony in green art canvas and white, with a deep crimson carpet and fine stained glass windows.' With palm court music a standard extra, the cossetting was complete. These great stores and their rivals on Sauchiehall St and Buchanan St became an index of Glasgow's stature as a great city, attracting window-shoppers from the country and admiring visitors from afar. They evoke all the comforts of the Edwardian era, a lost world.

"If you would be Graceful, learn to Skate."

American Roller Skating Rink,

Victoria Road (South-Side), Glasgow.

HIGH-CLASS ROLLER SKATING.

THREE SESSIONS DAILY.—10.30 a.m. to 12.30 p.m. ; 2 to 5, and
7 to 10. Military Band, Private Garage. Afternoon Teas.
Free Instructions. Five Books containing 60 Tickets for Admission
or Skates, £2.

43. Roller Skating had a sudden popularity *c.* 1909.

Indeed the fortunate had much to enjoy: more theatres and music halls
opened; activities like roller skating — with afternoon tea — had a sudden
vogue. Then came the craze for the new moving pictures. The first films
shown to a paying Glasgow audience were allegedly run in 1896 at the
Panorama building in Sauchiehall St. Towards the end of the Edwardian
decade cinemas, or picture houses as they were called, began to appear thick
and fast — though many of them were tiny by modern standards. The
Picture House opened in 1910 was on a more lavish scale, and immediately
became a great social spot. Taking tea among the palms, fountains and
caged birds of its salon was a way of prolonging escape from everyday life.

44. *Above*. Postcard advertising the Picture Salon Winter Garden and Tea
Lounge, opened *c.* 1912 at 92 Sauchiehall St. 'Specialities Afternoon Tea and
Teas à la fourchette. Ordinary City Prices. Orchestral Music.' The premises later
became the Picadilly, Glasgow's first night club.
45. *Below*. The tea room at La Scala Picture House on Sauchiehall St, opened *c.*
1912, from a postcard.

La Scala opened soon afterwards with the distinction of a tea room which extended over the back stalls on one side so that the pleasures of tea and the pictures could be combined.

Cinematographic shows and countless other amusements reflecting the gaiety of the period were major attractions at Glasgow's Scottish National Exhibition of 1911, which was expanded by the city's keenness for such things from the relatively modest conception of the originators into a full scale bonanza. Andrew Pettigrew brought all his skills in giving the public what it liked to the role of Chairman of the Executive Council, and was quite properly knighted in consideration of his labours. This time there was ample provision of refreshments.

Miss Cranston was to the fore again, 'catering in her inimitable style', with two tea rooms, named in accord with the patriotic spirit of the event, the Red Lion and the White Cockade. She was stoutly defended when general complaints were levelled in the press about the quality of some of the food on offer at the Exhibition — tired bread, coarse scones and un-attractive cakes at double price. It is probable that the offender was the Carlton Restaurant, classed as 'popular', run by William Kerr and named after his recently established Carlton Tea Rooms in St Vincent St: he had returned to Glasgow after learning sharp southern ways under Jo Lyons. For tea with an exotic touch visitors could try the Japanese Tea House by the river, where they would be served by 'dainty little ladies from the land of the Rising Sun' — or buxom Glaswegians in modified kimonos.

A promoter of tea drinking, and indeed of cinema-going, at the expense of alcohol was the Great War which broke suddenly upon a time of general prosperity in 1914. It began with confidence that it would take only months to show the Kaiser what was what: when adjustments were made for the young men who had volunteered, it was not too hard to say proudly 'business as usual'. The shipyards and foundries of Glasgow were busy, and so were its tea rooms; and it was during the First World War, according to Charles Oakley, that Glasgow opened its one hundredth cinema. One of these was Cranston's Picture House, shortly upgraded to 'Cranston's de Luxe Picture House'. In a final fling of entrepreneurialism, Stuart Cranston planned the reconstruction of his expanded Renfield St property round what he recognised as the key trend in leisure expenditure. The block from 13-17 was rebuilt by the leading Glasgow architect James Miller and opened in 1916, including a lower smoke room, a tea room, picture theatre, two-tier lunch room, roof smoke room and private rooms (p. 127 f.). Though its elegance later became shabby the cinema was a long survivor. Miss Cranston also managed to expand during the war, enlarging Ingram St and creating a new tea room in the basement of the adjacent building at Sauchiehall St in 1917: the 'Dug-Out' was topically conceived as a kind of war memorial (see p. 120).

The horrifying gap between the continuing comforts and normality of life at home and the living hell on the front only later became clear. But as the

NOTICE.

Public Meals Order, 1917.

On and after this date no Meals will be served in this Luncheon Room, the charges for which, as per Tariff Card, exceeds 1/3, exclusive of the usual charges for beverages, such as Tea, Coffee, Milk, &c.

TEA ROOM PRICES.

Plain Tea, Coffee, Cocoa, Small Cup	2½d
„ „ „ Large Cup	3½d
Chocolate per Small Cup	3½d
Extra Hot Water (per person)	1d
Clear Soup „	3d
Aerated Waters, Large	3d
Small Hot or Cold Milk	2½d
Small Glass Buttermilk	1d
Bread or Scone and Butter	1½d
Cakes, French or Plain	1½d
Hot Toasted Scone and Butter	2d
Slice of Toast	2d
Cheddar or Dunlop Cheese	3d
Jam or Marmalade	1½d
Ham Sandwiches	2d & 4d
Hot Mutton Pie	4d
Scrambled or Poached Eggs on Toast	8d
Small „ „ „	5d
Scrambled Egg and Cheese	7d
Welsh Rarebit	5d
Buck „	8d

SNACK TEAS from 3 till 7-30.

Fried Split Haddock	11d.
„ Whiting	10d.
Small Fish Cake	5d.
Kippered Herring	5d.
Small Potted do.	3½d.
Ham & Egg	8d.
Sausage & Bacon	8d.
Boiled Country Egg	4d.
Hot Mutton Pie	4d.
Small Cold Veal Pie & Salad	4d.
Potted Meat & do.	4½d.
Cold Roast Beef & do.	10d.
Honey Vanilla Ice	5d.

Cakes and Pastry Order, 1917.

Between the hours of 3 and 6, in the afternoon, the maximum amount allowed to be spent on a Plain Tea is 6d., but High Teas including Meat, Fish, Eggs, &c., are served as usual, as per Tariff Cards on tables.

HIGH TEAS from 3 till 7-30.

FIXED PRICE HIGH TEAS	
. . .	
PRICE	Ham and Egg or
1/3	Filleted Fish
	3 Breads Varied
	Pot of Tea
	. . .
PRICE	Ham and Eggs or
1/6	Filleted Fish & Chips
	3 Breads Varied
	Pot of Tea

A LA CARTE HIGH TEAS	
Cold Tay Salmon & Salad	1/1
Mayonnaise of Salmon & Salad	1/1
Fried Cod Steak	11d.
Aberdeen Haddock	11d.
Fried Haddock	11d.
„ Whiting	10d.
Baked Fish Custard	9d.
Kippered Herring	5d.
Potted do.	5d.
Fried Bacon & Eggs	8d. & 1/-
„ & Sausages	1/-
„ Sausages & Eggs	1/-
Wiltshire Bacon & Poached Eggs	1/-
Chicken & Ham Rissole & Sauce	9d.
Fried Turkey Egg	6d.
Small Cold Roast Lamb	10d.
„ „ „ Beef	10d.
„ „ Tongue	10d.
„ „ Do. & Ham	10d.
„ „ Round of Beef	10d.
Cup of Tea (small)	2½d.
„ „ (large)	3½d.
Pot of Tea (Newly infused) per person	4d.
Slice of Toast	2d.
Buttered Bread or Scone	1½d.
Cakes Various	1½d.
Preserves	1½d.

For HIGH TEAS and LUNCHEONS, see SEPARATE MENUS.

46. Miss Cranston's menu card for 1917, when various war-time restrictions were in force.

carnage dragged on, restrictions were introduced on various items, and difficulties in business began to be felt. The Government's first haphazard measures — voluntary rationing and meatless days in restaurants — were quite inadequate, and cumbersome food orders began to be issued: the cake and pastry order of April 1917, for instance, banned entirely crumpets, muffins and any decorated cake, and imposed a ration of 2 oz. per person on a meal begun between 3 and 6 p.m. The baking and confectionery business, very labour intensive in Scotland with the native penchant for fancy breads, cakes and sweets, was hard hit by shortages both of supplies and labour. It was slow to replace the men who volunteered with female workers, though commended them with apparent surprise where they were tried. Women, whose labour was always crucial to the tea rooms, were less easily exploited now with a whole range of new jobs calling them. Wages generally shot up, and while the price of materials rose their quality simultaneously fell — a trying combination. Businesses started to put up shutters.[28]

Even before the close of the war people were recognising that it marked the end of an era, and that life would never be the same again. On the tea room front this was symbolised by the withdrawal of both Cranstons, whose vigorous personalities had shaped and dominated the whole movement from its beginning forty years before. Stuart retired as managing director of Cranston's Tea Rooms Ltd in 1915, handing over the reins to his long-time right-hand man Robert Cairns. The company dropped 46 Queen St in 1918. Stuart died in 1921.

In 1917 Kate Cranston was still apparently going strong. But late in the year she was shattered by the death of her husband in October 1917. He was eight years younger than she, and the blow was unexpected. As the family biography records, 'They were a most devoted couple who lived for each other and life without her husband was something with which Kate Cranston could never come to terms.' She had leaned on him heavily in business, and clearly she could not face continuing without his support. She was anyway in her sixty-eighth year, and any slide from perfection was intolerable to contemplate. She began to withdraw, selling first Buchanan St, which became briefly a club, then a bank; then the Argyle St Tea Rooms, bought by her tenants Manfield & Sons, shoemakers, in May 1918. The Willow went the next year to the long-established Glasgow restaurateurs John Smith Ltd.[29] Only the Ingram Street premises ran on under the old regime, passing apparently as a gift to Miss Cranston's senior manageress and friend Miss Drummond.

Kate gave up too her lovely house at Nitshill, with its Mackintosh interiors, its gardens and strutting peacocks and fields of Cranston cows, and went to live in the North British Station Hotel, looking onto the site of the hotels where she had been born and grown up, for most of the remainder of her life. She wore black for the rest of her days, still in the style of 'extreme picturesqueness' which had always characterised her. Latterly her memory failed her, according to Hal Stewart, but she could be seen, 'a notable figure, flitting about the streets like some unhappy ghost from a happier time.' She died in April 1934, leaving an estate valued at £67,476: after various bequests[30] a third of the residue went to Stuart's daughter Sybil, and the remaining two thirds to the poor of the City of Glasgow.

But like her biographer, who prefers to remember her as she was when he first knew her, 'dark, petite, and graceful, with a ready wit and a happy smile', we should return to consider Miss Cranston at the height of her powers. The next chapter will be devoted to the famous interiors of her tea rooms, and to some other 'artistic' tea rooms in the tradition she pioneered.

47. A corner of the tea gallery at Miss Cranston's Willow Tea Rooms.

Miss Cranston and the
Artistic Tea Room

'I am reminded of the Londoner whom I took into Miss Cranston's first tea room. He sat down at the dainty appetising table, and exclaimed 'Good Lord!' — as well he might, poor devil, being used to nothing better than the cold marble slabs and canny methods of his London A.B.C. shops.'

This startled tribute from a stranger, here being introduced to the civilised side of Glasgow life by J. J. Bell, captures aptly the effect Miss Cranston and her tea rooms had on people. Glaswegians cherished their remarkable tea rooms with possessive pride and other cities were commonly compared to their disadvantage. As the expatriate artist Muirhead Bone wrote in the late twenties, 'Those Glasgow tea-rooms were things of extraordinary beauty and originality, and one cannot find any restaurants in London to-day comparable with them'.[1]

The southerner would have been flabbergasted not only by the fresh flowers and the quality of the cakes set out on the table, but by the evidence of progressive design all round him. In 1901 a new adjective was overheard on the site of the Exhibition: 'It is so kind o' artistic, ye know, wi' a' that sort o' light paint. Oh, it'll do A1! It's quite Kate Cranstonish!' And according to Neil Munro '"Kate Crantonish" became a term with Glasgow people in general to indicate domestic novelties in buildings and decorations not otherwise easy to define.'[2] The distinctive 'Glasgow Style' brought Miss Cranston fame, and she was in turn its most important single patron, starting at a period when it most needed support in her commissions to the young George Walton, and then to Charles Rennie Mackintosh, whom she continued loyally to use for the next twenty years, through some lean times for the artist. For this she truly, in Pevsner's words, 'deserves the art historian's unstinted gratitude' — as well as that of thousands of ordinary people who had their senses stimulated and horizons enlarged by the experience of interiors 'where everything was "different" and the whole atmosphere was one of gay adventure'.[3]

Although the story naturally focuses on Miss Cranston's commitment to Glasgow's 'new school' from 1896, the connection of tea rooms with 'art interiors' was well established before this. *The Evening News* in 1895 presents this picture of the typical tea room of the previous decade. 'Before the enterprising proprietor got hold of the place it was perhaps a cellar or a stationer's store, but the Artistic Decorator was called in and metamorphosed it in the twinkling of an eye, limning impossible sunflowers all round, touching in the roof with olives, azures, and chromes, and hanging up a Liberty Art fabric or two as curtains. After him, without delay, came

48. Artistic taste in the 1880s: the tea room at Miss Cranston's Ingram St premises, opened in 1886, with aesthetic sunburst on the ceiling, leaded glass, and touches of japonisme.

the Artistic Upholsterer with polished mahogany tables, a score or so of Chippendale and other weird chairs, a couple of luxurious settees; and a stock of buns, cigarettes, tea-boilers, and waitresses having been secured, and a cash-box labelled "Pay Here" fitted up, business was begun'.

Glasgow's restaurants spent money on interior decoration and often hung art on their walls. F. Stuart Bell's restaurant (the Queen Anne on Argyle St) described in 1908 is a good example: 'The walls are lined with crimson canvas, and studded with beautiful works of art, prominent among which we noticed a fine example of Alma-Tadema and two valuable Sam Boughs', while the smoking room to the rear with its stained glass roof was 'tastefully hung with Dutch watercolours'.[4] This tradition was continued by James Craig in later years (p. 140 f.). 'Valuable art' of this kind was mostly intended for male consumption, and where commissioned often followed the titillating classical tradition — as did, one assumes, Christopher Meadows'

15 ft x 9 ft 'The Lady of the Lake' for the back dining room of the Bank Restaurant in 1895. Pettigrew & Stephens' gents' smoking room of the 1920s was in the same line (fig. 100).

The tea rooms however introduced to public spaces a new, intimate, feminine note derived from 'artistic' domestic style at this period. These were years in which women were bombarded by books and magazines instructing them how to transform their homes into havens of comfort and art. Flint's tea rooms described in 1895 are representative of this taste: using oak furniture and 'real Japanese' papers and tapestry, they showed from umbrella-stand to doormat 'the latest improvements', which extended to clothing the attendants in a harmonious colour and design of dress.[5]

Miss Cranston's first modest premises, opened in 1878 at Argyle St, strange as it may seem in retrospect, used dark plush comfy chairs, and antlers over the fireplace for the contemporary baronial touch. The advertisement (fig. 12) for her new tea rooms at 205 Ingram St in 1886 reflects mainstream artistic taste, as does what we know of the decorators used there. By this time the influence of Whistler and the aesthetic movement, with its passion for things Japanese, was making itself felt. 'The painting of the walls and ceiling is of the most artistic charm,' opined *The Bailie*, 'and is altogether in the style of the "flowery land"'.[6] In choosing William Scott Morton, an Edinburgh-based decorator with strong Glasgow connections, to do the interiors at the lunch rooms added at 209 Ingram St in 1888, Miss Cranston was backing a Scottish firm much in vogue in the late 1880s.[7]

Miss Cranston's first interiors, which contributed to the journalist's parody quoted above, were thus in 'good' but not unprecedented taste. But in refurbishing her ten-year-old Crown Tea Rooms for Exhibition year in 1888, Kate turned to a young and largely untested designer working in a more innovative style. George Walton (1867-1933) was the youngest of a large and somewhat impoverished artistic family: his brother E. A. Walton followed his father into painting and became a leading 'Glasgow Boy', and his sisters Constance, Hannah and Helen were successful artists and craft workers. George attended evening classes at the Glasgow School of Art, but he was still slogging away safely as a bank clerk when Miss Cranston approached him.[8] His delicate, Arts-and-Crafts-influenced manner struck a fresh and appropriate new note, feminine yet sophisticated. This job seems to have given Walton the confidence to abandon banking once and for all, and he set up his own business in this year as Geo. Walton and Co., Ecclesiastical and House Decorators. Patronised by the artistic set in which his big brother moved, George soon built up a flourishing business, doing much to promote the emergence of a distinctive 'Glasgow' style of interior decoration which absorbed but was never dominated by English trends.[9]

Miss Cranston's satisfaction with her discovery is evident from work privately commissioned from Walton for her new married home at East Park in Barrhead, which the Cochranes rented from around 1893. But the real

49. A cosy corner in Miss Cranston's first tea rooms, the Crown Tea Rooms, Argyle St, redecorated by George Walton in 1888 with some characteristically tendrilly stencilling.

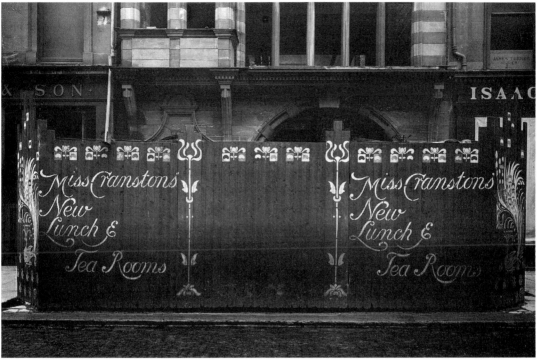

50. The unorthodox hoarding which piqued curiosity outside Miss Cranston's new Buchanan St Tea Rooms in 1896, boldly painted by George Walton.

plum she had to offer was the interior design job for her major tea room development on Buchanan Street in 1896. For this important venture into Glasgow's premier thoroughfare Miss Cranston played safe on the outside, commissioning the established Glasgow-trained but Edinburgh-based architect George Washington Browne, who specialised in banks and prestigious public buildings.[10] The result was a pleasantly revivalist addition to the up-market streetscape, in stripes of red and yellow stone, which won general approval: *The Evening Citizen* for instance thought it 'quaint-looking and artistic', while a visiting English journalist remarked on its 'pretty little gabled front . . . ; it is charmingly detailed in a very refined manner, and the two-storied oriel over the door is an exceedingly picturesque feature, notwithstanding its ugly-shaped pediment.'[11] (See fig. 20.)

This, Miss Cranston's first really big spend, embodied the transition in her tastes, from the conventionally 'artistic' exterior to the 'new art' surprises of the furnishing and decoration. There was advanced warning of originality from the hoarding which shielded the work from curious passers-by, perhaps the earliest hoarding to be given this aesthetic treatment, and a highly effective advertisement.[12] It was painted with a peacock design, acknowledging the powerful influence of Whistler in Glasgow, and the heart-shaped leaves which became a Walton trade-mark. Inside wonderful things were afoot, including something new to the point of weirdness, for it was now that Miss Cranston 'tried out' Mackintosh, just as she had tried out Walton eight years before, on some mural stencilling.

At first sight the middle-aged Kate Cranston with her peculiar fondness for the flounces of yesteryear seems an unlikely patron of some of the most strikingly 'modern' art of its time. But her bizarre personal attire is the key: this remarkable woman knew what she liked and was quite willing to flout convention in pursuit of it. The exceptional work of Mackintosh and three close School of Art friends, Herbert McNair, and Margaret and Frances Macdonald — the Four, as they became known — had become widely notorious in Glasgow at the end of 1894, when their contributions to the G.S.A. Art Club exhibition provoked a rabid reaction. The rumpus increased with a showing of posters in 1895, stirred by a gleeful press, relishing the language of spooks, ghouls and delirium tremens which had become attached to the style, and printing letters from members of the public left frothing by what they had seen.[13] Kate Cranston, with her instinct for something different, was doubtless attracted by this stir, and sympathetically drawn to these confident and unconventional young artists.[14] In 1896, the year in which Mackintosh exhibited at the Arts and Crafts Exhibition in London to more howls of rejection, she calmly handed him a commission which turned the tide of public opinion.

On his generous allocation of bare walls Mackintosh developed in a more decorative manner the arresting style of the recent posters, most notably in the frieze of stately white-robed giantesses schematically entwined in rose bushes and grouped with abstract tree shapes round the walls of the ladies' lunch room. Peacocks, taking a hint from Walton's aesthetic hoarding, together with stylised lollipop trees, were used in the scheme for the general luncheon room, blending well with Walton's elegant furniture. While the technique used was stencilling, there were many variations in detail, though characteristically the shapes and their placing maintained a clear rhythm in the overall design. The stylisation of organic forms towards abstraction went even further in the simple decorations of the smoking gallery. Where the three upper levels on which Mackintosh worked ran round a top-lit stair well towards the back of the building the schemes could be seen more or less together. A care for unity was evident in the alteration of the background colouring from green to 'greyish-greenish yellow' to blue, evoking a transition from earth to sky.

Gleeson White, editor of the immensely influential *Studio* magazine, was evidently excited by the murals when he visited Glasgow to do a piece on the new developments in 1897. He approved this 'honest attempt at novelty', seeing the work as the first notable example of permanent wall decoration evolved through the poster, and commented in detail on it. 'It is just because the means employed for these decorations are so simple compared with the result that it is essential to regard it as a very important enterprise', he says, remarking that as a rule plenty of money but little thought is lavished on the

51. The ladies' lunch room at Buchanan St, with Mackintosh's frieze of white ladies silhouetted against gold suns, and spotted with purple and pink roses.

52. The general lunch room at Buchanan St. Walton designed the elegant
chairs and table-settings, Mackintosh the stencilled wall decoration, which
incorporates a peacock motif.

walls of restaurants. His only cause for pain was the intrusion on the
schemes of some 'extremely irritating' ornamental features deriving from
the architect (whom he tactfully declined to name) — things like stone
coats-of-arms balanced on the bannisters, or a carved Rococo cartouche slap
in the middle of a gable end of the smoking gallery, a costly and superfluous
'eyesore' against the rarefied lines of Mackintosh's curious decorations.[15]

This uncomfortable transition from tradition to modernity within the
building was less noticeable in the areas handled by Walton — his wall
decorations used spriggy and delicate repetitive floral patterning, or elegant
panels of flower vases and fruit baskets, or in the case of the billiard room,
with its apple green panelling, a tapestry style 'medieval' frieze. His chairs
extrapolated traditional designs to new effect, and must have interested
Mackintosh, but even his slenderest high backed chairs were soundly made.
Though the effect of novelty produced by Walton's work should not be
underestimated, it was nevertheless visibly rooted in the Arts and Crafts and

aesthetic movements. Perhaps more importantly Walton was always prepared to adapt his style to its context — while Mackintosh was just as
evidently unwilling to compromise in his urge towards effect and originality.

Mackintosh's upstaging has too easily deprived Walton of his due recognition in the larger perspective of art history, and in particular for Miss
Cranston's first major tea room interiors. Buchanan St in all its careful detail
was very much his creation, apart from the wall areas handled by Mackintosh.[16] It must be said that Gleeson White, recognising Walton's work as
something distinct, planned to give him a separate write-up which would
have helped redress the balance, but he died the year after his first pair of
articles. It was something of a disaster for the 'Glasgow Style' that it lost this
friendly southern patron so early. White, like posterity, was magnetised by
the clear originality of Mackintosh and the Macdonalds and gave them his
first attention, seeing their special need of championship against the note of
ridicule and abuse in the common critical response to their work. So he
chivvied his readers with reminders that each season sees 'some artist
hitherto looked upon as a rebel, admitted into the ranks of "the advanced but
tolerated"'. In the case of Mackintosh he felt emphatically that intimacy with
his work would do the trick: 'when a man has something to say and knows
how to say it, the conversion of others is usually but a question of time'.

In Glasgow conversion to the possibilities of the new style followed hot
upon the opening of the tea rooms on 5 May 1897. *The Bailie* immediately
gave its seal of approval: 'Elegant as the new establishment is as seen from
the street, its interior is no less elegant, the decorations being in excellent
taste, and showing to much effect'. Indeed the press tumbled over itself: 'The
exterior of the pretty building in Buchanan Street with its aesthetic hoarding, has long piqued curiosity as to the opening of Miss Cranston's new
Luncheon and Tea Rooms, but one's highest expectations could not picture
anything more delightful than the reality of the interior'; 'Inside and out
Miss Cranston's new venture is unique ... Handsome, artistic, replete with
every novelty, these elegant rooms may well be numbered among the sights
of the city which no visitor will be justified in omitting'; 'Miss Cranston was
one of the pioneers, and the artistic taste, allied to homely comfort, which is
the characteristic of her other establishments, has been developed to a
remarkable degree in her new Rooms in Buchanan Street. Neither expense
nor ingenuity has been spared to make them one of the sights of the city'.[17]
The completeness of the effect was bewitching, as *St Mungo's* more pointed
reaction reveals: 'The latest addition to Glasgow's tea-rooms has all the
aesthetic wrinkles brought to perfection. The male attendants are clothed in
vestments of quaint and soothing design, the man who works the elevator
being a veritable poem. Even the spoons are fashioned upon a pattern that
will thrill with ecstasy the souls of the willow-pattern and sunflower
brigade.'[18]

The trade gave its own accolade: the *British Baker and Confectioner*
advised 'Everything in these Rooms, from the chairs to the china, bears the

impress of thought. Any member of the trade desirous of fitting up new luncheon and tea rooms would find the expense of railway fares to Glasgow amply repaid by the instruction derived from an inspection of *Miss Cranston's* premises'. The architectural press was less interested, apart from the *Studio's* keen approval, noticed already. But here is a nice informal tribute from the young architect Edwin Lutyens, in language which is a sensitive gauge of the extent to which Glasgow was in advance of even the progressive elements south of the border.

He was taken along in June by James Guthrie of J. & W. Guthrie, who presumably wished to show off his firm's work on the Mackintosh murals, 'to a Miss Somebody's who is really a Mrs Somebody else. She has started a large Restaurant, all very elaborately simple on very new school High Art Lines. The result is gorgeous! and a wee bit vulgar! She has nothing but green handled knives and all is curiously painted and coloured... Some of the knives are purple and are put as spots of colour! It is all quite good, all just a little outré, a thing we must avoid and shall too.' Lutyens, besotted with his forthcoming marriage to Lady Emily Lytton, was spending most of his spare time planning the marital home, and later accounts of its decoration show that elements of what he saw — including green-handled knives — found their way deep into his own work. On this visit he fell for Miss Cranston's 'most delicious blue willow pattern sets of china ware' and she generously made him up a set.

When Lutyens passed through Glasgow again the following June he returned for a wonderful breakfast (see p. 52) and further extravagant meditation on the interiors: 'Green, golds, blues, white rooms with black furniture, black rooms with white furniture, where Whistler is worshipped and Degas tolerated, Rodin ... admired for the love of oddity, sometimes called originality'. Walton's billiard room 'all clever and original' particularly absorbed him as he tried to fathom its influences, beginning with Egypt and travelling widely: 'There is tradition of every country and I believe planet! of the universe — yet 'tis all one.' His conclusion succinctly identifies Miss Cranston's unique and mutually beneficial combination of art, quality and value: 'So I am much amused and greatly entertained. The food! etc. at a third the cost and three times better than the ordinary hotel, and the surroundings full of space for fancy and amusement.'[19]

Miss Cranston's bold patronage of her young designers was perfectly calculated: it brought immediate 'sight of the city' status, and it is clear that respect for her business capacities was extended to respect for her tastes. After all this exhilarating 'uniqueness' was just the thing for tea rooms, where gazing around and assessing the decor was an important conversational standby. One can imagine the witty speculations on Mackintosh's 'greet white wummen', and in this context his work evidently went down very well, though the general tone of stabilising elegance which Walton provided was important. Glaswegians were soon proud of their special institution. By 1901 'J. H. Muir' could say 'It is believed (and averred) that

53. The billiard room at Buchanan St designed by George Walton. The startling fireplace and chairs use the flattened heart shape he liked. Through the doorway is the smoking gallery decorated by Mackintosh, with one of the architect's obtrusive baronial lumps on the stair.

in no other town can you see in a place of refreshment such ingenious and beautiful decoration in the style of the new art as in Miss Cranston's shop in Buchanan Street.' Art critics might still fume about 'the delirious phantasies' of the 'Scotto-Continental New Art', but Miss Cranston had made a major contribution to a breakthrough in taste.

The same design partnership, with Mackintosh as George Walton's junior, was set to work on Miss Cranston's next big project, to expand into the entire building at 114 Argyle St. This was presumably again at Miss Cranston's instigation. The relationship between the two designers is inscrutable: both were committed to perfection, and to the notion that every detail of an interior should receive creative attention, but they were temperamentally very different and must surely have found it difficult to share interiors. Walton, quiet and gentle on the surface, and more matter-of-fact about the commercial aspects of his art, nevertheless felt things strongly. When years afterwards both men were living in London they had no contact, and Mackintosh's name was allegedly never mentioned in the Walton household.

Work on Argyle St was not far behind Buchanan St and the new rooms opened in the autumn of 1897, another addition to the tourist map: *à propos* of the visit to Glasgow at the end of November of the eminent artist Walter Crane, *St Mungo* proposed that 'Walter should have coffee amid the weirdry of Miss Cranston's new tea howff. I will be pleased to hear from him afterwards.'[20] The 'deal' on the commission seems to have been done in tandem with Buchanan St, for while Mackintosh was there given a share of the mural decoration, at Argyle St he did a number of light fittings[21] and all the movable furniture, another major challenge which produced the first high-backed 'Mackintosh chair'.[22] However the lion's share of the work remained to the trusted Walton, since this time the

54. Exterior of the remodelled building at 114 Argyle St, opened in 1897, where Miss Cranston first began in 1878 beneath a Temperance Hotel.

55. One end of the billiard and smoking room at Argyle St, showing Walton's decorative stencilling on the beams and walls, and a striking fireplace design.

architect's hand was kept out of the interior and Walton had all the fire-places, doors, screens and so on to manage, as well as the general decor.

The brief was to reconstruct 'from the most commonplace of buildings, rooms to suit the most modern requirements and the most artistic tastes'.[23] David Barclay of H. & D. Barclay, a firm specialising in school buildings, was perhaps chosen to reflect Miss Cranston's increasingly austere tastes, as well as the less up-market location, after her experience with the lavish Washington Browne. The facelift job was very thorough: the front of the old tenement hotel was shaved of its mouldings, then rough-cast. Gables and dormers to the street and a quaint red-tiled turret behind were applied to create a fancy 'Belgian-like' effect. There were two entrances, a shop-front and a passage through to the tower (in Morrison's Court) which gave separate access to the different levels: men could thus bolt to and from the masculine haven of smoking, billiard and reading rooms on the second floor without inconvenience. The interior was gutted and left as a series of bare low interconnected rooms lit by regular windows, with prominent beams and central aisles of plain pillars.

In this scheme where Mackintosh's contribution was more pervasive his tendency to self-assertiveness is again noticeable. His designs were very strong, all in oak, mostly stained dark, relieved only by the simplest cut-out shapes, curved panels and subtle taperings. The furniture was mostly four-square and heavy to move about, a nuisance for those who had to sweep up the crumbs, but it was solidly made, and has lasted better than some of Mackintosh's later designs. Its 'masculine' strength was appropriate to the smoking room, where it nevertheless seems at odds with the dainty, spotty style of Walton's stencilling and his characteristic use of gathered fabric in

56. The lunch room at Argyle St, with screens and decoration by Walton. Mackintosh's tall chairs can dimly be seen standing sentinel at the tables.

the panelling. One feels that the result would have been better if one or other of the designers had had complete control. The lunch room shows more collaboration, with Mackintosh's excellent slat-backed chairs relating well to Walton's plain panelling and screens with vertical insets of stencilled decoration. Perhaps, as Roger Billcliffe suggests, it was a desire to dominate Walton's rather strong room divisions that led Mackintosh to design the first of his revolutionary high-backed chairs. He was evidently pleased with the effect, which achieved the clear spatial definition he always sought, and used these chairs in his own dining room.[24]

It is difficult not to be seduced by hindsight and talk first about Mackintosh. Again the overall effect owed most to Walton: his airy, repetitive wall patternings suffused the whole interior with an element of prettiness not found in the furniture, breaking away from the Victorian furnishing conventions which decreed dark sober colours and materials for male areas (which included dining rooms), keeping lightness and patterning for female preserves. It was Walton's work which confirmed the feminine, domestic style of the artistic tea room. Fireplaces often attracted his most original and effective ideas — note for instance the enormous baubles in the Argyle St smoking room. On this job Walton also made notable use of stained glass, combined in a new and effective way with beaten copper, in several excellent door designs. His luscious Eros panel (pieced together from green marble, slate, coloured glass, mother-of-pearl and the like) at the end of the lunch room was typical of Walton's widely liked decorative work; it was later duplicated for a commission in York. He also handled the shop

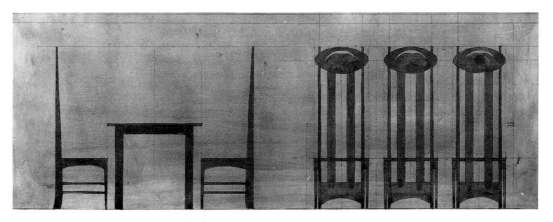

57. Mackintosh's design for the first of his famous high-backed chairs, 1896.

entrance with its wrought iron and repoussé copper fittings to great effect. Even the staircase in the turret, where simple designs were stamped into the wet plaster, shows traces of his inventiveness.

Indeed Walton's career was flourishing: in 1896 he was also commissioned by Rowntree's in Scarborough to decorate their Westborough Street Tea Rooms,[25] spreading the new tea room style to England, and there followed enough work to justify opening a branch of his firm in York. In 1897 Walton made a fruitful friendship with Kodak's European sales manager, George Davison, which led to the redesigning of Kodak's shops throughout Europe. Success beckoned him south, like other talented Glaswegians, and he moved to London: he had married a Londoner in 1891 and his brother had moved there in 1893. His firm retained a branch in Glasgow until 1905, and could still have executed commissions for Miss Cranston, but although she showed her confidence by investing £100 in Walton's company in 1897, she now put all her work in the direction of Mackintosh. Evidently she judged that he had proved himself in his trials under Walton, and probably felt that he was more in need of her support: Walton's individual but attractive version of advanced style, comparable with the work of such as Voysey and Baillie Scott in England, was clearly saleable. Her own instinct for keeping ahead of the competition, together with pleasure in using her money for patronage of this kind, turned her to Mackintosh.[26] He who truly felt the need to control all parts of a job must have rejoiced to be given sole charge, as first happened when Miss Cranston turned her attention to expansion and alterations at Ingram Street in 1900.

1900 was an eventful year for Mackintosh, for it saw his marriage in August to Margaret Macdonald, preceded by a burst of creativity in the furnishing of their new home at 120 Mains St; while later in the year his breakthrough to recognition on the continent was enforced by the brilliant showing of the Four at the Exhibition of the Vienna Secession, which he and Margaret visited to rapturous acclaim from young admirers.[27] The

58. The White Room at Ingram St, designed by Mackintosh in 1900. The gesso panel executed by Margaret Macdonald can be seen top right.

formalising of this important creative partnership was celebrated in Mackintosh's new White Room at Ingram Street, where they made two large gesso panels, 'The May Queen' (Margaret) and 'The Wassail' (Mackintosh), to face each other at the ends of the apartment. 'We are working them together and that makes the work very pleasant', wrote Mackintosh to Muthesius.[28] They also each worked a beaten silvered lead panel to go with the friezes, in another symbolic act of union.

Margaret's ideas were clearly fused with Mackintosh's at this period, which saw some of the couple's most successful work, including the designs for the 'House of an Art-Lover' competition. For some critics this has been a remarkably emotive issue: Margaret has come in for some venomous comment as a spoiler of Mackintosh's art, driving it temporarily down a road to trivial over-prettiness, though recent champions have reversed this tendency to denigration.[29] Although after marriage, as convention demanded, Margaret to a great extent pooled her identity with her husband's, she was an independently gifted artist; and theirs was an unusually deep and

59. Detail from a beaten lead panel worked for Ingram St by Margaret Macdonald, Mackintosh's 'muse', shortly before their marriage in 1900. Mackintosh did a matching piece.

supportive relationship, the closer for being childless. But many admirers of what they apprehend as Mackintosh's isolated genius have felt a need to protect it from all charges of 'lower' influence. Unfortunately Margaret is available to embody the invidious old opposition between 'masculine' architecture (pure, reasoned, essential) and 'feminine' decorative art (distracting, trivial, superficial).[30] But it was precisely its feminine quality that made 'Glasgow Style' design, to which women's contribution overall was very important,[31] so appropriate for domestic interiors and by extension the new kind of tea room. However Margaret's work is rated her importance as a source of inspiration to Mackintosh cannot be denied: his alleged remark that 'he had talent, Margaret had genius' is well known.

There is little evidence of any contamination at Ingram Street, rather an assured and delightful expression of Mackintosh's capacities in all fields: the thoughtful architectural management of given spaces, furniture design, decorative stencilling, leaded glass and metal-work. This was the longest surviving of Miss Cranston's tea rooms, not abandoned for restaurant use until 1950. There are sadly not many contemporary photographs, though some desolate pictures of the interior before final dismantling in 1971 add to the record of detail. Mackintosh's subterranean billiard room, appropriately masculine with dark stained panelling relieved by simply stencilled squares, and rush-seated settles, was judged 'a great success' and 'distinctly artistic'.[32] He also revamped one of the earlier rooms with stencilling of perfect elegance and new screens (he returned to do a more thorough job here in 1911). But his main work was in the new White Luncheon Room, with ladies' dressing room attached.

White paint was something Mackintosh had been using increasingly since his first white bedroom at Westdel in 1898 — notably in his own beautiful Mains St flat. At Ingram St the white enamelled paintwork was appropriate to an area intended mainly for female use, and enhanced the airy lightness of the apartment, with its high ceiling and large window area. The height allowed a mezzanine balcony along the back of the room,

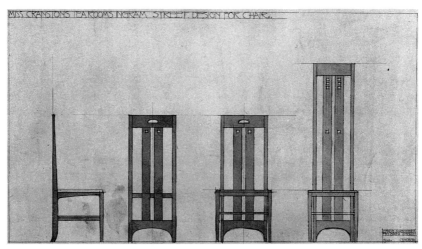

60. Design by Mackintosh for the chair used at Ingram St, in a standard and high-backed version. Some were later cut down for the new Cloister Room.

exploited by Mackintosh for spatial and social interest. For the furniture however Mackintosh kept to the strong dark-stained oak style established at Argyle St. The handsome chair with its back splats extended below the seat is clearly related to the Argyle St design: it also came in an astonishingly high-backed version, one of which Mackintosh did paint white for his own drawing room. The chairs were stronger in visual impact than fact, as the splats were not connected to the back of the seat — until many were screwed together for first aid in later years. The simple pierced square decoration was another motif Mackintosh was currently using: it reappears on cutlery perhaps designed for Ingram St. Many other details show his increasing fascination with the square, often used as a retaining frame for abstracted organic shapes, as in the leaded glass panels of the screen. The rich effect of coloured glass insets, perhaps influenced by Walton, was exploited in small squares of varied designs let into the balcony panelling. Stylised 'Glasgow rose' trees stencilled on the balcony wall were the only really 'pretty' decorative element, anticipating the rose fixation, attributed to Margaret's romantic influence, of designs of the next two years. An enormous lead-covered fireplace was another feature of the White Room which has lodged in many memories.

By the second Exhibition of 1901 it was natural that Miss Cranston should take a prominent place in catering. Who designed her Tea House is a a mystery: its front bore some stencilling in the Glasgow manner, and according to Neil Munro its 'architectural and decorative innovations created a sensation even among continental visitors'.[33] The decorative work at least is likely to have been by Mackintosh, though there are no surviving drawings. Both he and Walton were adept at producing striking effects with simple cheap materials — like the brown wrapping paper which Mackintosh used in his own dining room — and their style was eminently suitable for exhibition use. Exhibition premises were an important showcase for city-centre businesses, as Flint's also recognised in spending on their Exhibition tea room: with its clean lines, white finish and stencilled decoration it also attracted approving critical comment.[34]

With Glasgow showing itself to the world this is the point to interrupt the emphasis on Miss Cranston and consider some imitators. Though none wished or dared to go so far as to employ Mackintosh, 'artistic' is a word almost universally used of new restaurant decor at this period. Word had spread of the association of the Glasgow tea rooms with the New Art movement, and a full illustrated article appeared in the *Builder's Journal* of 1903.[35] Commenting on the extraordinary number of tea rooms in Glasgow, the author found them generally 'as interesting from an artistic and architectural point of view as they are useful'. They often tested productively an architect's ingenuity and ability to produce effect on a low budget.

Miss Cranston's adoption of the new school style is approvingly detailed; but the article begins with the reconstruction executed for Mrs Schiller, who had been operating for some years in what was originally the basement of a three-storey dwelling house in West Campbell St. The architect W. G. Rowan, known chiefly for his work on churches, referred apologetically to this sort of thing as 'bill-poster architecture'. A new doorway in ivory-painted wood, stencilled with thistle and rose, brightened and drew attention to the street entrance, while homely yet elegant simplicity was the

61. Mrs Schiller's Tea Rooms in West Campbell St, revamped inside and out by W. G. Rowan *c.* 1901.

hallmark within. The luncheon room and ladies' room were unified by the use of stylised tree and bird friezes, though in differing designs, and light bentwood chairs. Sturdier rush-seated chairs and darker colouring were applied to the masculine preserve of the smoking room, with a Persian-tapestry-effect frieze. A chic tapering line appears throughout the designs, in the wooden casing applied to the cast iron columns supporting the ceiling, in the panelling and the table-legs. An elongated chequer decoration on the beams of the luncheon room (perhaps picked up from Walton) was another smart touch.

Next mentioned were the Old Oak Tea Rooms opened in 1902 in one of Glasgow's best known buildings, the remarkable ten-storey 'Hatrack' at 144 St Vincent St: this was built by the young James Salmon, 'the wee Troot', a friend of Mackintosh and exponent of the Art Nouveau in Glasgow architecture. The large general luncheon room occupied the whole depth of the building, lit by an oriel at the front, and from a well at the back. Ingle nooks and 'upwards of seventy' old oak chairs, settles and cabinets evoked the olde-worldiness currently favoured in the English tradition. But the stencilled decoration in delicate colouring and the pronounced capitals of the columns — 'modern in detail' but 'Byzantine in feeling' — lent a distinctive atmosphere to the whole. The Regent Tea Rooms were also built into a new office block, by Burnet, Boston and Carruthers, and were likewise

62. Miss Schofield's antique-style 'An Old Oak Tea Room', opened in 1902.

An Old Oak Tea Room,
142ᴬ St Vincent Street.

63. 'Art' fireplace at the Regent Tea Rooms with Delft tiles and characteristic wall stencilling .

fitted throughout in oak, currently fashionable and appropriate to the predominantly masculine use of the rooms. The general luncheon room was the largest, with two contemporary fireplaces using delft tiles and painted panels in typical 'Glasgow Boys' style.

The article appeared before the opening of the Willow Tea Rooms on Sauchiehall St in November 1903, considered then and now the *tour de force* of Mackintosh's partnership with Miss Cranston. Here at last he controlled the structure as well as every detail of the interior decoration, and the effect was quite simply stunning. The Mackintoshes' current preoccupations — Margaret was obviously closely involved — were perfectly suited to the clientèle for these tea rooms, fashionable and largely female. Here is *The Bailie's* greeting: 'Hitherto Miss Cranston has been famous for the daintily artistical character of her several establishments. However her new establishment fairly outshines all others in the matters of arrangement and colour. The furnishing, besides, is of the richest and most luxurious character. Indeed Miss Cranston has carried the question of comfort fairly into that of luxury, when providing for the enjoyment of her friends and patrons. Her "Salon de Luxe" on the first floor is simply a marvel of the art of the upholsterer and decorator. And not less admirable, each in its own way, are the tea-gallery, the lunch-rooms, the billiard-room, and the smoking room.'[36]

64. Elegant hoarding designed by Mackintosh to cloak the construction of the
new Willow Tea Rooms on Sauchiehall St in 1903.

65. The Willow revealed. The long window of the Room de Luxe stretches above the lattice-paned shop front. The rooms were opened in November 1903.

The site was not unlike that in Buchanan St, a house-size plot between flanking buildings, tenements surviving from the residential use of this part of Sauchiehall St; but seven years later the result was very different. Mackintosh's sparkling little building is cut in half horizontally, the shallow curves of its front disobeying the rules of Glasgow street architecture without entirely ignoring the neighbouring buildings. The decoration of its face, with smart chequered edging and elegant looping ironwork announced again the combination of austere square with abstracted organic shapes which was currently so fruitful for Mackintosh. The motif of the willow lay ready to hand in the name of Sauchiehall Street, which means 'alley of willows', and appealed to Mackintosh's — and especially Margaret's — penchant for symbolism.

On entering customers were passed, just as at Ingram St, behind a white painted screen inset with leaded glass panels to the central cash desk and a choice of moves — into the tea room at the front or lunch room at the back of the ground floor, up the stairs to the tea gallery, built round a well over the back saloon, or to the Room de Luxe overlooking the street on the first floor, or further up to the male domain of billiard and smoke rooms on the second floor. The back saloon with tea gallery above was contained in a low extension to the rear of the building. It was open to the front saloon, the transition marked by a curious sculptural structure around an enormous flower bowl, suspended over two tables, and by the order desk for which Mackintosh designed in 1905 a high semi-circular chair. The staircase connecting the ground floor and the tea gallery was open too, screened by rods and dangling glass shapes. This distinctly modern interpenetration of related yet distinct spaces can never be fully captured in photographs, though Annan made a fine attempt at it.[37] The further visual interest of animated Edwardian figures glimpsed from different angles must be supplied by the imagination.

The front tea room was painted white, with dark-stained chairs, as at Ingram St. Its main decorative feature was a series of strange plaster relief panels, set in a frieze on the side walls. These can be decoded in terms of the willow's long oval leaves and whippy branches, but their transformation by abstraction went far towards modernism, as did Margaret's embroidery on the blowy curtains. The original panel designs show roses crammed over the top, a 'Margaretish' feature expunged from the final work. Indeed while the splendidly excessive Room de Luxe captured the precious, 'feminine' note of some recent Mackintosh designs, there was otherwise a certain turning back to austerity. Public tea-room usage of course demanded some sturdiness in the furniture — though Mackintosh achieved this more in effect than fact. The front saloon chair, with its curved rungs from top to floor, took the

66. *Opposite.* The great flower bowl marking the transition from front saloon to the back saloon beyond. The tall semi-circular order-desk chair can be seen, and the open-screened stairs leading to the tea gallery and upper floors.

67. The front tea room at the Willow, showing the plaster frieze panels and the screen behind which customers passed on entry. The table is set for tea.

68. The back saloon, a lunch room, with light falling from the central well of the tea gallery. The careful arrangement of furniture and the patterning on the carpet echoes the architectural structure of the room.

traditional ladderback to a new finality, but with a loss of traditional strength: the chairs were all later braced across the top. This was the basic chair for the three connected areas, contrasted in the back saloon and gallery above with a very boxy, smooth low arm-chair. Originally designed with sides sloping inwards at the bottom, it was modified between the drawing board and the cabinet maker's bench to make it less surprising but stronger.

The decor of these spaces was also related, though the effect was subtly different. In contrast to the white, light front room for ladies' tea, the back, for the service of more substantial food, was darker, with grey canvas panels on the walls, relieved by pairs of stencilled ladies peeping from behind enormous cabbage roses, a design which half-closed eyes can stylise into tall Mackintosh flower vases. Light here filtered down through the well from the overhead roof-lights and windows lighting the tea gallery. This upper area, a general tea room, was much lighter, panelled again in a pink and grey scheme with simple large stencilled roses and a ladder trellis motif which echoed the backs of the chairs.

69. The Room de Luxe, laid for lunch. Eight high-backed chairs stood at the centre tables. The carpet design echoes the formality of the room.

The Room de Luxe was — and is, for it has been restored to use as a tea room — something different, sumptuously extravagant and sophisticated. One wall is taken up by a long, low, slightly bay window looking over the street, set with a design in mirror glass; round the others runs a frieze of leaded panels of mirror, purple and white glass reflecting light, chairs and customers. The walls were originally lined with pale purple silk stitched with beads beneath the frieze. A pair of gorgeous glittering doors broke the side opposite the window, while the centrepieces of the other two walls were a fireplace, and opposite, in a matching frame, a panel by Margaret in a medium in which she excelled: gesso laid over string and set with glass jewels and beads, to give a richly textured finish. The panel, inspired by lines from a D. G. Rossetti sonnet, drew on the plangent associations of the willow, and the romantic imagery preoccupying Margaret, who had moved away from her 'spook-school' style by the time of her marriage. The chairs,

70. The chandelier of rose-coloured glass baubles which bewitched many young customers in the Room de Luxe.

astonishingly painted silver and upholstered like the fitted seating in purple velvet, came in two designs: a smaller chair with an elegant ogee curve to its back, used round the outside of the room, and dominating the centre, a set of eight of the famous high-backed designs. These were related to the recent white chairs, but substituted decoration of chaste squares of purple glass and ovals for organic shapes. The tables too, unusually, were decoratively embellished, with cloths trimmed short to show off the detail on their legs. And as a finishing touch from the ceiling hung a chandelier of dangling pink glass baubles, 'absolutely perfectly beautiful' to young eyes.[38]

The room was conceived as a select 'ladies' room, with a dressing room adjacent; and as something special. Its 'luxe' cost you an extra penny on a cup of tea. Miss Cranston's capital investment in the fittings was significant, though the sums are amusing in the light of their value today. Each of the fifty-eight leaded glass panels had cost £1. The eight high-backed chairs were £2 16s 0d apiece, the smaller ones (of which there were thirty four) a shilling less — this compared with 17s 6d for the ladderbacks (one hundred and thirty seven of them), while the fifty boxy armchairs were 18s 6d each.

Kate was quite prepared to go over the top to establish that she was *sui generis*. There were many who laughed at the result, or said tartly that it was 'not their cup of tea'; but after all the people came. And the amusement was unmistakably tempered with admiration. Neil Munro catches this note perfectly when he exposes two ordinary Glaswegians to the Willow in one of the 'Erchie' pieces he wrote originally for *The Evening News*: 'Erchie in an art tea-room'. Extracts put Mackintosh's decor in an entertaining contemporary perspective.

The hero tells how he met Duffy, a coalman in his Sunday best, flush with £3 10s insurance money for a dead horse, and deflected him from his path to a pub to 'thon new tea-room wi' the comic windows'. 'When we came fornent it, he glowered, and "Michty!" says he, "wha did this?" "Miss Cranston," says I, "Was she tryin'?" says Duffy. "She took baith hands to't," I tellt him. "And a gey smert wumman, too if ye ask me." He stood five meenutes afore I could get him in, wi' his een glued on the fancy doors.'

Overcoming Duffy's attempt to escape on the grounds that he wasn't well enough dressed, Erchie got him through the door, cap in hand. 'He gave the wan look roond him, and put his hand in his pooch to feel his money ... "It'll cost ye nae mair than the Mull o' Kintyre Vaults," I tellt him, and we began sclimmin' the stairs. Between every rail there was a piece o' gless like the bottom o' a soda-water bottle, hangin' on a wire; Duffy touched every yin o' them for luck. "Whit dae ye think o' that, noo?" I asked him. "It's gey fancy," says Duffy; "will we be lang?"'

Even the suave Erchie was a little overwhelmed: 'I may tell ye I was a wee bit put aboot mysel', though I'm a waiter by tred, and seen mony a dydo in my time. There was naething in the hale place was the way I was accustomed to; the very snecks o' the doors were kind o' contrary. "This way for the threepenny cups and the guid bargains," says I to Duffy, and I lands him into whit they ca' the Room de Looks ... There's whit Jinnet ca's insertion on the table-cloths, and wee beeds stitched a' ower the wa's ... The chairs is no' like any other chairs ever I clapped eyes on, but ye could easy guess they were chairs; and a' roond the place there's a lump o' lookin'-gless wi' purple leeks pented on it every noo and then. The gasalier in the middle was the thing that stunned me. It's hung a' roond wi' hunners o' big gless bools, the size o' yer nief ...

Duffy could only speak in whispers. "My Jove!" says he, "ye'll no' get smokin' here, I'll bate." "Smokin'!" says I; "ye micht as weel talk o' gowfin'." "I never in a' my life saw the like o't afore. This cows a'!" says he, quite nervous and frichtened lookin'.'

Something of Duffy's spirit returns as he eyes one of the comely waitresses (dressed by Mackintosh in white with chokers of large pink beads round their necks) approaching for their order. '"It'll likely be the Room de Good Looks," says he ... "I'm for a pie and a bottle o' Broon Robin." "Ye'll get naething o' the kind. Ye'll jist tak' tea, and stretch yer hand like a Christian for ony pastry ye want," said I, and Duffy did it like a lamb ... It was a real divert. It was the first time ever he had a knife and fork to eat cookies wi', and he thocht his teaspoon was a' bashed oot o' its richt shape till I tellt him that was whit made it Art. "Art," says he, "whit the mischief's Art?"' (Erchie then describes how Art broke out in his own home, and how it's now 'ragin' a' ower the place'.)

At this point Duffy repeats his wish for a pie. '"Ye'll get a pie then", I tellt him, "but ye canna expect it here; a pie's no' becomin' enough for the Room de Looks. Them's no chairs for a coalman to sit on eatin' pies." We went

71. Fresh roses and two of Miss Cranston's special waitresses in Duffie's 'Room de Good Looks': their dresses and chokers were designed by Mackintosh.

doon the stair then and I edged him into the solid meat department' (the back saloon). Erchie then describes the novel system of ordering food from the basement kitchen by means of colour-coded balls popped down a pipe. This was another source of wonderment to Duffy, but as Erchie continues "That's Art. ye can hae yer pie frae the kitchen withoot them yellin' doon a pipe for't and lettin' a' the ither customers ken whit ye want." When the pie cam' up, it was jist the shape o' an ordinary pie, wi' nae beads nor onything Art aboot it, and Duffy cheered up at that, and said he enjoyed his tea.'

After the Willow Kate expressed her appreciation of Mackintosh's work, just as she had of Walton's, with a substantial private commission: he was asked to decorate and to a great extent furnish the Cochrane's new mansion home, Hous'hill. There was some pre-existing furniture — including a Hepplewhite dining suite — to contend with, but this was an important job, showing Mackintosh's maturing domestic style moving further towards square-lattice-based simplicity.

He was recalled to the tea rooms early in 1906, to transform the basement at Argyle Street into 'The Dutch Kitchen'. This prompted another

72. Mackintosh's Dutch Kitchen at Argyle St, with the inglenook on the right.

article in the *Studio*, with the opening line 'Nowhere has the modern movement in art been entered upon more seriously than at Glasgow'.[39] Mackintosh's reference to the quaint concept was a delft-tiled fire place with rack for decorative plates above, and a large fake inglenook area.[40] But no Dutch kitchen was ever so smart and sophisticated. Mackintosh was well into his black-and-white-squares phase. The ceiling of this dark apartment was black, and gleaming black columns half screened the ingle. The floor was covered in stout chequered lino, traditionally woven in diamonds but laid at Mackintosh's behest on the cross to make squares, with smaller ceramic chequers on the diagonal to mark off the ingleneuk area. The dado was in tiny velvety checks, the walls white above. More vibrant chequers defined the square supporting pillars, and mother-of-pearl squares were set into the simple dresser. To all this black and white, sparkling under scantily shaded electric light, Mackintosh added a further dazzling touch: the chairs, a satisfyingly homely Windsor design — so normal that only one has been recently identified — were painted a strong emerald green. The only other touch of colour and survivor of organic motifs was a little pink in the weeping rose detail of the attractive leaded windows filtering light from the street grate above. Niches for the flower arrangements so characteristic of Miss Cranston's tea rooms made further points of relief. The result was pure urban chic, despite its allusion to the antique country style now established as a tea room norm. The modernity of the effect is noticeable in comparison with the rooms upstairs where Mackintosh had worked with Walton a decade ago, though his furniture design is now more traditional.

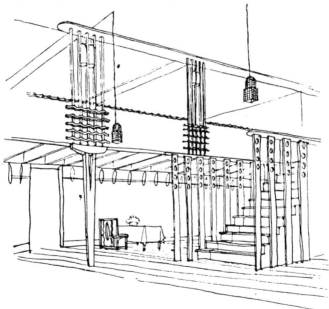

73. The Oak Room at Ingram St sketched by the young Hugh Casson in 1935 when it was operated by Cooper & Co.

Something similar can be discerned in Mackintosh's next project for Kate. In 1907 the 'Oak Room' was made on the ground floor of newly acquired premises forming an extension at Ingram St on the corner with Miller St. A ladies' cloakroom and an additional billiard room beneath were added at the same time. The Oak Room has much in common with the library, generally perceived as Mackintosh's masterwork, designed later this year for the School of Art, in a new style eschewing organic decoration for effects arising austerely from structure and spatial manipulation. At Ingram St Mackintosh was presented with a difficult long, tall, narrow space, and treated it again with a balcony around three sides. Decoration was of the simplest — squares of blue glass in the open screen of the staircase, and blue ceramic tiles round the serving hatch; cut-out or inlaid ovals; a wavy lath applied over upright ribs to make a series of lattice panels on the front of the balcony.

The new interest in wavy lines recurs in the back splats of a striking low chair of which sixteen were made for this room, and in a simple little dresser. Dark oak was used throughout. The main chair identified by Billcliffe is again traditional in concept and unusually strong, with its back sloping away from the bolt uprightness characteristic of Mackintosh's earlier designs. The chamfering of the back rails is another traditional detail which reappears as a decorative device in the G.S.A. library.

After the completion of the West Wing of the School of Art, work began to peter out for Mackintosh, and Miss Cranston's continuing commissions were doubly important. In 1909 he designed a card room at Hous'hill and two new rooms at Ingram St. Mackintosh's ingenuity was again tested with a most awkward space, a thin rectangular area adjacent to the Oak Room. His complex solution, based on the oval, with elements recalling Miss Cranston's own music room, is well described by Billcliffe.[41] Below was a rest room for 'business ladies', with two couches for those who needed to get their feet up. Supported above it, as a kind of mezzanine floor on free-standing pillars, was the Oval Room, an additional tea room area opening off the Oak Room gallery. Two carpets designed early in 1910 measured 19 ft 6 in. x 4 ft 6 in.: with wavy lines overlaid on checks for the Rest Room, and an oval design on checks for the Oval Room, they anticipated 'modernist' post-war design. Sadly the only photographs of these rooms show the bare interiors in miserable condition before dismantling in 1971.

The ladies' rest room was advertised on a menu card designed by Jessie Marion King, which brings us to the subject of Miss Cranston's commissions to women artists. These reflect the convention which tended to restrict women's capacity to make a living from their art to graphic and decorative work. Jessie King, the most successful female 'Glasgow Style' artist, well known as an illustrator and jewellery and pottery designer, did at least four designs for Miss Cranston, featuring variously aesthetic girls.[42] Margaret Macdonald, as we have seen, contributed decorative panels to her husband's tea room schemes, and we know of at least one menu, a striking design recalling elements of the Dutch Kitchen with its sophisticated black and white chequers and strong spots of red and green. This was for the White Cockade, one of Miss Cranston's tea rooms at the 1911 Scottish Exhibition; with admirable even-handedness Kate asked Frances Macdonald to do the card for the other.

74 and 75. Designs by Jessie King for the back and front of menu cards for Miss Cranston, *c.* 1911 and *c.* 1913. Two earlier designs are also known.

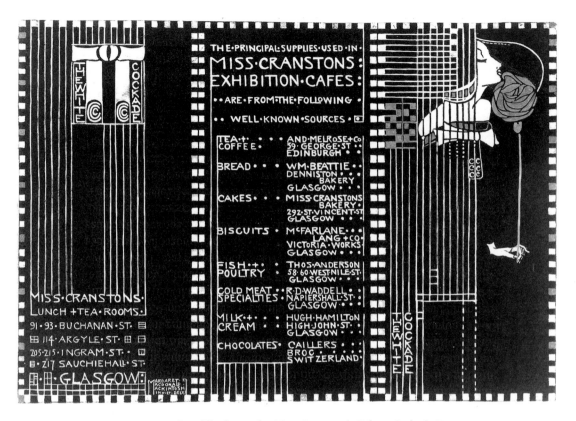

76. Margaret Macdonald's design for Miss Cranston's White Cockade Tea Room at the 1911 Exhibition. Note that Miss Cranston did not buy her brother's tea!

With the 1911 Exhibition marking another break-point we should glance at two new artistic tea rooms established towards the end of the Edwardian years. Jessie King was involved through the Scottish Guild of Handicrafts with the Arcadian Gallery, and designed a card for it (p. 65). Later called the Arcadian Vegetarian or Food Reform Café, this was a relatively short-lived attempt (1907-1912) to unite progressive eating with purchasable progressive art. The 'soothing' interior designed by another member of the Guild, the artist Henry T. Wyse, borrowed Walton-Mackintosh style — brown paper on the walls, a good background for the display of pictures, up to the continuous shelf for the display of art pottery, with a light-coloured frieze above, and white woodwork.[43] The Allander pottery contributed crockery. When Rose Rombach began business on her own account in 1910 (see p. 67), her version of Miss Cranston's style was more 'Viennese' in flavour, as befitted the German side of her background. The effect was 'less outré' than Miss Cranston's, but very striking, with beautiful brass wall fittings, fine leaded glass in pinks and greens in the office

MENU : MENU :

MISS ROMBACH

·LUNCH· ·AND·TEA· ROOMS··

5 WATERLOO ST.
75 & 79 HOPE ST.
GLASGOW 1

5 WATERLOO ST.
GLASGOW 1

CATERERS
FOR SOCIAL FUNCTIONS

ESTIMATES
ON APPLICATION

TELEPHONE
CENTRAL 4681

77. Stylish menu card for Miss Rombach, who opened her sub-Mackintosh tea rooms in 1910.

screen, and smart black and white china. Her first name provided the deep rose-pink of the scrim on the walls and her 'logo' — a flat dog rose, rather than the cabbagey 'Glasgow rose' favoured by Mackintosh. The general decor was maintained long after 'Miss Rombach's' had passed into her brother's and then her nephew's hands.

The 1911 Exhibition brought welcome extra work for Mackintosh, who apparently decorated Miss Cranston's two tea rooms there. The job books cover paintwork, lamps, screens and a pay-desk, but the only drawing to survive is for a plate rack for the White Cockade. The only photographs are of the terraces, where ordinary cheap bentwood chairs were used, though there are glimpses of an elegant pagoda-roofed cake stand, well designed to keep the sun off the scones. It seems likely, as Billcliffe suggests, that extra low wavy-backed chairs were made to the design used a little earlier for Ingram St, to be transferred there later as extras. A set of hitherto unattributable 'Mackintosh' settles seems very likely to have been made up cheaply from re-used School of Art panelling for one of the Exhibition tea rooms.[44]

78. The Chinese Room designed in 1911 at Ingram St, showing the cash box and the use of horizontal and vertical latticing. Photographed in 1971.

In the same year, 1911, Miss Cranston set Mackintosh to redesigning two earlier rooms at Ingram St, giving further stimulus to his search for a new style. The Chinese or Blue Room was a transformation of the old gents' tea room at 205 Ingram St, and its male clientele was reflected in Mackintosh's design. The square lattice dominated: it was applied against canvas-covered walls, varied with insets and niches of mirror, glass, and for the first time plastic; more lattice was supported horizontally by screens and the cash desk to hide the original ceiling, which was painted dark. Pagoda-ish finials, a strange door feature and dark polished step-backed chairs combined with the latticing to produce Mackintosh's personal version of the 'Chinoiserie' which waxed and waned in fashion. The most startlingly new element was that of colour, a powerful lacquer blue with touches of red.[45] Mackintosh was clearly moving in the same direction as contemporary designers in Paris, where the Ballets Russes were provoking a revolution of colour, stimulating the nascent 'Art Deco' movement.

79. The Cloister Room of 1911 at Ingram St before dismantling in 1971, a picture marred by the ugly settles introduced in later days.

The room already redecorated by Mackintosh in 1900 was now thoroughly transformed into the novel Cloister Room. A new barrel ceiling decorated with wide raised bands of plaster covered with a wagon-chamfering pattern hid the old embossed finish, which had previously been spared. Warm waxed wood panelling was run up and down all round, edged with double strings of a little diaper pattern picked out in strong colours — blue, green, red, and yellow. Panels were built out on the walls so that there was undulation everywhere, while niches of leaded mirror glass added spots of glitter. In a room without natural light this rippling pattern produced a bewitching, womb-like, and quite new effect.

While these two commissions show Mackintosh's creativity unabated, things were not going well for him in Glasgow: tensions in the office resulted in his resignation from the partnership in 1913, but he failed to win the commissions to support a solo practice. Heavy drinking compounded his problems, as did the outbreak of the First World War, and in 1914 he and

80. Mackintosh's design for the memorial fireplace in the Dug-Out tea room opened in 1917 at the Willow.

Margaret shook the dust of Glasgow from their feet and went to stay in Walberswick in Sussex. After the bizarre incident in which Mackintosh was arrested as a spy[46] they moved to London and lived modestly in Chelsea. Work was scarce, and Miss Cranston's commission for an underground extension at the Willow, for which plans were submitted on Mackintosh's behalf by James Carruthers in December 1916, must have been especially welcome.[47] Though alterations at Ingram St were carried out at this time apparently without Mackintosh's involvement,[48] a wish to put work in the way of the Mackintoshes may have been partly the motive for embarking on the 'Dug-Out' project, along with the novel idea of making it a kind of war memorial. A panel above the fireplace read 'This room was opened by Miss Cranston in the year 1917 during the Great European War between the Allied Nations and the Central Powers'.

A small lobby gave access to lavatories, a rest room, with comfy chairs, a writing desk and hanging flower basket, and the tea room. 'The Dug-Out' was completely without natural light but there its resemblance to a bunker ended. Against a background of shiny black paint Mackintosh developed the new style of geometric design he had recently evolved in the Derngate interiors for his other late patron Bassett Lowke in Northampton, using brilliant colour in stripes, triangles and squares. Two paintings executed by Margaret, 'The Little Hills', designed round some rather ugly fat children, were used as a frieze.[49] It is upsetting that this scheme, of which there are no photographs, has vanished without trace. It shows that Mackintosh and Miss Cranston still had new ideas. But it was her last commission and his last work in Glasgow. The death of Kate's husband later in 1917 snuffed out Kate's will to continue and she soon parted with the tea rooms and Hous'hill. Mackintosh struggled for some time to find work in London before abandoning architecture altogether and moving to the south of France, to live supported by Margaret's small private income in genteel poverty, painting watercolours. When he died of cancer in 1928 his entire estate, including watercolours, furniture and designs was valued at £88 12s. 6d.

This survey should support the *Studio's* judgement in 1906 that 'It is not easy to imagine what would be the position of modern decorative art in Glasgow to-day, apart from the group of tea-houses controlled by Miss Cranston': with the commission to Walton in 1888 'decorative art may be said to have entered on a new phase at Glasgow'. Kate effectively started Walton's career in 1888 and gave him an important push in 1896. But posterity owes her most for her sustained and loyal patronage of the Mackintoshes. The opportunities she gave Mackintosh under Walton at Buchanan St and Argyle St established the reputation for furniture and interior design which brought in an increasing proportion of his work, and she gave him all her major commissions thereafter. This was a continuous stream which produced work from all phases of his development, from the organically inspired to the severely geometric, from white paint to vibrant colour.

Mackintosh the supreme originator simply became Miss Cranston's house style, wherever he was going at the time.

Kate Cranston was for Mackintosh the ideal patron: for a strong-willed woman with absolute ideas about the running of her business she seems to have interfered remarkably little, and interference was something Mackintosh could not stand. It seems clear that her own perfectionism responded to that quality in Mackintosh which came close to making him unemployable. She presumably suggested certain ideas, but otherwise left him to experiment and refine freely. The two of them evidently developed a relationship of trust — Mackintosh was even content to let her do the flowers, not something he would trust to everyone. Her moral support must have been of inestimable value: in the same letter in which he wrote to Frau Muthesius of occasions when 'antagonisms and undeserved ridicule, bring on feelings of despondency and despair', he could say of his current project at the Willow 'Miss Cranston is delighted with everything I have suggested, she thinks this is going to be by far her first place'.[50]

As a complete controlled environment combining the qualities of a domestic interior with public use, a tea room brief was eminently suited to Mackintosh's talents, though it was regrettable that except in the case of the Willow he did not have full control of the architectural structure. The japanese influence on his approach — with its subtlety of spatial relationships, use of screens and refinement of line — is often remarked, and the element of formality in Scotland's own tea rituals doubtless appealed. After the early vying with Walton Miss Cranston offered him the total control he craved — from walls to cutlery, even the waitresses' dresses. Tables and chairs carefully ranged were part of the composition and he could be fairly confident that under Kate's eagle eye they would be kept tidy and not casually moved about: in domestic interiors it was only in the Mackintoshes' own home that living clutter and disharmony could be excluded. Elements of design that might have seemed too flashy or strong in a living space could be desirably bold in a tea room. The stimulation this gave Mackintosh is especially evident in the later interiors when he had little chance to develop new ideas elsewhere. With the strong streak of practicality that ran alongside his genius for invention Mackintosh was very successful in designing areas for people to use. Even his high-backed chairs, evolved as a way of defining space, gave a pleasant sense of privacy at the table. Their lack of comfort might almost be seen as an advantage in the context of a busy restaurant, and anyway this common complaint against Mackintosh takes no account of lamentable changes in posture since the beginning of the century: after all if one was an Edwardian lady one's back did not touch one's chair — in public at least (*cf.* fig. 41). More damaging is the charge of unsound construction in some cases, and unwieldiness in others — drawbacks avoided by George Walton's designs.

Miss Cranston was wealthy enough after marriage to do as she wished and to give free rein to her tastes; at the same time her tea rooms were not a hobby but a very successful business, catering for the general public, not a bohemian élite. As we have seen she was highly respected in Glasgow and thus shed a protective mantle over her progressive designers. If people were inclined to wry amusement at things which after all look pretty extra-ordinary today, at least they did not dismiss them out of hand, and most were prepared to admire the tea rooms as one of the special things about Glasgow. While there is some truth in the picture of Mackintosh as a 'prophet without honour in his own land', and he certainly felt himself at times beleaguered in Glasgow, an account of the tea rooms does something to modify the myth. The tea rooms gave ordinary people the exhilarating chance to experience a complete avant garde interior without having to live with it, and on those terms a lot of them loved it. Pretension, for sure, is one thing that Glaswegians won't tolerate, but equally they have always admired strong individuality. Perhaps nowhere else would interiors in a style so far ahead of the norms of taste have found such enthusiastic general acceptance.

It is true of course that the credit was often deflected from the designers to Miss Cranston herself; and how much work this brought Walton and Mack-intosh cannot be easily assessed. But the tea rooms were major show rooms for them, freely accessible, and well covered in the press. And while Neil Munro might imply doubt as to whether 'the refining and elevating influ-ence of Miss Cranston's beautiful rooms' would have a permanent effect on the taste of Duffy, the thing was catching. In a fascinating anticipation of the 'Mockintosh' rife in Glasgow today, Margaret wrote to Frau Muthesius in about 1904: 'It is very amusing — and in spite of all the efforts to stamp out the Mackintosh influence — the whole town is getting covered with imitations of Mackintosh tea-rooms, Mackintosh shops Mackintosh furn-iture etc. It is too funny — I wonder how it will end.' While Mackintosh himself became increasingly something of a loner, too difficult for any but the most daring clients, the tea rooms certainly played a major part in acclimatising the public to Glasgow's own school of progressive design and creating a market among the affluent middle classes for the less uncom-promising version of the 'Glasgow Style' marketed by firms like Wylie & Lochhead.

With Miss Cranston the Glasgow tradition of the artistic tea room was firmly established and a quality of decor related to the best contemporary domestic interiors became an accepted norm, only noticed by natives when they left Glasgow and could not easily find anything similar. Assisted by George Walton the style had spread to certain places in England[51] where it combined with the long-running design obsession with Tudor England to establish an Olde Worlde Tea Shoppe tradition. Edinburgh certainly had some elegant department store tea rooms, such as Robert Maule's, opened in 1894, but it was not until the 1920s that the artist Robert Burns installed a full-blown set of craft-based artistic tea rooms at D. S. Crawford's premises at Prince's St/Hanover St, painting decorative panels and designing furniture,

81. Stylish deco panel from Guthrie & Wells' scheme for the Ca'doro Buffet in the mid twenties: see p. 137.

while Georg Jensen provided tableware and the Bough studio some stylish pottery.[52]

By this time the lead in innovative design had passed to Paris. In Britain the shock of the First World War induced a general harking back to tradition, and a parallel desire to forget the past in an explosion of 'jazz' colourings. The new Glasgow tea rooms pursued a path of considerable taste overlaid from the mid twenties with the glamour of Art Deco, while a few 'picture galleries', chiefly those of James Craig, upheld in their own way, as we shall see, Miss Cranston's noble example of patronage of contemporary art.

The Second Age of the Tea Rooms,
1918–1945

After the flood of relief at the ending of the First World War and a brief boom while the merchant fleet and manufacturing industry re-equipped, Glasgow's industrialists had to face the hard fact that there would be no full return to prosperity: markets already slipping before the war had been permanently lost. Unemployment became an intractable problem, and the slow slide into depression began early in the 1920s. The decade saw a new flood of emigration, southwards or overseas, and as Oakley says of what he calls the 'years of disillusion', 1919-26, 'things went wrong for Glasgow'. Businesses began to be sold off, and some head offices to move to London. The economy picked up a little in the later twenties only to be submerged by the Great Depression. After this began to abate around 1935 Glasgow hauled itself optimistically towards reconstruction, only to have it shattered by another world war. It was during this period that the city began to appear to the outside world in colours which have clung tenaciously until very recently, with a reputation blackened by slum poverty, working class unrest, and horrific tales of razor gangs.

But through all this the Glasgow tea rooms quietly, or even ostentatiously, prospered, exemplifying the reassuring capacity of life to bob along above the swells of change. There was hardship for many, but middle class incomes were solid, and those with money could get a lot for a little. There was more leisure, and with rising wages more choice for more people. The manufacturing base might be crumbling, but the 'escape' industries, with some ups and downs, flourished. In 1922 the Book of Glasgow noted the 'prodigious outcropping of super-teashops, picture houses, and dancing palaces', while *The Bailie*, repeating sentiments voiced in 1897, asked 'where are all the Glasgow tea-houses and restaurants going to get their profits in the future? The supply of food palaces — each one more palatial than the other — must soon be in excess of custom'.[1] The reputation of the tea rooms remained something to cling to, and 1931's *Book of Glasgow* gave them a special mention: 'It has long been recognised that nowhere will one find restaurants and tea shops similar to those in Glasgow, and while this applies more particularly to the service, the same can be said about the architecture. The interiors are noted for their high standard of decoration and furnishings, and they are a distinct feature of the streetscape and of the social life of the city, and vie with the cinemas, of which there are many justly entitled to the name "super".'[2] There had been a great increase in tea-drinking during the war, and the strong prohibition lobby after it also gave the tea rooms a head start in the new era: this was the time when some

Sauchiehall Street, Glasgow

82. Sauchiehall St thronged with people in the late twenties. Beyond La Scala cinema is the distinctive outline of Copland & Lye and Pettigrew & Stephens.

areas used the local veto to go dry. Entertainment was usually found without alcohol, until the appearance of cocktail bars in the late thirties.

Despite great social changes the habits centred on the tea room had changed little and often caught the eye of outsiders. As the famous travel-writer H. V. Morton observed of Glasgow in 1929: 'She is the greatest, closely-knit community in Great Britain. She is the least suburban of all great cities . . . In no other city of this magnitude do more people know each other, at least by sight. To know a man by sight in Glasgow is to ask him to have coffee at eleven a.m. If the Clyde ever runs dry, sufficient coffee is consumed in Glasgow every morning to float the biggest Cunarder yet built.' He stood and watched the crowds pass later in the day, 'some to take the astonishing meal of high tea which Glasgow's cafés and restaurants have elevated to the apex of the world's pyramid of indigestibility (for I still cannot believe that tea agrees with fillet steak); some to dance ᵤr 3s. in surround-ings for which we pay 30s. in London . . .'³ In the late thirties J. R. Allan, an Aberdonian resident in Glasgow for eleven years, remarked again on the Glaswegian's 'genius for casual friendship', but speaking of the coffee rooms 'where business men gather for refreshment and gossip after a hard hour's work in their offices', he wondered subversively 'how the alleged rush and bustle of commerce allows so much time for coffee and discussion'. He picked out also the tea rooms 'where the ladies refresh themselves after an hour of shopping. The consumption of cream buns is enormous; éclairs die in thousands; chocolate biscuits melt away as in a thaw. It is perhaps not a wonderful thing that there are so many comfortable ladies in Glasgow when they do themselves so well in the afternoon.'[4]

Strangers visiting for the Empire Exhibition in 1938 were warned in their guidebooks that 'in many establishments tea is a fairly substantial meal, and might be regarded as the equivalent of a dinner elsewhere. It should also be noted that temperance hotels are by no means establishments of minor importance, as they often are in England and Wales.' The exceptional quality and range of Glasgow's restaurants and baking was noticed as frequently as in earlier decades.[5] In the interwar period Glasgow's family bakeries grew and prospered and it is they who dominate the second era of the tea rooms.

While the Cranstons were no longer active their name was still prominent. Stuart's business, well established as a public company, ran on smoothly after his retirement, expanding its catering to keep abreast of rival tea room–restaurant concerns, while the dry tea side of the business was wound down. Redecoration at Renfield St in 1923 showed an awareness of the need to keep decor up-to-date. The long-established artistic decorators Guthrie & Wells were called in and briefed to bring 'artificial sunshine' into

83. Advertisement of 1922 for Cranston's Picture House and Tea Rooms built in 1916.

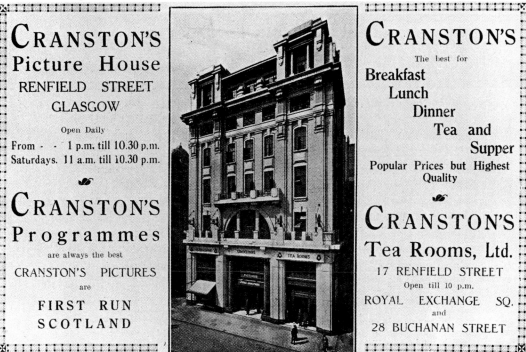

84. The Balcony Lunch Room at Cranston's Renfield St premises, colourfully redecorated by Guthrie & Wells *c.* 1924.

the large, rather gloomy ground floor tea room, in keeping with the new fondness for colour with which society was shaking off memory of the war. This they did with a ceiling in shades of yellow 'Duresco' with highlights of bright green, soft black and gold, red pay-boxes, and panelling decorated with moulded gilt festoons and masks; underfoot was an immense 56 ft square carpet in mulberry, green and gold on a fawn background, specially made by Templeton's. This evidently did the trick, and the firm was asked to redecorate the rest of the building except the cinema. The 'bright and even playful' use of colour was continued. The balcony lunch room had an orangey-yellow roof and glazed green walls, while private rooms were luxurious with fashionable Chinese gold-painted decorative panels. The roof smoke room with its fine views of the city bid to become a modish new venue for the business man with panelled walls in pale yellow decorated with the flower drops and swags beloved of Art Deco.[6]

Although Miss Cranston had retired she remained a visible and famous figure until her death in 1934. Her strange long flounced black skirts, or big black sombrero and cloak, left an indelible impression on many memories. The vestiges of her business, which had run on at Ingram St under Miss

Drummond, were taken over by Cooper's in 1930. They made small changes, including an up-to-date quick lunch counter, but otherwise respected the 'unique character' of these beloved rooms. The Willow too, rechristened the Kensington, was well looked after for a decade, before John Smith sold it on to Daly's next door. Much of the furniture was then transferred to Smith's recent acquisition, the Grosvenor, and found its way thence onto the market. But as Art Deco swept through restaurant design, Mackintosh's interiors began to seem an aging curiosity. Though affection and loyalty kept the Cranstons' name on people's lips the lead had passed to a new generation of tea room entrepreneurs, whose businesses, established before the war, now came into their own.

85. In 1930 Cooper's added to its original café Miss Cranston's Ingram St Tea Rooms in 1930, and also Wm & R. S. Kerr's Carlton in St Vincent St: both later came into the hands of Reo Stakis.

Chief among them were another brother and sister, who brought to the fore the bakery business established by their father James Craig as far back as 1870. They were rivalled by the two Urie brothers who developed their father's City Bakeries into another empire. But we look first at two more brothers, William and R. S. Kerr, who had first come to prominence at the 1911 Exhibition (p. 77).

William Kerr, the driving force behind this business, was an ambitious and able chef who had trained in two prominent Glasgow restaurants before moving to Birmingham with Mr Chatrian, who had been proprietor of 'F. & F.'s'.[7] He then moved still further afield, working for Lyons and Co. in London and Paris. He seems to have returned home with the ambition to become the Jo Lyons of Glasgow. Joined by a capable wife and his brother, who had been chef to De Beers in South Africa, he took over the Cabin Tea Rooms at $105\frac{1}{2}$ St Vincent St in 1906 and renamed them in accordance with his smart metropolitan ideas The Carlton Restaurant. By this stage he was also the author of *Practical Household Cookery*, and an invaluable volume on *The Art of Serviette Folding*.

The 1911 Exhibition was for Kerr a godsent chance to exploit his training under Lyons in profitable mass catering, and it evidently made him good money. He immediately rebuilt the Carlton at 111 St Vincent St and spread himself around the city by buying the Hydro Tea Rooms in Candleriggs, the 'artistic' Regent Tea Rooms in West Regent Street, and the Queen's Park Rooms in Victoria Road, all of which were reorganised. A second unrepeat-

86. William Kerr, the military caterer, in 1915. In this year he took over the Regent Tea Rooms, which he kept open for late suppers until 10.45 p.m.

able opportunity came with 'the grand burst-up' of the First World War, and Kerr seized it with both hands. When Lyons' contract for catering at the White City for 10,000 troops and 350 officers came abruptly to an end, he slipped in without a hitch and his Army contract business grew fast. By the time he was profiled by *The Bailie* at the end of 1915 there was a London office in the charge of another brother, Donald, with a staff of 300 to control this work alone. Meanwhile in Glasgow the firm was about to open the Grand Central Restaurant in Jamaica Street, 'the last word in restaurants', which Kerr proposed to open on Sundays (this *The Bailie* judged to be 'moving with the times'), and was building the palatial Marlborough at Shawlands 'to outdistance anything yet dreamt of on the South Side'.

The firm was at its height in the mid 1920s, briefly owning the Grand Hotel at Charing Cross, adding the poshly named Burlington House in Bath Street, and acquiring a licensed restaurant in Queen Street. It also operated the Kelvin Hall Tea Rooms, opened in 1927, which could allegedly seat 2000. But in the early 1930s the business collapsed, though an attempt was made to restart at the Gainsborough Halls in St Vincent St from 1932. William Kerr had brought back from his experience in the south ideas like late opening hours which pushed ahead the development of Glasgow's large tea rooms into major dry restaurants and function rooms. But along with this sort of chain catering went a certain ruthlessness in the treatment of staff. Glasgow tea room history after the First World War, accurately reflecting the new age, began with a strike at Kerr's restaurants in 1920, and this is an appropriate place to glance at working conditions for employees.

The excellence and low prices of the tea rooms had depended from the start on the exploitation of female labour. When Miss Margaret Irwin gave evidence back in 1901 on the conditions of women shop assistants in Glasgow[8] she revealed appalling hours, sometimes 14-16 per day, 80-100 a week, with girls obliged to stay late for special functions during the winter months. In the case of shops, many stayed open until eleven or midnight just because that is what everyone did; but the temperance establishments to which Miss Irwin confined her restaurant enquiries often used late hours as an advantage over their fiercely regulated licensed competitors. One woman, a proprietor helped only by members of her family, said that she opened every morning at five, and closed at midnight: 'she could not shut early because so many came in after the public houses were closed'. There was of course a reluctance on the part of the authorities to damage this competitiveness with legislation. An aggravation of long hours was that meals were taken on the premises, generally without any regular time being allowed, so that the girls 'have just got to snatch their meals when and where they can'. Such constant work in hot gas-lit interiors could be ruinous to health. As one poor girl summed it up: 'When I get home I just sit down and cry with fatigue.'

Some employers were more reasonable: Lockhart's cocoa rooms for instance operated a shift system, with girls alternating early and late weeks.

The tea rooms of the city centre, as opposed to the unlicensed eating houses where the worst conditions prevailed, generally closed at about 7 o'clock, and after high tea had been tidied up, waitresses might get some free time, though whether they had energy to enjoy it is another matter. Some kept later hours, like Kerr; and the demand for overtime to deal with private functions in all kinds of restaurants could not safely be refused — instant dismissal was a weapon readily used by some proprietors.[9] A twelve hour day was not unusual in the Edwardian years. How tolerable this was depended very much on the proprietor.

Miss Cranston for instance was regarded as a model employer, and so she evidently was, in the enlightened Victorian manner, combining a belief in the virtues of discipline and hard work with a paternalistic (rather than maternalistic) concern for the welfare of her employees. She liked to take on girls who were orphans or from single parent families; and she ran an insurance scheme for them, to cover medical expenses. But meeting the standards of her perfectionism meant hard work, and like all employers of the period she exacted long hours. Annie Quin recalled for *The Glasgow Herald* her days at Buchanan St, where she started at the age of fifteen in 1909, when it was the headquarters of Miss Cranston's empire with a very large staff. She worked from early morning sometimes until after eight in the evening, for a starting wage of 4 shillings a week, plus three good meals.[10]

Annie progressed from a lowly runner (a fetcher and carrier for a waitress), to menu-writer, and finally to cook, and is a fascinating witness to a highly organised business. She remembered rigorous hygiene and no waste: left-overs were served up as patties. Miss Cranston toured her establishments every day to oversee her administration. She took special care in the instruction of her manageresses, who presided over a scrupulously ordered hierarchy of staff running to hundreds of young women — waitresses, cooks, and carefully differentiated 'maids': potato maids, vegetable maids, stew maids, pudding maids. When Rose Rombach left her employment with Miss Cranston to set up 'Miss Rombach's' in 1910 she took these standards with her: the day's work for her staff began with an inspection of nails, hair, hosiery and the cleanliness of (unseen) petticoats. Such employers were certainly demanding, but there was a pride in working at the best places. As Annie Quin recalled, 'though it was hard work, we were happy. It was like a big family.' The loyalty of staff to proprietor in such establishments was very strong, and many served for decades.

Wages were indisputably low, but it is clear that for many girls, the gregariousness of the work clearly outweighed the isolation, subservience and even longer hours of domestic service, which was the main alternative. However the First World War asked women to do a whole range of jobs never previously imagined: they worked the trams and welded munitions — and were paid for it. Although society afterwards demanded that women again be excluded from such work, some of them at last got the vote. After such dislocation the old acceptance of exploitative conditions was passing.

The newspaper columns were packed with advertisements for cooks, 'generals', etc, but many posts remained unfilled, despite unemployment among women.

The angry stirring of Glasgow's working classes, marshalled by the 'Red Clyde' activists, had put terror into the whole country. Among the wave of post-war Glasgow strikes, was the action by waitresses affecting 'certain restaurants in the city centre', reported on 21 January 1920: *The Glasgow*

Sweated Workers in Glasgow

STRIKE OF WAITRESSES
AT KERR'S CAFES

Citizens of Glasgow, your attention is drawn to the conditions which prevail at above establishments:

Waitresses and Kitchen Staff are receiving the following Wages and Conditions:—

12/- per week for 12 hours per day

1/- deducted if girl breaks a plate			
9d	„	„	„ cup
6d	„	„	„ saucer
2/-	„	„	„ wineglass
3d	„	for being late in morning	

The Girls decided to join the Union, with the result that the Shop Steward was dismissed, which is quite evidently an attempt to undermine the Girls' Union.

Previous to joining the Union, the minimum wage of restaurant workers was 10/- per week, and they had to purchase uniform from the firm

We are asking the public to
SUPPORT THE GIRLS

87. Broadsheet stating the grievances of Kerr's waitresses, who went on strike in January 1920.

Herald would not name the employer concerned, but it seems certain that it was Kerr's. The employees, organising against oppressive conditions, had joined the National Federation of Women Workers, and the immediate cause of the strike was the dismissal of the waitress acting as shop steward, though the management naturally denied that this was why she was sacked. The pickets with their grievances attracted a good deal of public attention, but the strike was abandoned after less than a month when most of the strikers found alternative employment.

In the following year there was some agitation for the institution of a trade board for women in the catering business, but Glasgow 'labourists' found it very hard to organise the waitresses — partly because of the long hours they worked. Three thousand leaflets were distributed but very few girls turned up to the meeting called: those who did were mostly ex-munitions workers with some experience of trade unionism. Attempting to enquire into conditions the *Herald* got little co-operation from employers. Wages seemed to range from 10 to 25 shillings a week, with two meals a day, though there were frequent complaints about the quantity and quality of the food. No cases were found in Glasgow of the practice noted in some cities — Newcastle, for instance — of paying no wages and expecting the girl to live on her tips. Tea room waitresses, unlike those in licensed premises, had originally received no tips: *St Mungo* pointed out in 1897 that it was inexplicable and unjust that it was 'practically compulsory to leave a penny on the table for the girl attendant at the Pink Restaurant, but nothing for the equally hard-working and deserving young lady who does the same offices at the Buchanan St Aesthetic 'Alls and the tea shops'.[11] But by the twenties tipping was established as an important supplement to a waitress's income, ranging from 3s. to as much as 25s. a week in the best tea rooms. Tipping in the tea rooms often reflected the special relationships between regular customers and 'their' waitresses, and an awareness of how little the girls were paid. Altogether it seemed that waitresses in Glasgow after the First World War were no worse off than elsewhere, but from various points of view were 'in a more helpless position than probably any other class of women'.[12]

Conditions slowly improved, led by the great bakery businesses: as a large proportion of their employees were skilled workers — confectioners and the like — staff loyalty was valuable. James Craig's prided itself on the 'family atmosphere' which prevailed even in so large a company. In 1936 it had around 1,100 employees, many of very long service, and the oldest employees confirmed that there had never been a trade dispute at the bakery.[13] The rival City Bakeries was more innovative. Proposals for a profit-sharing scheme were drafted in 1914: employees' shares (which were non-voting and tenable only during employment) were given as rewards or could be bought by applicants ready to promise that 'they will not waste time, labour or money in the discharge of their duties, and that they will endeavour to check waste wherever found, and will seek to further the interests of the

88. John Urie, the ruling hand of the
City Bakeries, *c.* 1921.

company to the best of their ability and skill.' The company also operated a
suggestions scheme. By the mid thirties, when it had around 1000 employees, it was running a recreation ground with bowling greens, tennis
courts and putting green, laying on holiday camps and instruction in 'phys-
ical culture', and giving extra holidays for perfect time-keeping (for which
more than 60% qualified). Food at cost price was another perk. Staff welfare
was claimed to be as much the company's concern as profit; CB was to stand
for 'Cheery and Bright'. In this way the best Glasgow tea rooms set high
standards during this second major era of their history.

'Every true son of St Mungo' pronounced *The Bailie* in 1921, returning to
what the reader will now recognise as a well-worn theme, 'accepts it as an
article of his faith in the communal efficiency of the city, that Glasgow leads
the country in tea-rooms, and will continue to show the world how these
things should be done.'[14] In the year of Stuart Cranston's death, the magazine was celebrating 'another stage in the evolution of the art of popular
refreshment' in the opening of the Ca'doro. This was the magnificent flagship of the City Bakeries Ltd, and immediately the use of the word 'tea room'
had to be qualified, for the Ca'doro was seen as much more than that, 'a full-
fledged new type of restaurant'. This lavish suite of shop, tea rooms, restaurants and function rooms confirmed a new trend, followed later by James
Craig's and others.

The City Bakeries had been founded around the turn of the century when
Robert Urie, the son of a Paisley baker, took over the Friendly Bread Company at 37 Clarendon St, Glasgow. His son Willie, a quiet and not especially
ambitious man, carried on as a master baker the practical side of the
business, but it was another brother, John, who as managing director
shaped the business into one of Glasgow's foremost. He was a chartered

Ca'doro

for all

Social Functions

TEA ROOMS
LUNCH ROOMS
GRILL ROOM

Quick Service Rooms
for Ladies and Gentlemen

Telephone:
Central 6314

Corner of
GORDON STREET
and UNION STREET

89. Advertisement of 1922 for the Ca'doro, with its new top floor.

accountant before committing himself to the family bakery, and beneath his reserved exterior was a formidable financial brain and an energetic interest in business efficiency. During the war his cost accountancy work for the Ministry of Munitions had earned him an O.B.E.

The firm was a pioneer of baking centrally for a network of distributive outlets, instead of behind the shop in the old way. At the time of *The Bailie's* feature the Clarendon Street bakery at St George's Cross supplied thirty-six branches throughout the city. This had grown to more than sixty by the end of the 1930s, and City Bakeries claimed to be, after J. Lyons and Co., the largest private retail bakery in Britain. There were tea rooms, as commonly, above or behind all the larger shops, but the Ca'doro was something on a quite different scale, aiming to be when built 'the last word for a long time in restaurants'.

The beautiful building on the corner of Gordon St and Union St which the firm converted was designed in 1872 by John Honeyman as a furnishing warehouse and showroom for Gardner's, one of a series of innovative iron-framed buildings in Glasgow. Later it was adapted for miscellaneous use, including Mrs McCall's Victoria Restaurant from 1896 onwards, and there was some pleasure in seeing it restored to a unity, sumptuously refurbished. Its name derived from the supposed inspiration of the Venetian Casa d'Oro, or 'House of Gold', translated for publicity purposes as the 'House of Excellence'. The conversion was handled by J. Gaff Gillespie, a friend of Mackintosh's who had a reputation as one of Glasgow's more avant garde architects. The work took some time and was opened in stages. It included the addition of a singularly inappropriate top floor, and in the last phase *c.* 1925-7, an ugly-fronted extension in Union St by Jack Coia, both happily removed in the recent rehabilitation of the building.

The Shopping Hall at ground level described by *The Bailie*, with its 'beautiful porticos, stained glass windows, richly carved woodwork and ornate columns and pilasters', indicated the lavish style of the enterprise. A hall faced with fine marble and Caen stone, with 'artistic' kiosks for confectionery and tobacco, gave separate entrance to the restaurant floors. Downstairs, catering for business men, was the smoke room, and 'quite the latest in quick-lunch counters, run on the "help-yourself" principle', adorned with a view of Venice commissioned from J. W. Ferguson. The Venetian theme was continued in the first floor 'Venetian Tea Room'. There was a musician's gallery half way between this floor and the next, which was to be the luncheon room. Also still to come were the Smoke Room and City Business Clubroom on the third floor, the Reception and Dining Rooms on the fourth, together with the main kitchen, and a Banqueting Hall on the fifth. By the time the upper levels were decorated Glasgow was dancing mad, and the top floor was re-designated a Ballroom, and the fourth floor a 'Lounge' and 'Buffet' for use in conjunction with it. Guthrie & Wells' spectacular decoration reflected all the glamour and excitement of the new age,

90. The Ca'doro's splendid lounge and buffet area, decorated by Guthrie & Wells in the mid twenties.

using strong colours and geometric patterns, glossy varnish and lacquered metal, and decorative panels of stylised dancing figures (fig. 80).[15]

Altogether the Ca'doro was effectively planned to cater for a wide range of tastes and pockets. The slight flashiness of its decor appealed to people who more often used Italian cafés than tea rooms. Shop girls could dress up and go there in a gang on a Friday night, and it soon became a popular place for weddings and functions. As time went on it became looked down on by the 'better classes' who preferred the quieter atmosphere of Craig's.

James Craig's claimed a longer pedigree. Indeed when the firm first began to advertise itself seriously around 1910 it appeared as 'Jas Craig's Tea Rooms, estab. 1870' — perhaps an attempt to one-up Stuart Cranston, who was given to quoting 1871 as the date of his foundation. The original James Craig, who had worked for twenty years for James Boyd, in Renfield St, set up by himself at 19 Cowcaddens, opposite Buchanan Street Station, a shrewd location in the years before Central Station was built. Here he ran a small restaurant of the 'snacks of steak and chips and best pie in the city' sort, with a bakehouse below. Craig was a self-made man, committed to 'honest straightforward dealing', and he prospered. By the early 1890s he had built up a good line in catering for soirées, especially the 'conversaziones' popular in this era. His two elder children, James and Jessie, grew up in the business and soon became its driving force, though their father checked their more expansive ambitions, and it was not until his death in October 1908 that they got their heads.

The younger James was a master baker himself, but had in addition great business flair: he was well-known and gossipped about. Jessie, Mrs Wynd as she became, whose quiet but firm common sense complemented her brother's more impulsive nature, was the unseen hand in the success of the tea rooms. She was as painstaking and capable as Miss Cranston, but without her love of publicity. Indeed it was hardly known that it was she who ran and continued to enlarge the enormous business after her brother's unexpected death on 1 October 1933, at the age of 63. She steered it on through depression and war-time, a symbol of quality, comfort and excellence.

The first sign of the new generation's regime had been the big new bakery in Woodlands Road, at Charing Cross, which appeared with the adoption of the principle of centralised supply. The grandeur of its architecture was later, according to Charles Oakley, the object of John Urie's derision — though his own Clarendon St bakery, rebuilt as a seven-storey factory in the mid twenties, had baroque adornments on its brick front. By 1909 Craig's had a string of bakery shops, 'all noticeable by their lightness and elegance and the artistic character of their window-dressing', several including tea rooms 'which are among the most luxuriantly appointed in the city'. It was around this time that Harry Lauder would get a round of approving applause when he confided to his audience that he had been away buying 'a cookie frae Jimmy Craig in the Wood-lands Ro-ad'. From then on expansion

91 and 92. James Craig and one of the firm's wedding cakes *c.* 1909. The firm later boasted three challenge trophies and one hundred and fifty six medals and diplomas for its baking.

was steady: tea rooms were reconstructed and new ones added, all reflecting the Craigs' commitment to the best fittings and facilities.[16]

Top quality baking was the firm's other boast. It claimed among other things to have been the first to import continental pastry bakers to make 'French cakes', which soon caught on and were imitated throughout Britain. Woodlands Road pushed out extraordinary quantities of cakes, breads, biscuits and chocolates. Journalistic statistics gathered in 1936 when 400 staff were employed there on day and night shifts, quoted twelve Scotch ovens in continuous use; every week squads of girls laid out the shells for approximately 50,000 mutton pies, the staple of the Scottish high tea, while 300 gallons of cream were whipped up for the luscious confections which topped the cake stands. Behind this was the indefatigable managing director, Mrs Wynd, touring the shops, disposing of unsold tea bread to charitable institutions, attending to every detail of a huge but personal business.

93. James Craig's 'Gordon' in Gordon St, finished in 1933.

By this time Craig's had about twenty branches, including its two famous show pieces, the Rhul at 123 Sauchiehall Street, and the Gordon in the heart of the business centre on Gordon Street, not far from the rival Ca'doro. In the late twenties the building trade was in desperate straits, and Craig's was able to rebuild existing tea rooms on a lavish scale to make them 'the most luxurious and up-to-date restaurants in the City'. The Rhul opened in 1927, and the Gordon was finally completed only a few months before James' death in 1933. Both were designed by James Carruthers, who did a lot of restaurant work, and with their restrained, large-windowed facades, and their fine panelled interiors, they count among the best things built in Glasgow in these stagnant years.

It was in the Rhul and the Gordon that the majority of Craig's famous pictures hung, so that they became known as 'the unofficial Art Galleries of Glasgow'. Other restaurateurs had adorned their walls with pictures (see p. 82), but an undated manuscript in the papers of T. J. Honeyman, the eminent director of Glasgow's official Art Galleries, gives Craig's collection of 'first-rate examples of the work of well-known Scottish artists' a hearty commendation. 'Jas Craig's policy of exhibiting paintings so that all his

94. The Gordon's much-loved smoking room, not yet adorned with pictures.

customers might see them, has given delight to a great number of people. A visit to an art gallery and museum is a deliberate act, calling for a decision. A cup of coffee or tea has become, in Glasgow at least, almost a reflex action. Consequently when conversation lags or when the eye wanders in search of the overdue companion, if a painting comes within range of our vision it is just possible we may become aware of its significance and be made a little curious. Inasmuch as 'curiosity is the thirst of the soul', to quote that great tea-drinker Dr. Johnson, I salute the pictures and Craig's for the opportunity they give to enlarge our experience.' There were many who loved the paintings and would always try to get a table near their favourite.

Craig bought generously, and according to the *Daily Record* in 1932 the paintings hung in the smoke rooms at Gordon St were worth £3000-£4000.[17] The artists he bought included George Houston and David Gauld, who acted as advisers, Hornel, William Wells, Stuart Park, D. Y. Cameron, Zorn, James McBey and J. Campbell Mitchell. Sadly the collection was dispersed when the sale of the Gordon in May 1955 inaugurated the dismemberment of the firm. The pictures fetched prices that are agonising to recall today, and some had diminished in face value since they were first bought, reflecting the low esteem in which 'Glasgow Boys' painting was held after the war.[18]

Craig's was a worthy successor to Miss Cranston's, then, if in a less avant garde spirit, as a patron of contemporary artists and an enlarger of public taste; and also in its dedication to the highest quality. There was gleaming silverware, good furniture and deep carpeting.[19] There were waitresses, impeccably uniformed in black and white, standing in a silent row along the wall ready to dart forward to serve the tables. And of course there were the cake-stands piled high with irresistible currant bread and cream-cakes. Even Craig's pie and chips seemed to taste better than other people's. There was an enveloping sense of being well looked after, and it was a top place for a treat if you could not make a habit of it. The coffee rooms in particular were a favourite resort of business men keeping up the 'ancient custom' of business over coffee, and they could lunch there perfectly well for 9d. No wonder these places are so very fondly remembered.

95. Peacock's 'Georgic', designed by Whyte & Galloway, at 28 Union St, photographed after completion in March 1931.

Several other bakery firms founded in the previous century flourished at this period and followed the pattern of expansion during the hard times. R. A. Peacock & Son emulated Craig's by opening in 1931 a large modern restaurant with function rooms, The Georgic, at 28-40 Union St, and re-building at 149-51 Trongate in 1936 in similar style.[20] Its Peacock-blue cake boxes were well-known, but it never really competed on equal terms with Craig's. Walter Hubbard's (founded 1848) followed the same pattern away from the city centre, building an art deco gem to the design of James Lindsay on Great Western Road in 1931. Bill Crosbie, who painted some contemporary murals of 'spring lambs and such like' in the interior, was offered hard cash or free lunch for the rest of his life and sensibly chose the latter. Hubbard's rebuilt its shop and tea rooms on Dumbarton Road in similar style in 1937, and like Peacock's had many other local branches. Alex Colquhoun's was also prominent away from the city centre, its main luncheon and tea rooms at 225 Byres Road bidding for university custom with 'dainty afternoon teas and music from 3 to 5 p.m.'

Two other well-known tea room names, A. F. Reid and M. & A. Brown, descend from a bakery business founded by Robert Brown in Cumberland St in 1858. His daughter and her Aberdonian husband took over the original shop and expanded it into A. F. Reid & Sons, a sizable business by the end of the Edwardian era. They had bought up much of Wm & R. S. Kerr — its premises in Victoria Road, and the splendid function rooms, the Marl-borough and Burlington House, from which they operated a flourishing

96. Walter Hubbard's deco tea rooms at 508-10 Great Western Road, opened in 1931.

Meet your friends at

REID'S, Gordon Street

For your Morning or Afternoon Tea
or Coffee

Comfortable Tea Rooms and Smoke
Rooms

HIGH TEAS, SNACKS, TEAS

NOTE ADDRESS:—

30-34 GORDON STREET

———

Head Office and Bakery:—
78 VICTORIA ROAD, CROSSHILL
'Phone 1144-1145 Queen's Park

*Where estimates and particulars regarding all classes
of catering may be obtained*

---

97. Reid's, popular with men, advertising in 1929. As well as its city-centre tea rooms the firm ran a catering business from the south side.

catering business. They also ran tea rooms in a couple of cinemas. Their city branch and tea rooms opened around 1930 at 30 and 34 Gordon Street, opposite Central Station, were well placed for business men.

Meanwhile the original Robert Brown's sons 'M. and A.' had gone off to establish their own bakery at 277-9 Sauchiehall Street. In 1909 they were reported to have recently dropped their purveying business, but around 1930 the prospects for a new tea room seemed good enough for them to open at 283 Sauchiehall Street. In those days it was a classy place; later as 'Ma Brown's', beloved of students at the Glasgow School of Art, its atmosphere was more homely, and its reputation was for good helpings. It survived in family ownership until 1989.

Some firms hardly changed. William Skinner's, one of the oldest, founded in 1835, never attempted expansion, apart from a city branch at 30 St Enoch Square, but steadily maintained its old reputation for the elegance and class of its luncheon and tea rooms, which remained popular with ladies or with men wanting to take ladies somewhere nice. Good furniture in the French style, boule clocks and 'Louis' chairs, distinguished their well-loved premises at the Charing Cross end of Sauchiehall St, appealing over the decades to discriminating people who distinctly disliked anything 'modern'. Skinner's also rivalled Craig's in the matter of currant bread, shortbread and wedding cakes, and were a popular choice for refined teetotal wedding receptions. Latterly the firm was owned by John Sword, who

98. In 1922 the Royal Polytechnic added next to its restaurant a comfortable lounge area in the ever-popular 'Louis' style designed to appeal to women. Advertisement of 1923.

LADIES ARE INVITED TO ::
TAKE ADVANTAGE OF THE

Rest Room Louis XVI.

◇

Luxuriously Furnished.

ROYAL POLYTECHNIC, Ltd.,
65 to 99 ARGYLE STREET, GLASGOW.

dabbled in various profitable enterprises with the fortune he made from the SMT Bus Company after the First World War. He emulated Craig by hanging in the tea rooms many of the paintings he collected, mostly landscapes and seascapes: his tastes in general followed the current fashion for artists like Russell Flint and Laura Knight.

The great department stores felt the strains in the economy but bore testimony to the fact that despite bare-foot children and knots of suntanned unemployed on the streets there was good money around for the middle classes, even in the teeth of depression. On Buchanan St Fraser's star was rising under the control of the young Hugh Fraser. One of his first independent acts was to enlarge the tea room and install a restaurant, which soon became successful enough to turn customers away on market days. In 1931 a new smoking room and restaurant of 'modernist' design were opened.[21] Fraser's close rival Macdonald's (previously Stewart & Macdonald) was also popular, while on Sauchiehall Street shoppers were spoiled for choice: Trérons had rather lost standing at this period, and the smartest, by common agreement was Daly's — 'not a high tea place'. Pettigrew & Stephens held its own but Copland & Lye remained a common favourite because of the theatrical location of its tea room (fig. 37). Popular numbers from a string trio or a piano quintet were still part of the service: musicians ousted from the cinemas by the talkies were glad to find such work; those who couldn't played on the streets.

Both Copland & Lye and Pettigrew & Stephens created new men's departments in the early 1920s, with separate back entrances to their smoke and quick-lunch rooms, for shopping was still a strictly segregated business. Anderson's Royal Polytechnic on Argyle Street did not appeal to the 'better class' of fashionable lady, but its Louis XVI restaurant and spectacularly capacious Byzantine smoke room were popular resorts for business men after the First World War. Sir John Anderson's sell-out in 1929 to the firm founded in Liverpool by his father's contemporary Lewis, was an omen of things to come. The old building was dismantled and rebuilt over the next decades as 'Scotland's largest store'.

Where shall we Lunch?

or have Tea? The answer is Copland's, of course! Copland's have two restaurants (one for non-smokers, and one where smoking is permitted), and also a men's smoke-room where snacks can be had.

An excellent four-course Lunch, which costs only **2/3**, is served in both restaurants, and Teas—well, ask anyone who lives in Glasgow—Copland's Cakes are famous.

ORCHESTRA under the direction of JOHN MACARTHUR who broadcasts frequently.

COPLAND & LYE, LIMITED

99. Copland & Lye advertisement of 1938. A 2/3d (approx. 11p) CopLye lunch comprised grapefruit cocktail or soup — fish — stuffed duckling, or roast sirloin, or roast mutton etc. — hot or cold sweet — cup of tea or coffee.

100. Advertisement for Pettigrew and Stephens Man's Restaurant, 1930.
Paintings in the classical nude tradition — 'Aphrodite' is discreetly obstructed
by the artist — belonged to a long tradition of smoking-room decor.

101. The grandiose Byzantine Smoke Room at Anderson's Polytechnic in the
early 1920s.

102. Wendy's 'New Field' tea room incorporated fake stone-walling and gates, and her waitress wore homely clothes.

The smaller tea rooms also flourished in the hard times. During the world trade slump of the early 1930s a little clutch of new ones opened: with their friendly feminine names and pleasant atmosphere they met the need for comforting homeliness at this disturbing time. Reflecting the Americanisation of popular culture through the cinema, the new tea rooms were on first name terms with their customers: 'Wendy's', 'Jean's' and 'Rosalind's' succeeded the more formal 'Misses' of the pre-war era — though Miss Rombach's and Miss Buick's still thrived as family concerns.

Of the new rooms Wendy's, at 243 Sauchiehall St from 1931, and from 1933 also at 104 West George St (18 Bothwell St was added later), was particularly successful, shrewdly tapping the passion for the open air which characterised the thirties. Her trade mark was a very un-Glasgow little thatched cottage, and this little 'Wendy house' was built into the decor at the West George Street premises, along with other rural features. Her waitresses abandoned traditional black and white uniform for 'farmer's wife' clothes. She ensured country freshness by enforcing a no-smoking rule, not at all common at this period. 'The Green Twig' opened up a stair near Daly's on Sauchiehall Street in 1933 made a similar appeal — though judged by devotees better and cheaper than Wendy's. 'Trees' was opened by 'Rosalind's' sister Miss Gibson at the same time. These new tea-rooms, aiming chiefly at women, also showed a tendency to assimilate to English tea room style: Glasgow had not previously gone in for 'twee' names and the 'country goodness' image. The United Coop Baking Society's 'Wheatsheaf' Rooms on the Paisley Road, established back in the 1890s, and later run independently by Miss Martin and successors, were the rule-proving exception. In the grim and grimy urban depression of the thirties, however, the modest escapism of cottagey chairs and chequer table-cloths was welcome.

The spread of milk bars throughout the city at the same period was another symptom of this urge towards wholesomeness. This was so noticeable that it could be claimed in *Scotland 1938* that 'If whisky and beer are Scotland's two leading drinks, milk certainly is entitled to a third place'. An exaggeration perhaps, but there was a great boom in milk drinking, energetically promoted by the Scottish Milk Marketing Board and led in Glasgow by the chain of milk bars developed by the powerful Mrs Ross. Ross's advertised heavily to persuade the public that their Tuberculin-tested, pasteurised milk, presented in sealed bottles, was entirely safe and healthy. Their milk bars spread to become a popular chain, much as Lockhart's cocoa rooms had been in earlier days. Lockhart's Cafés, as they now were called, were declining to extinction: it was believed by those who would not have dreamed of entering them that their knives and forks were chained to the table. They were finally put out of business by the novelty and simple freshness of Ross's, which occasionally took over their premises. Like the tea rooms, Ross's pursued a well-publicised programme of building at a time of economic distress. 'The Optimist', proclaimed a billboard on their conversion of 294 Sauchiehall St: 'Our 1932 Slogan Was Spend. Our 1933 Spend Still More. Wise Spending Creates World Prosperity. Selfish Hoarding Creates Stagnation & Starvation. Watch Wise Spending Create This Lovely Corner House. It's Ross's — It's Right.' By 1938 it had almost fifty branches in the Glasgow district and several others in the west of Scotland. Griddles cooking in the window lured customers in for soda scones, sweet milk scones, oven scones, potato scones, and wonderful morning rolls with lashings of butter. A visit became a regular part of many people's day, en route to work or college perhaps. Later Morton's Milk Bar at Central Station introduced American style snacking, serving such novelties as waffles, and became madly popular with the young. But like the coffee bars of the fifties, the milk bars of the thirties were a relatively short lived phenomenon.

The Italian cafés of Glasgow were not so susceptible to fashion, and continued as a central feature of working class culture, in the hands of second or third generation proprietors, Scottish-bred. Bright, warm and long-opening, they remained a focus of cheerful neighbourhood life. They conformed to a common pattern: bars at the front stacked with confectionery, where wonderful ice cream would be ladled into any container you liked; and at the back the booths with long narrow tables where you could sit over tea or coffee or bovril, or the fish and chips which no native seemed to make as well as the Italians. Before teenagers were invented the local 'Tally' was a favourite place for sitting with the opposite sex, courting innocently over a 2d dish of hot peas and a bottle of lemonade or a lurid milk shake. Needless to say they were regarded as obscurely wicked by the upper echelons of society. They were forbidden territory for the well-bred young, though their ice-cream often tempted disobedience. The names of favourite ice-cream shops surface alongside those of the tea rooms in many people's memories.[22]

Café decoration had always been wonderfully colourful, so that 'just like an ice-cream shop' became a common disparagement of taste regarded as vulgar and gaudy. Back in 1897 *St Mungo* had commented that 'The Italian gentlemen who occupy ice-cream shops show considerable knowledge of human nature by lining the back and sides of their shop windows with mirrors, as there is no object in nature half so attractive to the average man as his own countenance'. The cafés took happily to Art Deco in the twenties and thirties, replacing the glitter of brass with chrome.[23] Their strongholds were were working-class territories where tea rooms were scarcely found. In the city centre, the domain of the tea rooms, they evolved greater pretensions, like the Café d'Oré on Dundas St, designed by J. Gaff Gillespie around 1930 and decorated by Guthrie & Wells.[24]

Tea rooms in these inter-war years were a ubiquitous part of daily life for the comfortable middle classes, a choice part of any treat for the less well off. These were of course also the great years of cinema, when Glasgow, with an astonishing number of cinemas all told, boasted in Green's Playhouse on

THE NEW SAVOY
GLASGOW'S SUPER CINEMA,
HOPE STREET.   Corner of SAUCHIEHALL STREET.

ORCHESTRAL CAFES, TEA LOUNGES, AND SODA FOUNTAIN.

Roumanian Orchestra every Afternoon, 3 till 5, in Upper Cafe.
Ladies' and Jazz Orchestras every Evening,
7.30 - 10.30 p.m.

OPEN DAILY 1.30 till 10.30   *OPEN DAILY—1.30 till 10.30*

103. Advertisement of 1922 for one of Glasgow's magnificent super cinemas.

Renfield St, finished in 1927 and seating near 4500, the biggest in Europe. All the 'super-cinemas' of the town centre had tea rooms, where you could wait for the second showing. Some of them — the Regal for instance, or La Scala — were very nice, a good place to take a girl on a date. Glaswegians' addiction to the cinema kept many other tea-rooms in business too, and induced late opening in some, like Miss Buick's, and Cranston's in Renfield St. Glasgow was also dancing crazy, and the necessary refreshment at all the dancing palaces, whether you sat out willingly or not, was non-alcoholic. You could get a good tea at the Locarno, or at the noisier Picadilly Club on Sauchiehall St, and if necessary a 'sixpenny' to dance with.[25]

104. 'Just Isn't Glesgow Fest? Rum (?) experiences in Glasgow's new night hells': cartoon of 1927, probably alluding to the Picadilly Club.

DANCING
AT THE
LOCARNO

Never before has the public been offered such ideal facilities for dancing. The musicians of the LOCARNO are drawn from the leading dance bands of London—The Savoy Orpheans, The Kit Kat Club, Ambassadors Club, and others. Theirs is a wonderful combination, and the ensemble gives full expression to that *throbbing lilt* so beloved by dancers.

The LOCARNO floor is of oak and is constructed on a unique system of springing. This floor has that smooth and delicate " touch " which is essential to dancing enjoyment.

The luxurious comfort of the LOCARNO charms everyone. Everything has been done to this end—the exceptionally lofty ballroom, the spacious lounges, the tasteful decorations, the perfect and regular ventilation, the novel lighting effects, the efficient service. All these in combination will enable the LOCARNO to give perfect dancing enjoyment.

THÉ DANSANT (2.30 p.m. to 5 p.m.)

Cultivate the vogue of the LOCARNO Thé Dansant, enjoy dainty afternoon tea and the entertainment of Scotland's leading dance band Dance in the afternoon.

MONDAY, WEDNESDAY, THURSDAY, FRIDAY,
2s. 6d. inclusive of tea.
TUESDAY AND SATURDAY, 3s., inclusive of tea.

EVENING SESSIONS

MONDAY, TUESDAY, WEDNESDAY, THURSDAY,
7.30 p.m. to 11.0 p.m., 3s. 6d.

FRIDAY (evening dress essential), 7.30 p.m. to 1.0 a.m., 7s. 6d.
SATURDAY (dress optional), 7.30 p.m. to 11.45 p.m., 6s.

Supper can be obtained every evening. Parties specially catered for.

Professional dancing partners will be in attendance and all tuition will be under the personal supervision of the LOCARNO Hostess, Mrs. J. BANKHEAD (Scotland's leading teacher of · dancing). Tuition, 7s. 6d. per half hour.

Ample garage accommodation for upwards of 100 cars.

Tables booked in advance. Telephone No., Douglas 4288-9.

105. The Locarno was one of Glasgow leading dance-halls: advertisement of 1927.

106. The Tower de Paris Tea Rooms at the Linn Park, from a postcard.

The city's magnificent public parks were well used for cheap days out: the Botanical Gardens, Kelvingrove, the Linn Park, Rouken Glen, Queen's Park, Hogganfield Loch — they all had tea rooms, and usually a bandstand too. And nearly everyone could manage the favourite Glasgow treat of a trip 'Doon the Watter' on the beloved Clyde steamers. Memories float back of the luxury of the plush cabin, with its starched damask cloths and smart stewards, slightly diminished by the mingled odours of tomato soup and engine oil. There was time for tea and cakes on the shorter trips, perhaps while the menfolk 'went to see the engines' — for a few of the stiff drinks with which the steamers were intimately associated.

Tea was by no means excluded from licensed premises, especially pubs in 'theatre-land', like Lauder's. Danny Brown's, one of Glasgow's oldest established restaurants, dating from 1846, was renowned for its two-course fish and meat high tea. On Wednesdays, market day, farmers would congregate there to eat enormous meals, washed down with tea and finished off with huge quantities of cake. Not far away was another venerable establishment, His Lordship's Larder. Or you could enter the magnificent portals of the Grosvenor and pass along the hall to the enormous tea room at the back: there, according to Jack House, all the good and the brave gathered; it was a famous trysting place and scene of many engagements. A separate tea room was opened next door under John Smith's proprietorship in 1934, supplying high teas. Ferrari's Globe, on West Nile St, long famous for its continental cooking, would do you a tea, and was open on Sundays too.

Miss **BUICK'S**
LUNCH and TEA ROOMS

SPECIAL
4 COURSE LUNCH - 1/6
HIGH TEA FROM - 1/3
COSY COMFORT
and
CHOICE COOKING
THAT'S MISS BUICK'S

19a RENFIELD ST.
Telephone—Central 1514
and
147 WEST GEORGE ST.
Telephone—Central 2465

:: GLASGOW'S ::
LEADING RESTAURANT
(LICENSED)

LUNCHEONS
DINNERS . .
and TEAS .

SNACK ROOM, LADIES' ROOM,
AND SMOKING ROOMS

DANIEL BROWN
——— LIMITED ———
79-83 St. Vincent St.

107. Miss Buick's advertising in 1930, emphasising homeliness and good value.
108. Danny Brown's, a long-lived restaurant renowned for its high teas (1929).

Many, then, were the tea rooms and their uses. They catered for all pockets, from a 'penny do' (an expression deriving from the 'ditto' prominent on the menu) at the cheapest on Argyle St, to Fuller's on Buchanan St with its cake forks and velvet chairs. They remained an invaluable resource for ladies with time on their hands, who could dress up of an afternoon and sally forth into town on the quick and convenient trams to a favourite tea room, not even needing to pre-arrange a meeting: they could enter quite comfortably and expect to see someone they knew. Experienced customers could stretch tea and a cake out to an hour, even beneath the eye of a waitress anxious to refill her tables. Men had their own tea room rituals to break up the long day in the office.

For the price of a cup of tea or coffee committee meetings could convene in the Ca'doro; Cranston's in Renfield St was the regular meeting place for the campaigning socialists of the ILP. Journalists wrote their columns comfortably in Miss Rombach's, handy for the newspaper offices; as the proprietor, David Rombach, was a renowned footballer, it also made an unoffical clubhouse. The rugby selectors meanwhile met in Rowan's gents' outfitters. Chess-players would converge on Miss Buick's, for Margaret Buick had married William Gibson, a Scottish champion chess-player. Mysie Ross, her niece, remembers as a child the mysterious clacking noise emanating from the male preserve of the smoke room, only later identified as dominoes.

Almost to the end of this period such entertainments were the preserve of tea rooms, as the Glasgow licensing authorities, still trying to minimise the attractions of drink, forbade games in pubs. And tea rooms were always invaluable to parents as bribes: Eileen Rombach's reward for co-operating during school uniform fittings was lemonade and currant cake at Cranston's.

But whose currant cake was the best? Cranston's, Craig's or Skinner's? All still have their loyal champions. Now that we are within the range of nostalgia it is favourite cakes that rise to the surface of people's memories. Fuller's éclairs, strawberry tarts, and marzipan and walnut cake with toffee topping; McKenzie's fruit slices; Daly's Albert cake; Craig's chocolate liqueur cakes; Hubbard's 'paving stones' (chewy, crisp gingerbread with hard icing)

109. Craig's shortbread was famous and travelled the world at Christmas in its tartan boxes (*c.* 1930).

and Swiss tart … Aah! Miss Cranston's young relative John Mackinlay still recalls his childhood longing for the French cakes at the top of the cake-stand, which at 2d were a forbidden extravagance.

If women's memories concentrate on cakes, men are as likely to recall their favourite waitresses. The fondness with which these Annies, Lilys and Pollys are recalled testifies to the comfortably close and solicitous relationships formed by the tea room habit — by regular appearances at the same time, at the same table.[26] Whether lively and chaffing, or firmly maternal, their waitresses dispensed the emotional cossetting which helped many a man through the stresses of a working life. How many scrawny young gents were brought extra portions, having been expertly judged to be in need of a 'fill up'? Looking back over the long history of the tea rooms it is clear that the couthy Glasgow waitress was one of their enduring special assets.

110. The traditional tea room scene, black and white waitress and male customer, updated to the 1930s by a flat chest and hand on hip. From an advertisement for the Ca'doro.

At the end of the thirties, as a new war gathered, Glasgow made an optimistic but doomed assertion that the bad times had been shrugged off. The clean pastel shades and ultra-modern architecture of the great Empire Exhibition of 1938 deliberately broke with the past.[27] Strenuous efforts were made to educate the populace and celebrate the power of planning, but predictably enough people remembered best the fun they had there, a gaiety enhanced by subliminal anxiety about events in Europe. The caterers, mostly Glasgow firms, did enormous business in relieving aching feet.

There were numerous milk bars, Ross's to the fore, and then sixteen restaurants to choose from, nine unlicensed. These included Peacock's

Georgic, the namesake of their main city-centre tea room. Wendy's had appropriately gained the contract for the refined restaurant in the Women of Empire Pavilion, the only haven for non-smokers. A popular attraction was the Treetops tea room, constructed on stilts at the foot of Tait's Tower on Bellahouston Hill so that growing trees were enclosed within it: this both placated the vociferous lobby against the desecration of the park for the temporary exhibition, and gave visitors an original tea-time experience.

EMPIRE EXHIBITION, GLASGOW

visit the
EMPIRE
TEA PAVILION
(Colonial Avenue)
for a really good cup of Tea

ISSUED BY THE EMPIRE TEA MARKET EXPANSION BUREAU

111. The pavilion of the Empire Tea Market Expansion Bureau at the 1938 Exhibition embodied the importance in the economy of the Empire of the tea produced by India and Ceylon for the mother country.

112. Ross's Dairies, with a widespread chain of milk-bars, continued to promote its public-spirited image in wartime: advertisement of 1940.

ARRANGE TO MEET YOUR FRIENDS HERE—

HENDERSON'S

Tearoom

for

MORNING COFFEE
•
LUNCHEON
•
AFTERNOON TEA
•

Dainty service and delightfully comfortable surroundings invite a welcome pause in the excitements of shopping.

ALEXANDER HENDERSON LTD. · SAUCHIEHALL STREET · GLASGOW

113. Henderson's advertisement in 1941 suggested that life could continue as usual. Its new 'moderne' tea room maintained the style of the 1938 Exhibition, and indeed re-used Nigerian pearwood panelling salvaged from it.

The Second World War was the temporary salvation of Glasgow's failing economy. After early panics it became clear that the city was not going to be seriously bombed: the Clydebank blitz in March 1941 was a searing experience fortunately not repeated. The ship-yards and munitions factories worked flat out, and Glasgow was crammed with people. Americans arrived with lots of money. Entertainments of all kinds boomed despite wartime shortages and restrictions.

The tea rooms were well patronised as an extra to rations, and these years saw their final doomed flowering. Craig's even in wartime managed to create an impression of luxuriant plenty. One journalist visiting in 1941[28] was evidently almost unhinged by his tour of 'gargantuan ovens specklessly clean, in whose shelves large fowls and plump turkeys lie sizzling and richly browning. Here the flanks of sirloins, of pies decked with the luscious stars and medallions of flaky paste, change colour with a becoming slowness ...' etc. The comfortable rooms likewise prompted a rhapsodic appreciation which makes a fitting close to this chapter of tea room history: 'There is, in truth, a golden bloom over everything, a lovely sheen as though a midsummer sun were shining, which turns your thoughts from the chilly world without and fills you with a new love of life.'

114. 'D' you think a Royal Scots Fusilier might have a cup o'tea?' Cartoon from
C. L. Davidson's Home Front series in *Scottish Field* (December 1941), alleging
corruption of standards by crowds of foreigners packing the tea rooms.

The Passing,
1945–1975

This chapter surveys the three sorry decades which saw the decline and disappearance of the tea rooms. The second great war of the century ruined the British economy; and it dislocated social mores to a far greater extent than the first. The problems left in its wake were enormous. Glasgow's traditional heavy industries, which had worked to capacity during the war and in the brief boom after it, soon went into sharp decline and were signed away to conglomerates. Almost all the enterprises established on the new light industrial estates were financed from outside, from the south or the United States, and they only scratched at the surface of the economic problem. Young men returned from national service, looked around and saw nothing for them; too often they headed off south, or overseas, in another flood of emigration.

Day to day life during the first grim period of readjustment to peace was pinched by shortages, rationing and the implacable rule of Utility. These were years when visitors touring again to Switzerland stood entranced by displays of cakes and confectionery which Glasgow before the war had matched. Such quality and range was never to return, even after the bickerings about sugar allocations had ceased. Proprietors large and small faced depressing difficulties in refurbishing and a continuous struggle against ever-rising costs and high taxation. But all in all the tea rooms survived quite well in the static years of the late forties, supported by staff and customer loyalty and an urge to get back to normal.

It was as prosperity returned to Britain at large that the tea rooms really began to go under, while Glasgow itself spiralled downwards into a trough from which it has only recently emerged. The Festival of Britain in 1951 was meant to mark emergence from post-war problems into a brave new era but the Exhibition of Industrial Power staged in connection with it in Glasgow was a flop.[1] Symbolically in the census of this year Glasgow lost to Birmingham its right to the title of 'Second City'. Faced with economic and social problems on a quite unmanageable scale the city surrendered its precious autonomy; and this was the period at which the cultural hegemony of Scotland passed clearly to Edinburgh.

From the mid fifties the march of progress became truly destructive in Glasgow, which like other British cities entered a period of rapid change. Though the drawbacks of uprooting people to housing estates 'without one picture house, laundry, pub, pool or anything else' were now thought to be widely known[2] it made no difference: the planners cracked on, sure they knew best. The process of flattening old urban areas and shifting thousands

115. 'Political' advertisement of 1947 urging eating out during the coal shortage. This group of licensed restaurants was owned by John Grant.

to bleak peripheral estates accelerated, as did the attendant social problems. Among the middle classes the drift to ideal homes in suburbia continued. Rationalisation was the new watchword in business life. The problems affecting the tea rooms came to the surface: they became increasingly run down and started to collapse and be swept away, along with other un-economic but much loved aspects of the old life — dance-halls, cinemas, steam-boats, trams. The next two decades saw many acts of vandalism and sad endings, haunted by an uneasy sense of loss.

The big bakery and confectionery businesses which had dominated the tea rooms between the wars succumbed like Glasgow's other great firms, most of them before the war still in the hands of the families whose names they bore, to the pattern of amalgamation and take-over by 'foreign' conglomerates. In the good old days Glasgow firms — Lipton's, Cooper's, R. S. McColl's, Birrell's — had colonised the rest of Scotland and lands south of the border too. The biscuit makers and the big bakers, pioneers of wrapped bread, sent trainloads of their products forth daily from Glasgow.[3] But the controls of war played havoc with businesses related to flour, and after it arrived the conglomerates — Cadbury's, Nabisco, United Biscuits and the like — buying up businesses weakened by the new conditions.[4] The Canadian-born bakery magnate Garfield Weston made a bee-line, as we shall see, for the over-extended tea room bakers.

The Glasgow tea rooms big and small had always been local family businesses. Fuller's was almost the only outsider to get a foot in; Jo Lyons apparently looked once at the Ca'doro for a corner-house, but was repelled by Glasgow's licensing laws.[5] This had been the tea rooms' strength, but it also made them vulnerable, when old proprietors retired without relations of ability and enterprise to succeed them. Loyal managers and manageresses were also crucial and sometimes irreplaceable. Worst of all was the problem of greatly increased costs: waitresses and kitchen staff demanded decent wages and reduced hours, and women had many other opportunities for employment. Everything became more expensive, and profits were not enough to support the commodious facilities offered by the old tea rooms, and to replace worn furnishings in anything like the same quality as before. Canned music replaced the string quartets: though the 'standard of living' had never been higher, the quality of many buildings and services fell to a prevailing cheapness and shoddiness.

The tea rooms had once had an almost continental centrality in a distinctive Glasgow way of life, but just as the city's big businesses fell under southern control, so too general tastes and patterns of life were increasingly assimilated to national norms. The strong tradition of a common public life was disrupted by many things: in the background was the dispersal of old communities and the transfer of their mutual support systems to the anonymous, if admirable, new Welfare State. The old segregation of the sexes for which the tea rooms had catered so comfortably was breaking down. Among the younger generations both men and women were smoking like chimneys, and drinking, flinging off in many cases the rituals and restraints of their upbringing, and their money was diverted to other ends.

The virtual disappearance of the traditional male 'coffee habit', had a devastating effect on the tea rooms. The pleasant old ways had continued before the war, long after the telephone had terminated any genuine need to congregate at the Royal Exchange or elsewhere. Men used to exit from their offices at 11 o'clock, leaving their secretaries to catch up, and go to chat over business, or golf, in a tea-room coffee room. After the war, with the end of Saturday working and a growing demand for efficiency, time was more pressing and the habit lapsed. At lunch-time too, with the constrictions of Temperance now largely abandoned, men were more likely to pop into a bar than to patronise the tea rooms.

Middle-class women also now had much less spare time. Domestic servants were definitely a thing of the past for all but the very privileged, and after the war women found themselves labouring almost non-stop in the isolation of their houses, trying to maintain their mothers' standards, while propaganda told them firmly that home was where they should be. The new domestic appliances were more than luxuries in these circumstances. At all events the home now became the focus of household expenditure, and as it became more comfortable it was increasingly the focus of leisure.

The television of course had a lot to do with this, though again the radio had started the trend before the war. The BBC came to Glasgow in 1923. Thirty years later the Coronation induced many better-off families to take the plunge into television ownership, soon followed by others keeping up with them. From then on it spread unstoppably to become, in Lord Reith's words in 1967, 'a potential social menace of the first order'. The television and new 'home-centredness' greatly altered the pattern of entertainment, so that attendance at all sorts of public venues fell off — football, lectures and church, as well as cinema, theatre and dance-hall. A strange exception was the popularity of Bingo in the later fifties, which gave some cinemas a lingering after-life.

Life before the war had been remarkably homogenous — within class limitations — and the tea rooms had catered for everyone except the very poor. Now everything was more mobile and a generation gap opened up in tastes and habits. Cocktail bars had begun to appear in the late thirties: now they proliferated to cater for women's new freedom to drink. Tea was also threatened as a social drink by coffee: after the invention of the Espresso machine in the early fifties, it became an in-drink, like milk in the thirties. Once instant coffee was widely available, making it a convenience drink, coffee overtook tea in domestic popularity too. A rash of coffee bars spread across the country, conventionally inhabited by talkative duffle-coated students, or by the disaffected, juke-box addicted teenagers who came into existence in the fifties. Glasgow's Italian cafés had always been popular with the young — now many of them took on new life. Others were newly opened, like the fashionably named 'La Causette' in 1957; or the Papingo coffee bar, 'purveyors of good coffee since 1958'.[6] But what might have seemed successors to the tea rooms were ultimately driven out of business by the same enemy: insufficient profit on the cups of coffee and occasional sandwiches consumed by idling customers.

From the mid fifties the affluent younger generations had the money to implement a natural inclination to cast off the past in favour of modernity.

116. A reflection of the new style in eating places (1961).

There was a passion for everything up-to-date. The stuffy old quality of the tea rooms — starched tablecloths and good furniture — was no longer wanted. Formica and leatherette were the thing, new, smart, easy to clean; and nice picture windows, not the old stained glass of Glasgow's distinctive decorative tradition. And to be really good food now had to be a bit foreign: after a long preference for the plain home cooking in which the tea room–restaurants specialised, the middle classes wanted to change their mince or fish and potatoes for something different. Glasgow had always had its good 'continental' restaurants — the Central Hotel's posh Malmaison, for instance, or the Restaurant Ferrari long in Swiss-Italian family ownership;[7] to these were added in the late fifties and sixties countless new restaurants with fancy names, and a growing number of Chinese and Indian restaurants as well as a few other ethnic specialities. For eating out, like entertaining in the home and holidays abroad, increased for those who had 'never had it so good', and many licensed restaurants were expanded or opened specifically to cater for new couple-based social patterns.[8] The emphasis was squarely on 'dining', with perhaps some dancing to a Latin-American quartet. A superficially sophisticated cuisine and ambience was de rigeur, a Spanish lounge almost obligatory. While the old tea rooms had almost universally changed their name to 'restaurant' by this period, they remained unlicensed and the public was not deceived.

This change of tastes was all personified in the emergence of Glasgow's post-war catering giant — indeed it was often claimed that he brought it about. At all events Reo Stakis, the Greek Cypriot who first came to Glasgow selling lace on a motorbike, made a very individual contribution to the end of the tea rooms. Like Miss Cranston and James Craig before him, he succeeded by giving people what they wanted. And because this 'contemporary' style was external, unlike the specially Glaswegian qualities of the tea rooms, it was easily exported, so that after building up his business in Glasgow, Stakis moved out in the old way to colonise the rest of the country. Knighted in 1989, he presided until very recently over an enormous empire of hotels and restaurants, casinos and nursing homes — though he still lives in Glasgow and the Stakis Organisation has its headquarters there.

After an experiment with a Greek restaurant at the end of the war, which was too early to 'take', Stakis bought a long established bakery, Fred J. Malcolm of Argyle St. The tea room side of the business was of no interest to Stakis: he 'didn't believe in tea rooms'. When he bought the venerable Ceylon Tea Room at the top of Renfield St, with the beautiful worked brass doors which many can remember, and reopened it as the Prince's Restaurant in 1949, he was resolved on something different. After a fire it was soon rebuilt on four storeys, like the Ca'doro aiming to cater for all tastes and pockets on different levels. The names tell all: in the basement the Taverna cocktail bar, above the Copacabana, the Calypso Bar, the Blue Room, the Rose Room, the Alpine Room.

When in Glasgow have lunch or dinner at the

IVY RESTAURANT

111 ST. VINCENT STREET

OPEN MONDAY TO SATURDAY
9 a.m. to 10.30 p.m.
Reservations — CENtral 7744

Special facilities available for parties : Ask for literature

117. The Ivy was opened by Reo Stakis in what had once been the Carlton Tea Rooms, then Cooper's. The graphics evoke the new style in dining, the antithesis of the high tea (1956).

'L'Aperitif', opened by Stakis at the eastern end of Sauchiehall St with the first new licence to be issued since the war, was described as 'a turning point in the quest for better eating houses for Glasgow'. After that all the premises were licensed. In the fifties and early sixties he opened more restaurants than anyone had ever done, tending to sell on one to buy two. Many were new, but other old locations which passed into Stakis' domain were William Kerr's Carlton Tea Rooms, at 111 St Vincent St, which had subsequently been operated as Cooper's 'St Vincent': this became the Ivy in 1951, later renamed the Alfa. The long-established Trades' House Restaurant in Glassford St was reworked as the 'Sans Souci' around 1960, and Stakis also took over various parts of the old Ca'doro to create new restaurants — El Guero, the Brasserie and the 'top-class' Tropicana. In the process he claimed to have introduced the licensed self-service cafeteria (though Lang's had effectively done this a century ago). In 1968 he bought A. F. Reid's Marlborough House on the South Side, which was shortly afterwards gutted by fire and redeveloped. Out of Wendy's Tea Rooms on Sauchiehall St Stakis made The Blenheim, and from her Bothwell St premises The Poseidon fish restaurant. Encouraged by grants from the Labour government he also moved into hotels in the 1960s, all 'ultra modern in the Stakis tradition': the most significant acquisition in this context was, around 1970, Miss Cranston's tea rooms at Ingram St.

Stakis' restaurants had exotic names (allegedly suggested by his children, who received prizes for their nominations), but their menus, though leavened with some unfamiliar, mostly Greek, dishes, were of general appeal. The chicken, newly popular with the growth of the broiler trade, was one of the foundations of Stakis' success. In 1960 the business was said to be selling seven thousand a week, about half of them in the Prince's — 'Where Dining Out Takes on a New Excitement'. The breakthrough came with the Stakis steak houses, which offered at a low price a 'night out' in up-to-date surroundings. High tea was absolutely banished. The interior design at all the restaurants (by Glasgow architects Tombazis at the Prince's and T. M. Miller thereafter) executed Stakis' conception of smartness and comfort in the contemporary manner.

The extent to which tastes had changed, and Glaswegians had been demoralised into forgetting that the city's tradition in restaurants was once of the best, was exemplified in panegyrics on Stakis' crusade to improve Scotland's catering and eating. In 1964 it was claimed that he had 'transformed a city's restaurants from meagre tea-rooms into restaurants whose decor, service and menus can rival any in Western Europe'.

Of course all these changes were at the time less perceptible than this account might suggest, and many personally-run businesses continued in the old traditions of the tea rooms, especially away from the city centre. In the comfortable middle-class enclave of Hillhead, for instance, many will remember from the 1940s the tall aesthetic Miss Mackenzie and her Greengates Tea Rooms on Bank St:[9] passing through the little cottage gate in its

118. Wendy's advertisement from a 1950s tourist guide, still projecting a distinctive image.

special shade of green one entered a tasteful interior in cream and green, with parchment-shaded lamps. It later became an Indian restaurant. On Byres Rd University wives lined up their prams outside a longer-lasting establishment, Barclay's. This notable business, begun in the thirties, was run at two locations — a shop and tea room, and a separate restaurant at the corner of Ashton Rd — by two Bettys (they were cousins, both named Bethiah). Betty Barclay knew every artist in Glasgow and staged exhibitions of work she liked: she generally took a painting in lieu of commission and thus built up her own excellent collection. Several artists got a useful start in her tea rooms. Barclay's ran on through the sixties until a compulsory purchase order demolished the restaurant and the business with it.

In the centre of town Glasgow's big department stores, a large number of them brought into Hugh Fraser's voracious House of Fraser group since the war, fought on in the fifties and early sixties, ceaselessly up-dating to reflect current tastes: Muirhead's on Sauchiehall St, for instance, was modernised in 1954, with a restaurant seating five hundred on its fourth floor, designed to tempt in office girls for lunch and a spot of impulse buying. The stores still featured significantly in family life, often in a complex hierarchy of preferences. Naturally however many of the older generation maintained that things were not what they were, lamenting falling standards of service and decor. They remained true to the old ways, and many younger people today remember being taken to tea rooms by their grannies. Even at the end, old ladies in old furs could still be seen in Fuller's drinking Russian tea the proper way, through a sugar lump between their teeth; and elderly lawyers might still disappear mysteriously in the middle of the morning to G. M. Frame's dark basement coffee room.

119 and 120. Rivals to Wendy's from the 1930s still going in the 1950s: Jean's and the Green Twig, both on Sauchiehall St.

But from the swinging sixties the end was certain. The new spenders spurned the tea rooms and old department stores in favour of pizza, which took Glasgow by storm, and boutiques. A rash of 'Easy Eats', 'Super Eats' and 'Snax' had appeared in the fifties, presaging Wimpy's appearance on Sauchiehall St around 1960. They were direct contenders to the tea rooms' cheap quick service, but brighter and more casual. Once the tea rooms had been mainstream and up-to-the-minute: now they seemed old hat and peripheral, altogether lacking in glamour.

Now we must trace the demise of individual businesses which illustrate this story of decline. Miss Cranston comes first: her name was still alive in popular memory, and the Ingram Street Tea Rooms still in operation after the war in the ownership of Coopers. But Mackintosh was largely forgotten and his aging interiors looked battered and strangely dated. Ordinary chairs replaced broken originals, and tables were set with a disconcerting mixture of Mackintosh cutlery and standard cafeteria ware.[10] Nevertheless the bulk was undamaged when under pressure the Corporation bought the tea rooms for £23,000 in 1950. Nothing could be more significant of prevailing tastes than the destruction which occurred during the city's ownership over the next two decades, when the premises were let to an outlet for tacky tartan souvenirs. The Oak Room was painted and grained, with silver- and gold-flecked insulating tiles stuck to the roof; doors were moved, tiles smashed, the gesso panels of the White Room 'brightened up'. Finally the building came into the hands of Stakis, but an application to revive the interiors for restaurant use was foiled by fire regulations and rampant dry rot. The remains were dismantled in 1971, and spent some years in limbo, before passing into the care of Glasgow Art Galleries and Museums, while the building was largely demolished.[11] It is a chastening tale, only too characteristic of the bad old days before Glasgow woke to its architectural heritage and the benefits of taking care of it.

The Willow had been sold to Daly's next door in 1927, and over the years the store was ruthless in converting the premises to shop use, breaking through the party wall and smashing away Mackintosh's frontage at street level and much of the interior. With the revival of interest in Mackintosh in the late sixties, cognoscenti penetrating Daly's to see what was left of the Willow might surprise a bride-to-be in her underwear in the Room de Luxe. Meanwhile refittings to keep the Clydesdale Bank and Manfield's shoe shop up-to-date had removed nearly all traces of the original interiors at 91 Buchanan St and 114 Argyle St (from which the People's Palace Museum salvaged what it could in the 1970s).

Stuart Cranston's company had made it through to this postwar period. Like other tea rooms it had done well enough during the war, but afterwards was a typical casualty of the unequal battle against rising overheads and dwindling profits. The Cinema in Renfield St was sold off and became the Classic, while R. S. McColl, for some time tenant of 13 Renfield St and

at your
SERVICE
LYRIC
RESTAURANT
62 SAUCHIEHALL STREET

MELODY
RESTAURANT
38 ST. ENOCH SQUARE

AND THE

CLASSIC
RESTAURANT
17 RENFIELD STREET

The ideal meeting places for :
★ MORNING COFFEE
★ LUNCH
★ AFTERNOON TEA
★ HIGH TEA

R S McColl RESTAURANTS

121. The successful confectionery company R. S. McColl moved into tea rooms, though using the word restaurant. It took over Cranston's tea rooms at Renfield St in 1953. Advertisement of 1964.

like Lang's an old business associate of Cranston's, took over the tea room side, operating the main restaurant at 17 as The Classic Cafeteria.

The closing in April 1954 of Cranston's premises on the corner of Argyle St and Queen St, the very first Glasgow tea room, inaugurated the real end of what had begun there. There was a regretful, if detached, awareness of the passing of something special, bound up with the greatness of Glasgow's past: 'We have often heard the claim made that this was the original tea room from which all other tea rooms in the country have been derived. Certainly it was always a pleasant reminder that this was one of Great Britain's many institutions which had their beginnings in Victorian Glasgow.'[12] The freehold was acquired for over £200,000 by a Scottish insurance firm and the building was leased to a multiple furnishing business. The company went into voluntary liquidation in 1955.

In this year Craig's delivered even more of a blow to Glasgow's businessmen when the company sold up the Gordon and its famous pictures, leaving countless regulars shattered and disoriented by the loss of their beloved smoking rooms. The large Union St premises went in the same stroke. The original premises at 19 Cowcaddens where James Craig senior had set up baking pies in 1870 had been closed two years after the war. The firm's crisis in the fifties was precipitated by the death in August 1953 of Mr W. Watt Hepburn, a baker who had established himself in Aberdeen in the 1890s and built up an enormous provisioning business. Among his many investments he had quietly acquired a controlling interest in James Craig's. His death evidently left the Craig family shareholders in an impossible position, compounded by high taxation and the crippling overheads of running such elegantly spacious premises. The business had also depended very much on the energy of Jessie Wynd, and ran down without a vigorous and committed individual at its head.

Craig's Gordon St building was acquired by Thomas Cook and Son, whose general manager James Maxwell had joined the firm in Glasgow and nurtured an ambition to create there 'one of the finest travel centres in Europe'. But even this ruthlessness was not enough, and two years later, on 17 May 1957, the firm closed its other flagship, the Rhul on Sauchiehall Street. Late the following year the diminished remains of the company suffered the indignity of being bought up by its once lesser rival Peacock's — which was by now a front for Associated Bakeries and General Investment Co. Ltd, a Scottish conglomerate.[13] Conscious of public feeling they promised to 'maintain the tradition established by Craig's and so far as possible retain present staff'. However the company wound down and was liquidated in November 1962, though a business continued at a few minor branches as 'James Craig Bakers' until the complete disappearance of the name by 1970.

1958 saw the final end too of the old Ca'doro, which had dwindled into a low grade shadow of its former self. The 'real' City Bakeries had fallen to outside takeover just before the outbreak of the war: the elder Uries were in a quandary about which of the next generation might succeed to the administration of the empire when Garfield Weston offered them more money than they could refuse. John Urie remained however as managing director until 1945; he died in 1956. When Weston established himself firmly in London at the end of the war he made other large tea-room bakers his quarry. Walter Hubbard's and Alex Colqhoun's were gathered into his net. So too in 1955 was Cooper's, becoming Coopco Stores Ltd, part of the FineFare group (now Gateway); and eventually Peacock's and a few last shreds of Craig's.[14]

The Ca'doro was sold off after the war to the Scottish Cooperative Wholesale Society. In April 1958 they announced that it would close 'in view of the increasingly unsatisfactory economic position in the catering trade' — though to avoid disappointment for summer weddings it continued to do functions until October. It was broken up for letting: Reo Stakis, equal to the economic situation, established himself in the basement and the two upper floors. It also accommodated Clark's shoes, Lilly White Frowd's sports goods and a shipping agency, and became increasingly a mess.

By the end of the fifties nothing old was safe: everywhere the past was being dismantled in favour of modernity.[15] In 1957 the old Corn Exchange restaurant and tea room opposite Central Station, founded in the 1880s and a favourite place for high teas, was bought out and closed by Grosvenor Caterers Ltd, who owned the big Grosvenor next door. Two of its waitresses had been there for forty years. Meanwhile, just round the corner in Hope St, British Railways was converting the quick lunch bar affectionately known as the 'Ratpit' into the air conditioned 'La Fourchette'. Its 'fully contemporary' style mixed primaries with pastel shades and 'vogueish, coloured, lagerglass shapes to add fancy to a crisply functional design'.[16] The new Gay Gordon was similarly up-to-date, done out in Gordon tartan with vibrant yellow seats to David Hicks' design around 1959. Where the tea rooms had done good pre-theatre high tea business, the late-opening Gay Gordon filled a new demand for post-theatre suppers. The kitchen fronting onto the restaurant let customers, once shyness wore off, chose their own steaks; there was taped music during the day, and dancing nightly to Geraldo's band. The owners were optimistically planning expansion as the sixties dawned.[17]

Equally typical of the mood of the era was the 'transformation' in 1959 of the Grosvenor Restaurant itself. This 'dignified relic of Edwardiana' established in 1898, was now to be marched into the modern world. The process began with the smashing of its magnificent marble staircase, which would have been an intolerable intrusion on fifties chic. The tone of lament is clear in the account of a *Glasgow Herald* reporter on this 'melancholy but inspiring' occasion. The old restaurant with its marble pillars and curlicues 'did not merely belong to Glasgow, it was a period piece of which all Britain could be proud. Its loss (modernisation proceeding) is severe.' But, he goes on stoutly, 'the new Grosvenor rises gloriously, like Venus from the sea, and in elegance, comfort, and mood will hold its own against anything the rest

122. The Grosvenor, in Greek Thomson's magnificent building on Gordon St, included a large tea room at the rear. Photographed in full grandeur in 1935, with the new Tea Room annexe on the left.

of the country can offer.' The large downstairs tea room was treated in 'Regency effect' aquamarine and rose, with silver architraves and quilted turquoise leather on the doors. A cocktail bar was installed where the large fireplace used to be. Sadness resurfaces: 'going upstairs has lost its pomp and circumstance. The marble staircase with its drugget, up which generations of Glasgow and West of Scotland mothers have ushered their daughters to wedding parties, will shortly be no more. Now you nip up a simple modern flight, or pop out of one of two lifts.'[18] By September the job was done. Most of the old dining room became a lounge, the rest of it, together with the floor space which had been occupied by the famous staircase and the old Grosvenor Tea Rooms annexe, became the new dining room. (The whole thing was burnt in the late sixties, and at time of writing is a mere facade with prestigious office redevelopment proceeding behind it.)

The closing of hotels was another sign of an ailing economy.[19] Among them was another relic of Glasgow's prosperous past, the Grand Hotel at Charing Cross. By the end of 1959 the United Coop Baking Society was negotiating to sell it off. This magnificent building had always been a little too far from railway stations to be a real success, but it had its regulars and its grandeur had great appeal to those wanting to feel a bit posh. It had

THE GRAND HOTEL, GLASGOW.

123 and 124. Charing Cross before the motorway. Above, the Grand Hotel sketched in the days of its Edwardian opulence in 1906, demolished 1969. Below, the view down Sauchiehall St, with Charing Cross Mansions on the left (preserved) and Skinner's beloved tea rooms on the right (demolished).

never recovered from requisitioning and invasion by squatters at the end of the war, and afterwards became a white elephant, increasingly shabby and impossible to run. It was eventually put out of its misery in 1969 to prepare for the motorway crashing through Charing Cross. This blight also carried away Skinner's, which had maintained its standards impressively to the end.

125. Miss Rombach's was still going strong in the fifties, emphasising the continuous service that was the key to survival.

MISS
ROMBACH RESTAURANT
CORNER OF HOPE STREET
& WATERLOO ST. GLASGOW
Telephone Central 4681

CONTINUOUS
7-30 SERVICE 7-00
A.M. P.M.

Parties after 7 p.m., by Arrangement

It must not be thought, however, that the tea rooms went down without a fight. Miss Rombach's is a good example of successful adaptation. In 1953 its smoking room, which though popular was no longer profitable, was converted into a function suite with an excellent dancing floor, to meet the increasing demand for dinner-dances and buffets. The breakfast room began business early in the day. At midday many leading businessmen who retained their sober habits were to be seen at the 'Top Table' in the lunch room. Afternoon and high teas followed. After the main restaurant closed at 7 o'clock the suite would be open until midnight, licensed as required. This was punishing work for David Rombach, nephew of the original Miss Rombach, but it achieved continuous use of compact premises. The business fell in the end to larger economic forces, when the building in which it was housed was demolished along with the fine old Corn Exchange, which was no longer filling its original function, to be replaced by a particularly unattractive specimen of shoddy contemporary architecture, in 1962. This was indeed a dire year for Glasgow: the City lost the last of its trams, the Empire music hall, and St Andrew's Halls, gutted by fire.

Miss Buick's, founded like Miss Rombach's in 1910, plugged on through the hard work of two branches of her family, serving good plain cheap food, resisting pressure to modernise, faithfully supported by regulars. In 1959 Miss Buick's nephew Robert Buick closed 19a Renfield St, which become the Excelsior Chinese restaurant, and joined forces with her niece Elizabeth Fraser (Mrs Rae), who had entered the business in 1926, at 147 West George St. There Miss Buick's continued until in 1967 'the ever-increasing burden of the city's rates' forced closure on a business with low profit margins. 'We are sorry the news has got out', said the proprietors; 'We have not yet told our customers, many of whom have been our friends for more than thirty years'.

Wendy's finally closed its West George St premises in 1972, when Miss Irene Cooper, managing director, had to say likewise that she was sorry, but the continuously rising overheads had become intolerable. Pettigrew & Stephens and Copland & Lye were demolished in the same year to make way for a new shopping mall. Indeed few tea rooms survived the decade from 1962, when the process of shedding the past was drastically accelerated, with massive, often savage redevelopment plans, bleak tower block estates, and eventually the implementation of the motorway plan, which cut ugly swathes through old areas of the city.

While Stakis was at his height, moving into casinos and opening more steak houses, the newspapers were carrying reports lamenting 'Scotland's eating out desert', the disposable age in catering, the cost of eating out, and so on. In 1974 *The Glasgow Herald* began a long, nostalgic correspondence about Miss Cranston. A hundred years after the tea rooms began, they were virtually extinct. If you wanted anything like a proper Glasgow city-centre tea room your choice was limited, with the closing of Fuller's, to M. & A. Brown or the tea room in Trérons, both on Sauchiehall St. People began to realise that something they had taken for granted was gone, and they missed it.

Epilogue

In the last chapter we set the virtual disappearance of the Glasgow tea room one hundred years after the first was opened. But 1975 might also be picked, again a little arbitrarily for neatness' sake, but not unreasonably, as the beginning of the recent upturn in Glasgow's fortunes. In the mid seventies the first stone-cleaning programmes began the process of revaluing the nineteenth-century past. Tenements stood a chance of being rehabilitated, rather than automatically flattened; buildings in the city centre began to have their facades propped up while rebuilding proceeded behind them. The losses continued of course, and the motorway programme cut an unstoppable swathe of destruction, but attitudes changed. By the time this reached its apogee in Glasgow's year as European City of Culture in 1990, the building activity and air of prosperity and confidence in the city could be likened to the bustle of the 1890s — though now as then the city has its appalling black spots hidden from middle-class view.

Economic revival spawned a rash of wine bars in the seventies, accommodating women in the way that traditional Scottish pubs still did not. In the eighties evolved the phenomenon of the café bar, serving the new class of properous 'hot-croissants-and-Chablis' consumer anatomised by Ian Jack in 1984 in his essay on the 'Repackaging of Glasgow'.[1] Run typically by stylish youngsters, detached and casual, who have little in common with tea room waitresses, these places are nevertheless in a sense successors to the tea rooms, with their designer decor and convenient flexibility. Afternoon tea has lost its place in common routine, and patrons are more likely to dawdle over a capuchino than a cup of tea; but the demand for a good quick lunch in attractive surroundings during a working day remains, albeit undermined by the take-away sandwich.

The restoration to tea room use of Mackintosh's pièce de résistance for Miss Cranston, the Room de Luxe at the Willow Tea Rooms on Sauchiehall Street, perhaps symbolises this change of attitude. A new appreciation of Mackintosh, fired by the final loss of the Ingram St Tea Rooms, was mobilised by the foundation of the C. R. Mackintosh Society in 1973. In the mid seventies the society watched anxiously over the fate of the Willow with Daly's imminent departure from the building. When it was acquired by the Arrowcroft Development Group in 1978, restoration as far as possible to its original structure was made a condition of planning permission. Fittingly it was Mackintosh's old firm, now Keppie Henderson, which was called in to consult on the complex task.[2] The destruction of the past decades was carefully undone: the party wall rebuilt, the ugly plate-glass shop front removed, the columns and beams and false ceiling of the gallery replaced, casts made of the strange plaster panels of the frieze, and so on — though the now beneficent planning authorities perpetrated a different kind of wrecking when fire regulations enforced the glassing in of Mackintosh's open stair and gallery.

The Room de Luxe had survived almost intact — it was perhaps just too exquisite to smash — and tea room business was re-opened there in 1983. Mackintosh would be upset however by the disorderly modern arrangement of the tables and the free use of replicas of the high-backed chairs as the basic seating, which confound his original conception: the high chairs were intended only for the centre of the room, now occupied by some odd small pieces derived from designs for other tea rooms. The billiard room on the next floor up now houses a gallery, and the rest of the building is occupied by the clutter of a jewellery and Mackintoshiana business. Despite a lack of refinement in the restored decor, one can only be thankful that so much of this intimate little building can be once more appreciated. The queues of enthusiastic tourists on the narrow stairs, waiting to take tea and try out a Mackintosh chair, suggest that more of the premises might profitably be restored to their intended use.

Exploitative appreciation of Mackintosh, now neatly known as Mock-intosh, is today rampant in Glasgow. The Sauchiehall Centre shopping mall, unworthy successor to the grandeur of Pettigrew & Stephens and Copland & Lye, is a particularly crass example. Crude application of Mackintosh motifs to its open-plan 'food court', including an 'echo' of the Argyle St high-backed chair, in plywood, metal tubing and naked screws, serves only to highlight by contrast the old quality of the tea rooms.

The fate of James Craig's 'Rhul' is typical of the vandalising of Sauchiehall St in the sixties and seventies: the facade survives, but it has had all the quality stripped out of it, and is a hollow shell for a cheap clothing company. Craig's other flagship in Gordon St is slightly better off: the tiled sign for James Craig, somewhat defaced, is visible in the passageway next to the main building. Though Thomas Cook's has reduced the ground floor and old smoking room downstairs to anonymity long since, the art deco lift of polished wood and brass which rises to the upper floors recalls another age. On the first floor, now occupied by a bridal-wear company, many traces of the fine panelling, fireplaces and cornices are preserved.

Craig's rival, the Ca'doro, had become by the seventies a commercialised shambles. Its gutting and refurbishing, assisted by a fire in 1987, allowed the building to arise like a gleaming phoenix, no longer housing any restaurants, but a fine bookshop and offices above. The ugly top floor added by City Bakeries in 1922 was removed, and the equally ugly extension in Union St was replaced with a seamless addition replicating the bays of the original.

When this book was first thought about 'Ma Brown's' survived on Sauchiehall Street, with its bakery shop at the front, tea room behind, and cash box at the top of the stairs leading down to the capacious restaurant, once the smoke room, below. Then in 1989 the family tradition ended and it was taken over by the Pars Delta bakery, by whom it was operated briefly in the

126. M. & A. Brown on Sauchiehall St, photographed in 1934 not long after opening; by 1975 the sole tea room listed in the *Post Office Directory*; closed during the writing of this book.

same manner until closure in 1991. At the time of writing it is undergoing refurbishment for a licensed restaurant.

Attempts to reintroduce tea rooms have not been entirely successful. In 1989 'Miss Pink's Tea Parlour' was in business — its name had the wrong reverberations but its basement location in Bath St was classic — indeed there had been a tea room there during the First World War. Recently it revised its name to The Glasgow Tea Room, and applied the ubiquitous Mackintosh iconography. But at the time of writing it has closed.

We end with two more hopeful establishments that evoke the old nature of the Glasgow tea rooms. One is a modest long survivor, the other a glossy reintroduction. On Union St Trees Tea Room, now called Trees Restaurant, runs on in a big first floor room: no frills, and no licence. It opened in 1933, and the present proprietors the Lamarras, father and son, moved to it from the family fish and chip business in 1963. Regulars, many at their tables every day, are its life blood. They let the staff know when they are going on holiday, so that no one gets worried. And they dictate the good plain dishes of the menu.

Bradford's coffee shop opened in 1989 is a smart recreation, next to Wendy's old address on Sauchiehall St, of an old pattern of city-centre tea room — with a bakery and confectionery shop on the ground floor, and black-and-white waitress service for tea and light meals above, non-smoking. While at first the clientèle was mostly elderly, mobile phones are now appearing on the tables as business people start to use the place. The decor is 'tasteful' and spotless, and the company trades on top quality in baking and service. Paintings by members of the Society of Women Artists hung on the walls for sale evoke another tradition of the Glasgow tea rooms. Perhaps best of all, they can produce a cake-stand if you order afternoon tea.

Note on Sources and Brief Bibliography

The Glasgow Post Office Directory, supported by its rival, Kelly's Directory, has been an essential tool of research. It is a mine of information for most of this period, though towards the end of its life in the 1970s, increasingly marginalised by the telephone directories, it becomes sadly inaccurate and incomplete.

The Bailie, Glasgow's answer to *Punch*, published from 1872-1926, is an excellent source for advertisements and gossip. Its shorter-lived rivals *The Quiz* (1881-1898) and *St Mungo* (more sporadic) are equally good for the years they cover. Advertisements have been a key source of information, and other magazines such as *Scottish Field*, *Glasgow Illustrated*, *Glasgow University Magazine* and *Ygorra* have all been helpful, together with temperance society magazines and theatre programmes.

Guide books and the various special publications which were a vehicle for the pride of Glasgow's business community have been very useful: Kirkwood's *Dictionary of Glasgow* (1884); Baddeley's Guide (1888); *Glasgow of To-day* (1888); Stratten's *Glasgow and its Environs* (1891); *Glasgow To-day* (1909); *The Book of Glasgow* (1922); *The Book of Glasgow* (1931); and various later tourist guides. I have also made use of the *Journal of the Glasgow Chamber of Commerce*, and the *Victualling Trades' Review*, the journal of the licensed trade in Glasgow.

Newspapers are valuable though hard to search. Here should be mentioned Alison Downie, whose article 'Kate Cranston by those who knew her', *Glasgow Herald* 13 June 1981 p. 9, collects some fascinating testimonials about this remarkable woman. Alison Downie was in fact planning to write a book on Kate Cranston at the time of her sudden death in 1986, but I have not been able to discover whether she had collected any material. Another tantalising source mentioned to me too late to be found is George Blake's novel *Westering Sun* (London 1946). It apparently concerns a daughter who rescues the failing fortunes of her family by opening successful artistic tea rooms towards the end of the nineteenth century. I look forward to reading it for unreliable novelistic insights into Miss Cranston, on whom the character is evidently based.

The notes give details of specific sources, but I list below for convenience a few articles and books. Further information has been collected from the many people who have kindly talked to me, including such Glasgow authorities as Charles Oakley and the late Jack House.

Berry, Simon, and Whyte, Hamish, eds, *Glasgow Observed* (John Donald 1987)

Campbell, John McNicol, 'Memories of Glasgow Tea Rooms', in *Glasgow Illustrated* June 1974

Cunison, J. and Gilfillan, J. B. S., eds, *The Third Statistical Account of Scotland. Glasgow* (Collins 1958)

King, Elspeth, *Scotland Sober and Free: The Temperance Movement 1829-1979* (Glasgow Museums and Art Galleries 1979)

Muir, James Hamilton (=James Bone, Archibald Hamilton Charteris & Muirhead Bone), *Glasgow in 1901* (Glasgow/Edinburgh 1901)

Oakley, C. A., *'The Second City'* (Blackie 1946; 1967; 1975; 1990)

Oakley, C. A., *Dear Old Glasgow Town* (Blackie 1975)

Oakley, C. A., *Our Illustrious Forbears* (Blackie 1980)

'The story of the Glasgow Tea Roooms', in *Glasgow To-day* (Glasgow 1909) supplement, on Stuart Cranston

   For Miss Cranston and Mackintosh:

Billcliffe, Roger, *Charles Rennie Mackintosh: The Complete Furniture, Furniture Drawings and Interior Designs* (John Murray 1979, 2nd edn 1980, 3rd edn 1986)

Glasgow Girls, ed. J. Burkhauser (Canongate 1990)

Howarth, Thomas, *Charles Rennie Mackintosh and the Modern Movement* (London 1952; 2nd edn 1977; repr. 1990)

Mackintosh Architecture: The Complete Buildings and Selected Projects, ed. Jackie Cooper (Academy Editions 1978)

Munro, Neil ('Hugh Foulis'), 'Erchie in an art tea-room', originally published in *The Evening News*, republished in *Para Handy and Other Tales* (Edinburgh 1931; repr. 1972)

Robertson, Pamela, 'Catherine Cranston', *Journal of the Decorative Art Society* 10 (1986) 10-17

Waddell, J. Jeffrey, 'Some recent Glasgow tea rooms', *The Builder's Journal and Architectural Record* 15 April 1903, pp. 126-31

White, Gleeson, 'Some Glasgow Designers and their work', Part 1, *Studio* 11 (1897) pp. 86-100

Notes

INTRODUCTION

1. 'J. H. Muir', *Glasgow in 1901* (1901) p. 166.
2. *Glasgow To-day* (1909). Tea rooms in the Glasgow style were reported from fashionable resorts like Nice, as well as corners of the Empire.

THE BEGINNINGS, 1875–1888

1. George Square was Glasgow's hotel centre between the opening of the Queen St Station in 1842 and the redevelopment of the square in the late 1870s with large civic buildings, including the Municipal Chambers.
2. 'The Story of the Glasgow Tea Rooms', *Glasgow To-Day* (1909).
3. John Burnett, *Plenty and Want* (2nd edn 1979) p. 146: tea in packets began with Horniman in 1826, but was brought to a wider market by the Mazawattee Tea Co. in 1884. See also Alec Waugh, *The Lipton Story* (1951).
4. Andrew Aird, *Glimpses of Old Glasgow*, p. 15, quoted in D. Macleod Malloch, *Book of Glasgow Anecdote* (1913) p. 82, noting tea gardens at Bridgeton, on ground later occupied by Robertson's mill; the Rosehall Gardens, New City Road; and Roseneath Cottage, Paisley Road.
5. Burnett (n. 3) p. 133. The impoverished urban diet of tea, sugar and bread (with perhaps a scrape of margarine or jam) tended to replace in Scotland a healthier reliance on oatmeal.
6. Average annual consumption per head of tea rose from 2.25 lbs in 1850-9; to 4.28 lbs 1870-9; to 5.59 lbs 1890-9; and continued rising to 9.68 lbs in 1930-5: George B. Wilson, *Alcohol and the Nation* (1940) p. 242, and Burnett (n. 3) p. 131 f. Cocoa showed a similar strong increase, until finished off by instant coffee after the Second World War.
7. T. C. Smout, *A Century of the Scottish People, 1830-1950* (1986) p. 125. Average annual per capita sugar consumption in 1880-4 was for Spain 5.1 lbs, France 22.6 lbs, U.S.A. 38 lbs, and Great Britain 68.8 lbs: Burnett (n. 3) pp. 132, 190.

8. Report of the Royal Commission on the Scottish Poor Law, quoted by Smout (n. 7) p. 141.
9. *Victualling Trades' Review* 1895, p. 10.
10. Select Committees as far back as 1834, reporting on the 'Causes and Consequences of Intoxication among the Labouring Classes', had noted the need to tackle the housing problem, and to provide for public leisure facilities. See also e.g. Joseph Rowntree and Arthur Sherwell, *The Temperance Problem and Social Reform* (1899); and Sherwell's lecture on *The Drink Peril in Scotland* (1903), which urged the view that 'while it is unquestionably true that Temperance sentiment is much more advanced in Scotland than it is in England, it cannot be said that the country has made any substantial progress during the last forty or fifty years, and the gravity of the evil is as evident in the national life of Scotland to-day as it was two generations ago.' Consumption nationally was falling from its peak in the 1870s. Glasgow easily topped tables for overcrowded living conditions: Sherwell quoted 26% of families living in one room, 70% in one or two rooms. See also J. Cunison and J. B. S. Gilfillan, eds, *The Third Statistical Account of Scotland: Glasgow* (1958).
11. 'J. H. Muir', *Glasgow in 1901* (1901) p. 176 ff. The pseudonym was a cover for three bright young men: A. Hamilton Charteris, James Bone and his brother Muirhead Bone.
12. Elspeth King, 'Popular Culture in Glasgow', in R. A. Cage, ed., *The Working Class in Glasgow, 1750-1914* (1987).
13. *Glasgow of To-day* (1888): Lockhart's chain run from Glasgow comprised at this time 11 branches in Glasgow, 3 in Leeds, 9 in Newcastle, 3 in Sunderland, 2 in Southshields and one each in Gateshead, Jarrow and Darlington; the outlets were 'commodiously arranged' and well fitted, employing five to six hands. Profits were reported in *Victualling Trades' Review* 1895, p. 203. Cocoa later gave place to tea and in concession to the Glasgow tradition they changed their name to Lockhart's Tea Rooms, then Lockhart's Cafés. They finally disappeared in the 1940s.

14. Aytoun Ellis, *The Penny Universities: A history of the coffee houses* (1956). Coffee houses are generally regarded as extinct by the beginning of the 19th century, but in London the directory listing of coffee rooms still far outnumbered that of refreshment rooms in 1900.

15. The family originated in Jedburgh and moved to East Calder at the request of the Earl of Buchan *c.* 1778. Besides keeping an inn, Robert's father James also worked as a stone mason, like his own father before him. This account draws heavily on *Through Four Reigns: The Story of the Old Waverley Hotel and its Founder* (1948), by Hal D. Stewart, great-grandson of Bailie Cranston, and other family papers, now in the possession of Dr C. J. Mackinlay, for whose help I am most grateful.

16. There is a nice example in the 'fearful' warning to be derived by teetotallers from the report of an artery slashed by a gingerbeer bottle: 'such occurrences ought to plead more eloquently with the misguided "abstainer" than all the sermons spoken and written by social reformers like the Bailie; yet alas, still the "league" flourishes', *Bailie* 7 Nov. 1886, p. 3. The magazine kept it up across the years: e.g. 3 Apr. 1901, writing against the Scottish Temperance Federation; 21 Nov. 1923, calling for a vote against prohibition.

17. Muir (n. 11) p. 173.

18. *Quiz* 18 March 1881, p. 4; *Bailie* 28 July 1880, p. 1; 'Mr Incognito', *Daily Record and Mail* 16 Apr. 1929.

19. Businesses listed under 'confectioners and pastry cooks' back in 1863 which then or later operated as restaurants include Ancell's, Daniel Brown, Wm Brownlie, Henry Calderwood, F. & F.'s, John Forrester, Thos Gemmell, Walter Hubbard, Wm Lang, John Scott, Wm Skinner and Chas Thornton.

20. The *Glasgow Post Office Directory* introduced a 'restaurant' listing as early as 1865, after which it gradually grew at the expense of the old 'eating house' category. Edinburgh had 'refreshment rooms', opening a 'restaurateur' listing in the late 1890s. London did not have a 'restaurant' listing until the next century, earlier referring enquirers to Hotels, Dining Rooms and Refreshment Rooms, while the Coffee Rooms category remained enormous.

21. Miss Cranston was in fact the first to use the description 'Tea Room'. Stuart at first referred to the sample room, and did not employ 'tea room' in the *Post Office Directory* until 1887.

22. Stuart lived at his father's hotel in the 1870s and was probably involved to some extent in that business, just as George seems to have been briefly involved in his son's tea business before he retired in 1873. The demolition of the Crown Hotel cut the knot and the younger Cranston felt no obligation to continue in hoteliering.

23. 'p.p.c.' = 'pour prendre congé', leave-taking: Hal Stewart, biographical notes (n. 15).

24. Robert (b. 1843) later Sir Robert, Lord Provost of Edinburgh, opened three Temperance hotels in London on his own account between 1900 and 1906, which caused some coolness with Mary, though the breach was later healed.

25. Mary Mason's daughter Elliot, a founder member of the Scottish National Players, is remembered as a 'super person': theatrical friends like Tyrone Guthrie were among those who came to tea.

26. Miss Jessie Macdonald for example took over her father's 'Dining and Celebrated Fish Supper Rooms' at 86 Glassford St *c.* 1870 and ran them successfully for over twenty years until Miss Agnes Steel succeeded in 1892. (Edinburgh had a notable female fish restaurant dynasty in its 'far famed Clark family', advertising in 1875 'Fish Dinners established upwards of 100 yrs, now removed to the Peacock Hotel. Proprietor Mrs Main, daughter and only successor to the late Mrs Clark.') Boyd's Restaurant in Renfield St lost James Boyd in 1876, but ran on in the capable hands of Mrs Boyd. A little later David McCall's Victoria Restaurant (estab. *c.* 1880) was successfully transferred by Mrs McCall to the splendid building subsequently occupied by the Ca'doro in Union St, when its premises on the corner of Renfield and Gordon Streets were taken into Forsyth's in 1896. Similarly the Bank Restaurant run by Peter Hamilton was taken over by Mrs from 1900-14.

27. Jane Murdoch interestingly started listing herself as plain J. F., with similar effect, from 1889.

28. Miss Buick also continued in business under her maiden name after marriage; Miss Rombach retired from hers a few years after her late marriage, but the business was continued by her brother as Miss Rombach's. See further p. 67.

29. The tea rooms at 205-9 Ingram Street are listed under Stuart's name along with his premises at 2 and 46 Queen St in Baddeley's 1888 guide. They first appear under C. Cranston in the restaurant directory for 1889.

30. Restaurants prominent at this time include McDonald's and the Trades House Restaurant (Glassford St); Wright's and Blackadder's (Hope St); the Lorne (Howard St); Stewart's Royal, Stark's, and Scott's (Queen St); McCall's (Renfield St); His Lordship's Larder (St Enoch Sq.); Watson and Blane (W. George St); and the Royal (W. Nile St).

THE FIRST AGE, 1888–1918

1. For a full account and illustrations of the exhibitions mentioned in this chapter, including further detail on catering, see Perilla & Juliet Kinchin, *Glasgow's Great Exhibitions: 1888, 1901, 1911, 1938, 1988* (1988).

2. China tea held 90% of the British market before 1870. By 1900, aided by mass-marketers like Lipton, the scales had tipped completely and China was down to a mere 10%: J. Burnett, *Plenty and Want* (2nd edn 1979) p. 131.

3. Picken began around 1881 after training under John Forrester: Stratten, *Glasgow and its Environs* (1891) p. 194; *Victualling Trades' Review* 2 Jan. 1893.

4. Away from the centre the Sorn Dairy Supply opened a 'Ladies' Tea Room' in Grosvenor Place off Byres Rd, carrying the new fashion to Glasgow's residential areas.

5. *Draper's Record* 14 July 1888, 13 Oct. 1888. Some London stores had instituted refreshment rooms in the mid 1880s. See Michael Moss and Alison Turton, *A Legend of Retailing: House of Fraser* (1989) p. 60 f. on department store tea rooms.

6. *Glasgow of To-day* (1888) p. 137. Thiem had left Germany in 1868 and worked as a chef in various hotels, moving north from London to Edinburgh where, like his brother, he established himself in the hotel business. He became

a naturalised Briton, and after the Panorama interlude returned his energies to hotels, running the Windsor Hotel in Glasgow and the Peebles Hydropathic.

7. Nine years earlier Leopold Schostal, an importer of foreign wines, beers and cigars, had experimented briefly with the Alexandra Restaurant, but soon decided that there were better entrepreneurial prospects in artificial slate. Otto Bergner ran the Victoria restaurant for a couple of years from 1888. H. Schnake was at the Pavilion from 1888-92. G. Brunfaut took over Andrew Stark's smoking rooms and restaurant at 35, 41 Queen St (later the Bank Restaurant) until transferring to the Royal from 1894-6. P. Chas Rupprecht, with relations in the Glasgow hotel business, was at 183 Hope St *c.* 1889-96: he had worked for Thiem and then in the South of France before remodelling this restaurant (later The Strand), introducing waitresses and a ladies room. Sautermeister, 'Vienna and foreign bakers and confectioners', on W. Nile St from *c.* 1896 might also be mentioned, and Alfred Hugon, 'restaurateur and chef de cuisine' at a somewhat unfashionable address, 606a Gallowgate, *c.* 1892-3. 'Foreign' chefs had a general cachet: the Royal Restaurant in 1897 was advertising 'French, German, Italian and English cooks'; M. Chatrian became the city's darling after he took over F. & F.'s in the same year.

8. First at 93 Sauchiehall St in 1887, early in the 1890s moving to 110, which had a long history under the Ferrari name: see further p. 165. Pianta, Annovazzi, Fondini and Zanetti also appear in the 1890s, running restaurants in combinations too complex to detail.

9. The tea room listing was joined in 1897 by Miss Cranston, Flint's and the Govan British Workman Coffee Tavern. From then on it grew rapidly. Approximately twenty businesses were listed in 1901. No such category appeared in the Edinburgh directory until 1909, or in London until even later.

10. *The Letters of Edwin Lutyens to his Wife Lady Emily*, ed. Clayre Percy and Jane Ridley (1985) 1 June 1898, p. 56 f., quoted by kind permission of Harper Collins Publishers Ltd.

11. Hal Stewart, *Through Four Reigns* (1948) p. 5.

12. *Bailie* 13 Oct. 1897, p. 10. Seven years later Mattie was still plugging Cranston's, re-

commending his Japanese nick-nacks and confectionery for Christmas presents: *Bailie* 21 Dec. 1904.

13. *Victualling Trades' Review* 1895, p. 33: the journal did not normally deal with unlicensed businesses, but presumably hymns the arrangements because Thos W. W. Flint was an established wine as well as tea merchant. Designed by Dykes, the premises had separate gentlemen's and ladies' rooms on the first floor, and a smoking room downstairs, and included niceties like electric brackets combined with gas fittings for use when the new lighting collapsed.

14. Share offer 28 April 1897 (the papers were full of share offers for expanding businesses this year, including the well-known Danny Brown's). In 1899 the Hall and Library of the Aberdeen Society of Advocates were converted into shops and the Queen's Restaurant, with tea room above, at a cost exceeding £6000.

15. Also Miss Carswell at 121 Renfield *c.* 1892, then listed under Mrs C. Kidd 1893-98; Mrs Jessie Mackenzie from 1900 at 6 Maxwell St, followed by Mrs Lawson; Miss Davidson at 92 Dundas St from 1900; Misses Findlay & McDowall at 116 W Nile St from 1903.

16. Further examples are Carrs, Lacey, and Calderwood: it is difficult to discover when bakers and confectioners began what might be called tea rooms, as most had a long history of purveying. William McCreadie at 444 Argyle St (predecessor of Fred Malcolm) is typical, advertising in 1889 'Tea, coffee, pies and tarts served with promptitude'.

17. U.C.B.S. which had run tea rooms at 62 Renfield St from before 1893 later listed four tea rooms at 102-4 W. Nile St, 9 London Rd, 119F Main St Gorbals (next to the Royal Princess Theatre), and 263 Paisley Rd.

18. Whitelaw was at 76 Gordon St from *c.* 1886, then added 58 Jamaica St in 1896. He moved from Gordon St to 105 Hope St in 1898, and also ran 'Scott's' at 90, 98 Queen St around this time.

19. This modestly remarkable institution metamorphosed later into the Café de Luxe, which, run by Miss Mary Wilkinson, continued on from 1933 into the 1960s.

20. The Grosvenor was opened in Alexander 'Greek' Thomson's Grosvenor Buildings in 1898: see fig. 122. Metropolitan names can be seen replacing the old penchant for royalty at this period.

21. *Bailie* 20 Oct. 1897, p. 13. See also *Bailie* 30 Mar. 1898, p. 7 on a customer in love with Mabel. *St Mungo* ran another rhapsody on the tea room girl on 21 Dec. 1905, p. 272. Miss Cranston's waitresses were usually something special.

22. Judged 'quite the best piece of architecture among the minor buildings', *Architectural Review* 9 (1901) p. 250: The architect was A. N. Prentice; interior design by Guthrie & Wells; furnishing by Wylie & Lochhead.

23. Built by John Campbell *c.* 1802 in a street full of Campbells: *Regality Club* 3 (1899) p. 123.

24. Plans for 'Tea Rooms' for Dr Walker, 137-45 Sauchiehall St, submitted by Honeyman, Keppie, Mackintosh on 3 Oct. 1904 are in Strathclyde Regional Archive. A narrow entrance past plants, confections and cash girl and across a marble floor led to a lounge area and then into a sizable tea room on the street floor, with smoking room above and ladies' room in the basement, together with ladies', men's and girls' retiring rooms.

25. *Glasgow Herald* 13 June 1981, reporting the recollections of Robert Grier, the driver of the donkey-cart: Kate's soft spot for the donkey is also recalled.

26. Rose was the daughter of Karl Rombach, a German master clockmaker, and Annie Calder Sutherland, whose parents had kept the Sutherland Arms at Golspie.

27. See the magnificent book by Michael Moss & Alison Turton (n. 5) for a history of Glasgow's department stores.

28. The United Coop. Baking Society wound up its tea shops during the early years of the war; Thos Robertson's Mercantile Tea Rooms went; and Ed. Lipsett's Cocoa Rms. Cameron's closed, and Jules Boullet who had added tea rooms at 294 Sauchiehall St in 1911 disappeared from the directory.

29. John Smith had a long history in Glasgow's restaurant business: he bought Stark's in Queen St, then in partnership with Thomas White took over Ancell's Trades' House Restaurant in Glassford St and Forrester's at 7 Gordon St in 1895, and later the Corn Exchange in Gordon St. Later acqui-

sitions as Smith (Glasgow) Ltd after the partnership split were the Athenaeum in Buchanan St, 19 Renfield St *c.* 1915, Miss Cranston's Willow in 1919, and the Grosvenor Restaurant in 1924, to which was added a Tea Rooms annexe at 80 Gordon St. These were later sold off until the company was left with only the Athenaeum in the 1950s.

30. Miss Cranston's bequests included sums for her former assistant Miss Mary Sharp, and for Thomas Erskine, baker; and large amounts for Saltcoats Mission Coast Home and Saltcoats Child Welfare Home.

MISS CRANSTON AND THE ARTISTIC TEA ROOM

1. J. J. Bell, *I Remember* (1932) p. 33; Muirhead Bone quoted by Neil Munro, *The Brave Days* (1931) p. 199.

2. 'J. H. Muir', *Glasgow in 1901* (1901) p. 167; Munro (n. 1) p. 198.

3. Nikolaus Pevsner, 'George Walton: his life and work', *JRIBA* 46 (1939) p. 538; and Munro (n. 1) p. 199.

4. *Victualling Trades' Review* 1908, p. 120.

5. *Victualling Trades' Review* 1895, p. 33; designed by the architect Dykes. For Flint's see also p. 99.

6. *Bailie* 15 Sept. 1886, p. 5 attributes the painting to Henry Christie of Christie & Henderson, not otherwise known. A copy of a miniature illustrated booklet of 1897 in the possession of T. & R. Annan & Sons attributes work at 205 Ingram St to the architect Kesson Whyte, also mysterious, and Alexander & Howell, established Glasgow furniture makers and decorators, who specialised in revivalist styles; the lunch room at 209 is credited to Scott Morton. These were almost certainly the original schemes. For japonisme in the tea rooms *cf.* the new Colosseum tea rooms of 1888 (p. 45) and the Mikado *c.* 1893 (p. 57); Cranston opened a Japanese and oriental dept at 43 Argyll Arcade *c.* 1896; similarly Madame Bain at 184 Sauchiehall St in 1901 opened tea rooms which also sold oriental curios, cabinets and pictures.

7. Scott Morton was born near Glasgow and trained there as an architect, founding his firm in Edinburgh in 1870. The Glasgow carpet

Templetons were major backers of his development of Tynecastle Canvas, a heavy embossed wall and ceiling covering fashionable at this period, and shown off spectacularly in the reconstructed Bishop's Palace at the 1888 exhibition.

8. *Studio* 39 (1906) p. 33 speaks of a commission for stencilling in the smoking room, but the job seems to have included other areas too, to judge by illustrations in Annan's booklet (n. 6).

9. A major study of George Walton by Karen Moon to appear in conjunction with an exhibition of his work at Glasgow Art Gallery and Museum in 1993 will give Walton the attention he deserves.

10. See in general Pamela Robertson, 'Catherine Cranston', *J. Dec. Art Soc.* 10 (1986) pp. 10-17.

11. *Builder* 75 (1898) p. 23. The building is dubbed 'Francois I' by A. Gomme and D. Walker, *Architecture of Glasgow* (1968) p. 198 n. 3, 'North German Renaissance' on second thoughts in the 1987 edn, p. 258 n. 3 (under Free Style).

12. Pevsner (n. 3) p. 538. Shades of conventional reaction to the Glasgow Style occur in the notice in *St Mungo* 13 May 1897, p. 4 after the hoarding was removed: 'The "artistic" barricade which so long decorated Buchanan St in front of Miss Cranston's tea-rooms is now doing duty in front of a railway operation in Gibson St, Hillhead, but as the planks have been put on any-how the *ensemble* suggests a nightmare of the new poster designer after a supper of lobster and stout.'

13. See Elizabeth Bird, 'Ghouls and gaspipes: public reaction to early work of the Four', *Scot. Arts Review* 14 no. 4 (1975) pp. 13-16; also *Glasgow Girls*, ed. J. Burkhauser (1990). One of the posters was commissioned by Drooko Umbrellas, later Miss Cranston's tenant at Argyle St.

14. How Miss Cranston came to meet Mackintosh is not clear. It is likely to have been through Fra Newbery, Headmaster of the Glasgow School of Art, always energetic on behalf of his best pupils; or his wife Jessie (Rowat), herself a leading member of the 'advanced' school of Glasgow design, noted particularly for her art embroidery (which she applied like the Macdonalds to making her

own unusual clothes). She was a tireless champion of Mackintosh: see the reminiscences of Mary Newbery Sturrock (Fra and Jessie's daughter) in *Connoisseur* Aug. 1973, pp. 280-8. The other possibility is that he was brought onto the job by Walton, who had certainly met Mackintosh before this. According to Pevsner (n. 3) p. 544 Keppie drew his attention to a young draughtsman 'very much in your style. You should meet him'. However as Mackintosh's murals were executed by J. & W. Guthrie, whereas Walton's company employed its own craftsmen to execute designs, the commission seems more likely to have originated from Miss Cranston. Walton would presumably have kept the whole interior to himself if he could have.

15. Gleeson White, 'Some Glasgow designers and their work' (Part 1), *Studio* 11 (1897) pp. 86-100. White pays full tribute to the quality of the execution by Messrs Guthrie (shortly afterwards renamed Guthrie & Wells).

16. Roger Billcliffe, *Charles Rennie Mackintosh: The Complete Furniture, Furniture Drawings and Interior Designs* (3nd edn 1986) p. 258 withdraws his earlier suggestion that Mackintosh may have designed some light fittings also. The sketch D1896.14 inscribed for Buchanan St is not in fact the same as the fitting shown in Walton's lunch room (which is by Walton). It seems likely that Mackintosh provided extra lights a little later: he designed several fittings for Argyle St. Billcliffe's magnificent book gives a full record of the tea room interiors.

17. *Bailie* 5 May 1897, p. 6; *Evening News*; *Hamilton Advertiser*; *Evening Times*, quoted in a publicity booklet (n. 6).

18. *St Mungo* 13 May 1897, p. 4: the cutlery was presumably by Walton, including the green- and purple-handled knives mentioned on p. 90. A piece published on 29 July 1897, p. 8, doubtless from the same hand, mentions 'Waltonesque spoons'. This is a revealing spoof, looking back from the future, on the new era of aesthetic eating which Miss Cranston was ushering in. 'For the first time no one was allowed in a dining or tea room unless his or her costume harmonised with the colour scheme of the mural decorations, and there are many among us who remember the *cause celebre* Craibe Angus v. The Crown, the case of a well-known art dealer of the period whose

bottle green tweed suit was adjudged by a jury sufficient to justify his ejection from the splendid Lobster Salad and Old Cork Saloon of a Buchanan St tea-room', etc.

19. *The Letters of Edwin Lutyens to his Wife Lady Emily*, ed. C. Percy and J. Ridley (1985) 17 June 1897, p. 49 f.; 1 June 1898, p. 57. See p. 53 for the decor Lutyens installed at home.

20. *St Mungo* 25 Nov 1897, p. 4. Photographs of the interiors fairly complete were apparently taken as early as April 1897, if Howarth's note of Annan records now lost is correct.

21. Several designs for light fittings survive accompanied by notes like 'leaded glass in rich colours, glass jewels leaded into reflector', 'decorated with green beads', but the interiors were photographed before the wiring was completed.

22. This design was soon referred to as a 'Mackintosh chair': e.g. *St Mungo* 21 Dec. 1905, p. 272. See Billcliffe (n. 16) pp. 43-52, 258-9. Mackintosh had previously designed only a few private and exhibition pieces, some plain furniture for Queen Margaret Medical College, and some bedroom furniture for Guthrie & Wells in 1896. He had been employed by Honeyman & Keppie since 1889, and sallies into applied art were incidental to his developing architectural career. Work at Buchanan St and Argyle St was undertaken on the side.

23. J. Jeffrey Waddell, 'Some Recent Glasgow Tea Rooms', *The Builder's Journal and Architectural Record* 17 (1903) pp. 126-31.

24. Billcliffe (n. 16) p. 47 discusses this chair in detail, emphasising its newness, where Mackintosh's previous furniture had had clear links with Arts-and-Crafts and traditional designs. All the furniture for Argyle St catalogued by Billcliffe shows shared features of design.

25. Karen Moon, 'George Walton & Co.: Work for Commercial Organisations. The Rowntree Firms', *J. Dec. Arts* (1981) pp. 12-22; and see her forthcoming book (n. 9).

26. Walton's connection with Miss Cranston was soon lost to view: the *Builder's Journal* (n. 23) commended Walton features at Argyle St without mentioning him by name, and spoke chiefly of 'Mr. Macintosh, who together with Mr George Walton is responsible for the decoration and furnishing' at Buchanan St.

However an article in *Decorative Kunst* 1900 discussed Walton's work at Buchanan St without mentioning Mackintosh.

27. The international penetration of the *Studio*, consolidated by an article in *Decorative Kunst* in 1898, paved the way. Later articles, e.g *Ver Sacrum* 1901, *Dek. Kunst* 1902, 1905, spread knowledge of Mackintosh's work widely on the continent. At home he became a partner of Honeyman & Keppie in 1901 despite his jilting of Jessie Keppie to court Margaret.

28. 24 Jan. 1900; correspondence from the Mackintoshes to Hermann Muthesius and his wife, who became valued friends, is now in the West Berlin Werkbundarchiv, and is quoted by kind permission of Frau Vera Muthesius. *Studio* 28 (1903) pp. 287-8; Billcliffe (n. 16) p. 86 ff.: the panels were exhibited in Vienna.

29. E.g. P. Morton Shand's letter to William Davidson, 31 Mar. 1933, about the proposed Mackintosh memorial exhibition: 'I hope that the exhibition may not be so arranged or announced as to give the impression that Mrs Mackintosh was in any sense considered her husband's equal or alter ego ... the future is scarcely likely to see her rather thin talent restored to a place of honour.' This is quoted by Pamela Robertson, whose essay 'Margaret Macdonald Mackintosh', in *Glasgow Girls* (n. 13) p. 109 ff. is a valuable reassessment. Timothy Neat, *ibid.* pp. 117-21, proclaims 'Margaret Macdonald is the spiritual key to Mackintosh's greatness — the importance of her role in his personal and intellectual development cannot be over-emphasised.'

30. Billcliffe narrows Margaret's greatest influence on Mackintosh to 1901-2, which saw the development of a fluid new style — hard white enamel denying the wood beneath, insisting on the chair as a sculptural form, luxurious insets of purple, rose and green glass. This allows him to connect the 'less experimental', 'limited', 'over-refined' features of this work with Margaret's 'predictable' imagery and over-pretty later style.

31. The green and purple so characteristic of Glasgow-Style colouring, while perhaps influenced by the soft heathery hues of the Scottish landscape, surely had feminist added value from the suffragettes' use of the same colours. The Glasgow School of Art was an unusually liberal institution, offering excellent opportunities to women in art: see *Glasgow Girls* (n. 29).

32. *Builder's Journal* (n. 23). See also *Studio* 28 (1903) pp. 286-8.

33. Munro (n. 1) p. 197. With its square towers and big round headed windows it harmonised, though much plainer in effect, with the ornate main building and was possibly by James Miller himself. Mackintosh's entry for the Exhibition buildings competition was predictably unsuccessful, and apart from some privately commissioned stands Mackintosh had little to do with the Exhibition, looking rather to his growing reputation abroad.

34. *Studio* 23 (1901) p. 45: designed by Dykes & Robinson; decorative work by J. B. Bennet & Sons; fittings by Wylie & Lochhead.

35. *Builder's Journal* (n. 23) p. 126, with several illustrations.

36. *Bailie* 4 Nov. 1903, p. 6. The Willow has usually been incorrectly dated to 1904.

37. For a full set of photographs and careful discussion see Billcliffe (n. 16) pp. 128-38 and 262.

38. Thus remembered by Mary Sturrock (n. 14).

39. J. Taylor, 'Modern Decorative Art at Glasgow. Some notes on Miss Cranston's Argyle St Tea House', *Studio* 39 (1906) p. 31 ff.

40. Probably Miss Cranston's idea, and perhaps inspired by long memories of the enormously popular Dutch cocoa house at the 1888 Exhibition. Delft had been a popular constituent of 'Old English' artistic style for some years.

41. Billcliffe (n. 16) p. 201-4; carpet designs p. 212.

42. Colin White, *The Enchanted World of Jessie M. King* (1989) dates the designs to 1903 (a design related to an opulent binding for the High History of the Holy Grail); 1906 (more pastoral, with shepherdess's crook and ribboned bonnet); and 1913 (two girls: fig. 75), designed when Jessie was in Paris. A fourth design (fig. 74) in the stronger, later style, *c.* 1911, was used in conjunction with the second on a menu card.

43. *Studio* 41 (1907) p. 70, noting the opening in June, with illustration.

44. The Ingram St chair is illustrated by Billcliffe (n. 16) p. 203. Other furniture and fittings may have been designed to move to the

new Ingram St rooms after the exhibition. Two oak settles bought by the Mackintosh collector George Smith were allegedly acquired by William Whitelaw, a tea room proprietor, who had four, from 'Cranston's' (meaning Miss Cranston's) before the First World War; decorative motifs relate them to the School of Art (*Glasgow Herald* 20 Aug. 1983). Material was jettisoned from the G.S.A. during building of the second phase *c.* 1909. Temporary exhibition use for the settles makes sense of the clues: the settles would be cheap but distinctive, and not needed later.

45. Perhaps not so startling as the repainted remains at Glasgow Museum and Art Gallery suggest. George Smith recalls the colour as less bright, though allowance must be made for dim light and darkening by smoke.

46. Story told by Mary Sturrock (n. 14): a letter from Vienna, Mackintosh's spiritual home, didn't help.

47. See Billcliffe (n. 16) pp. 235-8, and on p. 271 the plans which turned up in Strathclyde Regional Archive, showing that the extension was made in the basement of the adjacent building to the west: the fireplace of the front saloon was removed to make way for stairs leading down to it.

48. In a 'Note to Visitors' (coll. People's Palace, Glasgow) announcing closure of the Argyle St Tea Rooms (on 18 May 1918), Miss Cranston says 'Since this time last year I have completed commodious extensions both to my Ingram Street and Sauchiehall Street premises ...'; see also *Bailie* 15 May 1918, p. 11. It is not clear what was done at Ingram St.

49. Mary Sturrock (n. 14) remembers Margaret working on them at Walberswick, therefore in 1915 or before. Billcliffe (n. 16) argues Mackintosh's hand in the design on the grounds that it is 'too controlled' for Margaret.

50. Mackintosh to Frau Muthesius, 27 March 1903. Other letters allude to the amount of work involved in the tea rooms. Of Ingram St he wrote on 24 Jan. 1900 that the work would take three to four months; on 12 July he wrote 'I am not nearly done with 'Miss Cranston's yet[:] it has involved a great lot of work', and projected the opening for late September. Kate evidently had to accept slipping schedules in the cause of getting things right.

51. See for instance Mawer & Collingham's

1910 tea room illustrated in M. Moss & A. Turton, *A Legend of Retailing: House of Fraser* (1989) p. 98.

THE SECOND AGE, 1918–1945

1. William Power's somewhat unenthusiastic comment in *The Book of Glasgow* (1922) p. 77 (accusing Glasgow of not realising its metropolitanism: it needed an opera house and repertory theatre); and *Bailie* 1 Feb. 1922, p. 6.

2. George Boswell, President of the Glasgow Institute of Architects, in *The Book of Glasgow* (1931) p. 69. The book was produced for Civic and Empire Week, and strove to project the belief 'that history will repeat itself' and that prosperity would soon return. It was explicitly designed to stir Glasgow pride and combat its poor name, recognising an urgent need to attract new industries.

3. H. V. Morton, *In Search of Scotland* (1929), a penetratingly sympathetic piece: 'Glasgow is a mighty and inspiring human story. She is Scotland's anchor to reality.'

4. J. R. Allan in *Scotland 1938* (1938) p. 70 f.

5. E.g. 'Glasgow is famed throughout the country for her magnificent baker's shops and tea rooms and for the excellence and infinite variety of cakes and other bakery products which they supply', *Evening News* 12 June 1936.

6. Brochure in Strathclyde Regional Archive. The design is attributed to John Ednie by Elizabeth Williamson *et al.*, *The Buildings of Scotland: Glasgow* (1990) p. 231. See Ann Wyllie, *Guthrie & Wells: Interior Decorations 1920- 30* (U. Glasgow Decorative Arts Course thesis 1988). Lang's smoke room was similarly updated by Guthrie & Wells in 1929, with walls of metallic old gold above a broad turquoise stripe over a red dado, and broad lampshades with chevrons of purple, orange, turquoise and blue. The firm also did designs for tea rooms for J. Smith, Wools, next to the Willow on Sauchiehall St, and Lauder's on Renfield St: see n. 24.

7. Kerr began with Joseph Ancell at the Trades House Restaurant, and was then with John Smith at the Athenaeum. Profiled *Bailie* 3 Nov. 1915, pp. 3-4.

8. 'Women Shop Assistants: how they live and work. Evidence given by Miss Margaret H. Irwin to House of Lords Select Committee on

the early closing of shops', 29th April 1901. I thank Eleanor Gordon for this reference.

9. *St Mungo* 19 August 1897, p. 4 reports the conditions of a lady waitress at 'a certain city restaurant': 70-80 hours a week for 8 shillings, supplemented by tips; hours from 8 a.m. to 6 p. m. or 11 p. m. alternately; often kept late on 'early' nights, but docked 3d if a minute late in the morning. The girl lost her job for innocently communicating this information.

10. Alison Downie, 'Kate Cranston, by those who knew her', *Glasgow Herald* 13 June 1981, p. 9.

11. *St Mungo* 5 Aug. 1897, p. 3: the Pink Restaurant is unidentified; the Buchanan St Aesthetic 'Alls must refer to Miss Cranston's, always first choice as a representative tea room.

12. *Glasgow Herald* 27 Aug. 1921, quoting a labourist view.

13. *Evening News* 28 Feb. 1936, p. 9.

14. *Bailie* 13 July 1921, p. 3.

15. See Ann Wyllie (n. 6). Strathclyde Regional Archive holds Guthrie & Wells' designs for the 'New Course' interior.

16. James Craig was featured in *Glasgow Today* (1909). It was not until 1910 that the firm entered the *Post Office Directory* tea room listing with seven branches, headed by the newly acquired premises at 19 Gordon St (the kernel of the later Gordon restaurant), followed by 51-3 Union St, 10, 12, 16 Woodlands Road, 219 New City Road, 19 Grosvenor Place, Byres Rd, 653 Great Western Road, Hillhead, and lastly the original shop at 19 Cowcaddens. The firm became James Craig (Glasgow) Ltd during the First World War and added four new tea rooms, including 123 Sauchiehall St, later rebuilt as the Rhul. Three tea rooms, including 44 St Enoch Square, the address where Stuart Cranston first began, were added around 1934, after James jun.'s death.

17. *Daily Record* 15 Jan. 1932: for this reference I am grateful to Liz Bird, whose research on Glasgow collectors is deposited in the Special Collections of Glasgow University Library. There were 34 pictures in the main smoke room, 21 in the smaller. Some of the best were hung in the Rhul. There were also pictures at St Enoch Sq., Union St and The Cross, Paisley.

18. Hornel fetched the best prices: 'Blossom Time' made £97 10s, 'Spring Time' £80, but 'A Japanese Tea Party' only £22. Park's flower paintings were fetching between £16 and £20. Examples of diminished value included F. P. Martin's 'Summer Morning', bought in 1931 for £60, sold for £41: this painter, evidently once esteemed, has now disappeared from view.

19. Craig's claimed to have been the first in Glasgow to carpet their tea rooms. Decoration was handled by the Glasgow firm of George W. Sellars & Sons.

20. Designed in 1929 by Whyte & Galloway, with diffused lighting a feature of the interior: there was a ground floor shopping hall, and tea room, restaurant and ballroom on three upper floors. Rudolph Kenna, *Glasgow Art Deco* (1985) p. 35. Peacock's was founded in 1857 and built up effectively by Mrs Peacock and her son A. G. Peacock in the 1880s. It grew greatly after the First World War and by 1938 had 24 branches.

21. See M. Moss & A. Turton, *A Legend of Retailing: House of Fraser* (1989).

22. Rossi, di Simoni, Biondi, Coia, Jacutti … The University Café on Byres Rd, with counter stuffed with sweets and cigarettes, Edwardian panelling, deco advertisements, and hot peas on the menu survives as an example. During and after the War Italian names were prominent in the tea room listings.

23. Several are recorded in Rudolph Kenna (n. 20).

24. Another branch at 14 Killermont St opened in 1936: Kenna (n. 20) p. 24. Guthrie & Wells' designs for other such interiors, including the Rialto Tea Rooms at Kirkcaldy, are held in the Strathclyde Regional Archive: see n. 6.

25. From 1928 the Locarno opened its new tea rooms and smoke room to the general public during the dead hours of 10 a.m. to 2 p.m. Around 1930 it also operated a roller skating rink.

26. E.g. in print John McNicol Campbell, 'Table d' Hôte or à La Carte', *Glasgow Illustrated* June 1974.

27. See Neil Baxter, in P. & J. Kinchin, *Glasgow's Great Exhibitions: 1888, 1901, 1911, 1938, 1988* (1988) pp. 127 ff.

28. *SMT Magazine* 1941, pp. 78-9.

THE PASSING, 1945–1975

1. Glasgow's Empire Exhibition of 1938 had been trying to express something similar, and anticipated the Festival of Britain in many respects. See P. & J. Kinchin, *Glasgow's Great Exhibitions: 1888, 1901, 1911, 1938, 1988* (1988) pp. 127-67.

2. *J. Glasgow Chamber of Commerce* Feb. 1954, writing of the Pollok estate.

3. E.g. Bilsland Bros, Montgomerie Bread Co., Beattie's, Macfarlane Lang & Co., Gray Dunn & Co. and Wm. Macdonald (inventors of Penguin biscuits): see Charles Oakley, *Scottish Industry Today* (1938); reprinted as *Glasgow Made It: How Glasgow came through the 1930s depression.*

4. *J. Chamber of Commerce* Aug. 1959: approximately 250 pre-war businesses had been reduced to 30 by amalgamations and takeover.

5. According to Charles Oakley. The Adelphi Hotel was however Lyons-built.

6. *Glasgow University Magazine* Apr. 1957, p. 319: 'The Expresso Bar Type', on Glasgow's coffee bars. At the same time the old night coffee stalls in St Vincent Street and St Vincent Place, open since the mid twenties, serving it was estimated 600,000 snacks a year, were closed down, having become a focal point for undesirables.

7. See p. 45 ff. Ferrari brothers arrived in 1890 to join the Globe at 110 Sauchiehall St, then opened the Adelphi at 10 Sauchiehall St, later renamed Restaurant Ferrari and licensed in 1933 under the next generation. The Malmaison was prominent after the War.

8. In 1949 the new One-O-One in Hope St and the adjacent Ninety-Nine cocktail bar, were opened by the proprietor of the neighbouring Blythswood Bar. Similarly Guy's, famous for its Horseshoe bar from the mid 1920s, opened the Superbe upstairs in 1951 specifically to be able to cater for women.

9. Connected by more than one informant with Jessie King's house, 'Green Gate Close', in the Scottish artist's colony of Kirkcudbright. She sometimes used a green gate as a signature on her pottery.

10. See Thomas Howarth, *Charles Rennie Mackintosh and the Modern Movement* (1952, 2nd edn 1977) preface to 2nd edn p. xxii f.

11. Roger Billcliffe, *Charles Rennie Mackintosh: The complete furniture ...* p. 86. Much of the furniture had gone to the Glasgow School of Art when Cooper's closed the tea rooms in 1950. A small section of the Chinese Room has been recreated at Kelvingrove, and one end of the Cloister Room was reconstituted for the Glasgow Girls exhibition in 1990. There are plans for a fuller recreation.

12. *J. Chamber of Commerce* Apr. 1954, p. 37.

13. Associated Bakeries also owned Alex Currie & Sons and Hannah McMillan & Co. at this time. *J. Chamber of Commerce* Nov. 1958, p. 447.

14. In 1975 downgraded CB Tea Rooms or 'Lite Bites' were operating at 494 Dumbarton Rd, 225 Byres Rd, 147 Trongate and 44 St Enoch Sq. which had been Hubbard's, Colqhoun's, Peacock's and Craig's respectively. Some CB bakery snack-rooms have survived until recent years, but chain identity has swept away any traces of the past.

15. This applied to the late Victorian and Edwardian interiors of which Glasgow had such a wealth. Rogano's stylish thirties decor was spared as 'not unattractive' to the younger generation in 1960.

16. *J. Chamber of Commerce* Apr. 1958.

17. *J. Chamber of Commerce* 1960, p. 298.

18. *J. Chamber of Commerce* 1959, p. 157.

19. One of the most recent was among the first to go, when the Beresford, built originally for the 1938 Exhibition, was acquired by ICI in 1952 for offices. It had been popular with American servicemen during the war and had gained a rather doubtful reputation. It now serves as a student hostel for the University of Strathclyde. In 1957 the Adelphi closed.

EPILOGUE

1. Ian Jack, *Before the Oil Ran Out* (1987) p. 200 ff.

2. See Geoffrey Wimpenny, 'Reconstructing the Willow', *C. R. Mackintosh Soc. Newsletter* 24 (1979/80).

Street Directory of Tea Rooms and Restaurants in Central Glasgow

This directory gives addresses and some dates for the main tea rooms of the city centre, together with many restaurants. It is often difficult to make a distinction, as unlicensed premises popularly known as tea rooms would often call themselves restaurants; and many licensed premises did good tea business. The list is inevitably a little arbitrary, and certainly incomplete: it has been impossible to list, e.g., all branches of Lockhart's or Ross's, all cinemas and all bakers who may have had tea rooms. A fuller version is deposited in the Glasgow Collection of the Mitchell Library.

ARGYLE STREET

11	Smith, The Argyle c. 1888; C. Mackenzie, baker, confect. 1893-1958
26	Lockhart's Cocoa Rooms c. 1886-27
31	Pope's Eye (lic. rest.) famed tavern, mid 19th c. to 1913
34	Wm Logan, Mercantile Dining Rooms (prev. 21-3 Maxwell St) 1875-1919
41	A. Pollok 1886-1925, Jas B. Young 1925-7; D. H. Munn, confect. c. 1930
42	Matthew Waddell, City Commercial (temperance vegetarian rest.) 1880-86
58	H. Farrell, c. 1917-29 (also 17 Hope)
76	Cranston's Tea Rooms Ltd (corner with 2 Queen St) 1875; whole block acquired; shared with R. S. McColl from 1930; closed 1954 (demolished)
86	Peacock's Tea Rooms (rebuilt as 80-90 in 1931) 1926-62
97,99	John Anderson's Royal Polytechnic (est. 1837), expanding to 69-99; bought by Lewis's 1929 (rebuilt, 65-117)
108	(Morrison's Court, = Argyll Arcade) Cranston's Tea Rooms Ltd, smoke room 1896-1948
114	Miss Cranston's Crown Tea Rooms 1878, beneath Aitken's Temperance Hotel; c. 1892 acquired lease of whole building, 108-14, redeveloped it, opening 1897; Manfield & Son 1918-90 (redeveloped 1991)
115	A. T. Assafrey, confect. 1890-1909
117-19	(= 3, 7 Maxwell St) Wm 'Pie' Smith, baker c. 1880; Helen Barton 1903-9
137	St Enoch Picture Theatre
147	Lockhart's Cocoa Rooms, later Lockhart's Café 1896-1935
146	Stewart's Tea Rooms c. 1940, later Stewart's Restaurant
149	The Angus Restaurant 1939
166-8	Wm Skinner's, baker (prev. at 472; also 477 Sauchiehall St) from 1880s, tea room by 1897; city branch moved to 30 St Enoch Sq. 1925
186	Eden Vegetable Restaurant (prev. 6 Jamaica St) 1911-15; Grant Arms 1939-63
191	St Enoch and Logan's Tea Rooms 1912-50
191a	King's Café 1901-51
193	Lockhart's Café 1927-40
197,199	Walter Gibson's (lic. rest.) est. 1834; Matthew Paxton c. 1888; Finlay Stuart Bell, Queen Anne Restaurant, 1906-51 (fire; Bell moved to 247-9 St George's Rd)
206	Great Western Tea Rooms 1898-04

219   A. Sibbald, baker, confect. c. 1881; Victoria Restaurant 1890; Swanson's Tea Rooms, later 217-219, 1911-50s

251   C. Thornton, The Merchants Dining Rooms, (lic. rest.) c. 1875; W. H. Wilson, Clarendon Luncheon Bar 1881-1900s (now Blue Lagoon)

269   Wm Whitelaw Tea Rooms 1905-21

276   Peter Hamilton (prev. 259a) 1899-1906; other proprietors to c. 1925

295   R. Elliott, 1883; Todd 1885; Agnes Edgar 1886; Jeanie Fletcher 1888; Lockhart's Cocoa Rooms 1900-27

336   Alston's Tea Rooms 1916-55; Copra Restaurant 1960s (now Amber Royale)

311-13   Clark's Restaurant (lic.) c. 1932, Bell's Restaurant from 1935

355a   J. H. Johnstone, Tea Coffee & Cocoa Rooms 1888-1900

412   K. McKenzie 1870s; Maggie Campbell 1879; Annie McDougall 1883; Wm McIntyre 1884; T. Fusco, confect. c. 1900

444   Wm McCreadie, baker, confect., tea room 1889; Fred J. Malcolm 1903; bought by Reo Stakis 1947

471   D. McGowan, cocoa rooms (prev. 34 High St, also 488) c. 1917

ARGYLL ARCADE (between 108 Argyle St and 26 Buchanan St)

42-3   Cranston's Tea Rooms Ltd 1892-54

62   Restaurant (lic.) est. c. 1825, David Sloan prop. from 1900 (still Sloan's)

BATH STREET

21   Linda's Tea Rooms c. 1940; Betty's Tea Rooms c. 1947

38   Howie's Tea Rooms 1913-18; Miss Pink's Tea Parlour 1989; The Glasgow Tea Room 1991 (closed)

183   Burlington House, Wm & R. S. Kerr 1915; A. F. Reid & Sons 1931-1950s

BOTHWELL STREET

17   A. Stout (prop. of The Garden Vegetarian Restaurant 14 Adelphi St from 1887) & A. Moffat, Tea Rooms; Cabin Tea Rooms Ltd, Mecca 1897-1903

18   The Hubb, Misses Marshall & Cairns, c. 1940; Wendy's Tea Rooms 1954-69; Stakis' Poseidon (fish rest.) 1970s

70   Matthew Waddell from 1882 (Christian Institute Building, demolished)

BUCHANAN STREET

8, 10   Arthur & Fraser (est. 1849), Fraser Sons & Co. from 1875, department store

20   Wyllie Hill & Co., store

21-31   Stewart & Mcdonald Ltd (est. 1826), later Mcdonald's; then House of Fraser 9-61

26-28   Cranston's Tea Rooms Ltd 1889; rebuilt 1903; closed 1954

36   Ferguson & Forrester (popularly 'F. & F.s') lic. rest. 1863-1931 (now Prince's Square)

37-45   Wylie & Lochhead (est. 1829); absorbed by House of Fraser 1957

68, 74   Rowan's, gents outfitters (est. 1840) 1921-57-

70, 74   The Queen's Restaurant 1876-1902

71   Alex. Manson, confect. c. 1886; A. Ferguson confect. c. 1905; G. M. Frame c. 1935

87   Great Western Dining Rooms c. 1864 (one of 19 branches in this year)

91   Alexandra Café 1878-93; rebuilt for Miss Cranston's Tea and Luncheon Rooms 1897-1918 (now Clydesdale Bank)

99	Fuller's Tea Rooms 1914-75 (now Thornton's confectioners)
106-8	Duncan's Restaurant 1870s; Thornton's Restaurant 1880-87
123	Kardomah Tea Rooms and Restaurant, 1960s, 70s
175-9	Athenaeum Restaurant; under John Smith from c. 1910-55
185	Cranston's Waverley Temperance Hotel 1860-85 (sold, became Old Waverley; the Ivanhoe c. 1920 to 1977; then Friar Tuck licensed rest.; now the Buchanan
197	Easy Eats (also at 226) 1951-75; then Scot Bar
222	Temperance Hotel c. 1886-1920s; Ferrari Corner House, from 1939; Buchanan Restaurant c. 1960-70
249	Sefton Tea Rooms c. 1917
266	Super Eats c. 1955
286	A. F. Reid & Sons 1939-75

CANDLERIGGS

35	Wm Black, pastry baker, rest. c. 1860; John Stewart, c. 1931; Mrs McGrady 1940-55
59	Lockhart's Cocoa Rooms, then Tea Rooms, then Café c. 1908-32-
64	Clydesdale Restaurant 1888; Wm Mackenzie (prev. 155 Queen St) 1893-1912
90-98	City Hall
93	City Hall Rest. & Dining Rooms c.1865; Fruit Exchange Tea Rooms 1926-63-
97	Rathie's Tea and Luncheon Rooms c. 1898; Hydro Tea Rooms 1902; Wm Kerr 1912-19 (now The City Merchant)
99	Miss Gibb, tea rooms 1915-19
113-15	Thos Gemmell's, baker, confect. from c. 1860, rest. listed 1879-94 (then at 127)
127	Ramshorn Restaurant from 1877; Gemmell's 1894; W. L. Edgar 1911; Miss Reoch 1929; refurbished 1936, then listed as 93 Ingram St to 1960s

COWCADDENS

| 19 | James Craig (the original shop, opp. Buchanan St Stn) 1870-1947 |
| 102 | Clarkson Tea Rooms c. 1900-53 |

DUNDAS STREET

1b	Rosebery Tea Rooms c. 1903; J. Gibb c. 1908
15	John Marletta c. 1955; Moka Coffee Bar & Restaurant c. 1965-77-
19, 23	Jas Ancell, rest., confect. c. 1882 (J. & G. Ancell at 27 c. 1863)
33, 35	F. Smith 1890; Alston & Lamb Tea Rooms 1898, Jas Lamb 1903-8
56	Celeste Zaccharini c. 1952
58	F. Fersichini, Tea Rooms c. 1940
83 & 97	K. Cameron, dining rooms 1880; K.McKenzie c. 1886; J. Bannerman from 1892; J. Thomson 1920s
92	Miss Davidson c. 1900
101,3	Café (later Restaurant) d'Oré (Cocozza) c. 1930-65-
141	Clark's Dairy & Tea Rooms c. 1935, refurbished 1938

DUNLOP STREET

| 7 | Queen's Restaurant (lic., est. 1863)1886 Richd Prosser; R. Graham c. 1903; Trocadero Restaurant, R. Ford c. 1920 (Greek Thomson building, demolished) |
| 23 | Royal Dining Rooms next to Royal Music Hall, c. 1880 |

EXCHANGE PLACE

11 Rogano (orig. prop. John & D. C. Grant) 1935- present

GALLOWGATE

46 Mrs Niven c. 1900; Great Western Dining Rooms c. 1908; Hugh Stewart Tea Rooms 1913-16
96 Mrs Lloyd c. 1903; R. & A. McLellan c. 1907; R. Morrison c. 1916-27
99 Glasgow National Restaurant 1939-63
149 Jas Crocket c. 1916; Wm Caulfield c. 1921; J. Holmes c. 1931; L. McCallum 1934
465-7 Wm Orr c. 1894-1920
594a Miss A. Walker 1886, D. Walker 1890; Wm Nimmo 1893; R. Stirling 1902-8

GEORGE STREET

24 Miss Annie MacGregor c. 1940
145-7 Jas Campbell Tea Rooms c. 1900
260 Alex. Maitland's Tea Rooms c. 1891

GLASSFORD STREET

20 Steele & Thomson, rest. c. 1880; Jas Campbell Luncheon & Tea Rooms 1908-35-
39 Steele & Thomson c. 1886; Hamilton & Russell 1895; Thomson & Blain 1900 (then at 60)
41 Cabin Tea Rooms 1905-6
60 Hamilton & Russell (lic.) c. 1890; Thomson & Blain 1903-34; then Capaldi
79 Miss Barbara Fergus, Tea Rooms 1889-1929
86 John McDonald c. 1865, Miss Jessie McDonald 1870; Miss Agnes Steel 1892-1902
87,89 (= 88 Virginia Place) Trades House Restaurant, Jas then Jos. Ancell c. 1870-95; Thos White & Smith 1895-08, then John Smith (later Smith's (Glasgow) Ltd) 1909-24; R. Paterson c. 1929; Stakis, Sans Souci c. 1960; The Rooster c. 1975

GORDON STREET

7 John Forrester, pastry cook, confect. from c. 1835, lic. rest. enlarged by John jun. c. 1863; Thos White & Smith 1895-1909, then White's 1909; absorbed by James Craig's 1930; Fuller's 1951-74; then Quality Inn (now Pizzaland)
14 City Café (temperance) 1888; Cabin Tea Rooms 1898; Savoy Tea Rooms 1902
19 James Craig 1910, rebuilt as The Gordon, 7-19, 1932, closed 1955 (then Thomas Cook)
30, 34 A. F. Reid & Sons, Tea & Coffee Rooms 1912-60s
33a Rosalind's Tea Rooms 1933-59
40 Seaton, Turner & Co. c. 1895; Cabin Tea Rooms Ltd, The Anchor 1897-1904
52 Lockhart's Café c. 1927; Ross's Dairies from 1931
62 M. Wylie 1870s; McCall & Ferguson, then D. McCall, Victoria Restaurant (lic.) 1880-96 (became Forsyth's, Mrs McCall moved to Ca'doro building 130-2 Union St)
71-91 Central Station Hotel, built 1879-83, inc. lunch rooms for city gents; Malmaison Restaurant prominent from 1940s
74 The Grosvenor Restaurant, J. & W. McKillop 1898; John Smith 1924, adding bakery and Tea Rooms adjacent at 80; Grosvenor Caterers Ltd c. 1945-68 (tea rooms removed 1959; fire 1968; rebuilding 1991)

76   Wm Whitelaw, pastry baker 1886-98 (then 105 Hope St)

78   Lockhart's Cocoa Rooms c. 1905-1920

84   Corn Exchange Restaurant, -1874; Thos White & Smith 1903-9, then Smith (Glasgow) Ltd from 1909; bought by Grosvenor Caterers, closed 1957; Scottish Milk Centre, coffee lounge 1960s; Dairy Fare c. 1975 (now revived as Corn Exchange, bar with diner)

HIGH STREET

3, 5   Jessie McHardie 1900-14 (then at 28)

27   Lockhart's Cocoa Rooms c. 1900

25   Finlay McHardie 1927; Wm Wylie 1947-60s; then The Colonial (now Colonial India)

28   L. Thurgo 1901; Jessie McHardie 1914-25; Wm Wylie 1950s,60s

34   D. McGowan, Cocoa Rooms 1899-1913; Lockhart's Tea Rooms 1915-20

177   Crossmyloof Bakery c. 1886; A. Cordner 1901, then Mrs 1936-42 (Jas Adam building, demolished)

176   Alston's Tea Rooms 1926-35-

185   Alston's Tea Rooms 1916-29

185½   Miss Marshall c. 1901; Mrs M. Hamilton 1907

200   Alston's Tea Rooms 1925-65

257   Jas Rollo 1902; A. & C. Kirkwood 1935-43; Marina Restaurant 1970s

HOPE STREET

17   H. Farrell (prev. 7 Trongate, also 58 Argyle) c. 1928-33

75-9   (= 5 Waterloo St) Miss Rombach's Tea Rooms 1910-62 ('Miss Rombach Restaurant' from 1945) (demolished with Corn Exchange)

91   Cabin Tea Rooms, The Orient, c. 1895-1908 (opp. Central Stn)

97   Walter Wright's (lic. rest.) c. 1884-1905; then Blythswood Bar, to present

101   One-O-One 1949-75- (now Godfathers Italian restaurant)

105   Wm Whitelaw Tea Rooms 1899-1908

111   The Glasgow Dairy Co. Tea Rooms c. 1945-60s; Ad Lib Restaurant 1970s

176   John Armour 1897; Miss Rombach's Tea Rooms 1911-21 (also at 75-9)

183   Wm Blackadder 1884; P. Rupprecht 1889; Wm Todd 1897; The Lansdowne, Vallance, 1900-20s; Kelburne 1929; Barrett's 1932; The Strand (lic.) 1938-77-

186   Dene's Tea Rooms 1888; 184-6 Daniel Walker 1893-1909

188-96   Guy's Restaurant 1925, adding the Superbe 1951-70s

261-3   Stakis' Acropole c. 1947

HOWARD STREET

17   The Bungalow Tea Rooms 1888; Dene's 1889; Wm Whitelaw Tea Rooms 1890

29   Cabin Tea Rooms 1890-1906

30,32   Cooper & Co.'s Tea Room 1903, later Cooper's Café (Cooper & Co. at 12 Howard St from 1872, later expanded; demolished 1966, now Gateway)

40   The Lorne Restaurant 1879, The Lorne (Bar) 1970s

46   St Enoch Café, G. Lemmi 1930s

HUTCHESON STREET

19   Miss Gillies Tea Rooms 1892; Walker 1893

42   Thos McLaren Tea Rooms 1900

INGRAM STREET

59 Miss E. Hudson & Jane Reid, rest., pastry cooks c. 1870

65 J. Shankland, rest. 1883; D. McDonald c. 1920; Miss Isa Barr Tea Rooms 1929

93 Ramshorn Restaurant 1936-65 (prev. listed at 127 Candleriggs)

155 Jas Steel, Temperance Restaurant before 1882 (moved to Athenaeum)

201 Alston & Lamb Tea Rooms 1892, Alston's 1902-65 (also High St, Argyle St)

205 Miss Cranston's Tea Rooms 1886; Lunch Rooms added at 209 in 1888; expanded to 217 in 1900; 104 Miller St added 1907; run by Miss Drummond 1919-1930; taken over by Cooper's 1930-50; bought by Corporation and let as souvenir shop; stripped 1971; rebuilt as Stakis' The Ingram Hotel

233 R. Calderwood, confect., rest. 1883-95

245 Burn's Tea Rooms 1888-1903

JAMAICA STREET

6 Caledonian Restaurant, Jas Arbuckle (prev. 292 Buchanan) 1880; Eden Vegetable Restaurant, L. McCaughey 1895-1911 (then 186 Argyle)

20 Grand Central Tea Rooms, Wm & R. S.Kerr 1915-32; Grand Central Restaurant and Picture House to 1960s; Stakis, Voll Cafeteria c. 1963; Jamaica Inn c. 1975

21a Mikado Tea Rooms, Wm Lee 1893-1910

58 Wm Lee, Tea Rooms c. 1895; Wm Whitelaw 1896, Mrs J. Whitelaw c. 1923

60-70 The Colosseum, department store

69 Lockhart's Cocoa Rooms, later Café c. 1895-1947

71 McHardy 1893; Wm Lee 1895; J. Johnston 1898; Agnew 1903; D. Gillio c. 1920

72-96 Paisley's Store

77 Lord's, confect., rest. to 1908, then G. Capaldi; Betti & Co. 1921, Café de Paris 1932

MAXWELL STREET

3, 7 'Pie' Smith's, see 117-19 Argyle St

6 G. Wraight c. 1896; Mrs Jessie Mackenzie c. 1900; Mrs Lawson 1903-12

21-23 Wm Logan, Mercantile Dining Rooms (temperance) 1856-75 (then 34 Argyle St)

MITCHELL ST

41 Clarkson's Tea Rooms c. 1926-50

92 D. Munro c. 1885; Margaret Grant 1888; G. Ralston 1898; The Garden House, Marshall 1931; later L'Ariosto c. 1970 to present

QUEEN STREET

2 Cranston's Tea Rooms Ltd (the first tea room, corner with 76 Argyle St) 1875; later extended to 2-10; closed 1954

8, 10 Times Restaurant, John Campbell 1877; Royal Restaurant, Stewart's 1881; Hinshaw 1914-21; absorbed by Cranston's

12-16 Craig's Lunch and Tea Rooms, 1904-22

39, 41 A. Stark, Smoking Rooms, lic. rest. c. 1870; Bank Restaurant 1889 under a series of proprietors: Brunfaut, McLean, John Smith, Hamilton, Maley, Myron

43 Mecca Coffee Room c. 1950

46 Cranston's Tea Rooms Ltd c. 1886-1918

60	Daniel Brown, confect., rest. from 1846 (also at 79 St Vincent St); Miss M. Sillars 1906; Hugh McCallum, Tea Rooms 1912; Crown Restaurant, Jas McCallum 1925; D. Church to 1946-55
73	Lang's luncheon bar c. 1845; extended to 79 with coffee and smoke rooms; closed early 1970s
90, 98	Scott's Restaurant ('est. 1796', lic.), under Wm Whitelaw c. 1897, A. McKenzie c. 1905-7
138	W. Davie, rest. c. 1870; Miss M. Sillars c. 1912; The Ingram (lic. rest.), John Caldwell to 1925, Wm & R. S. Kerr 1926-32; D. S. Smith c. 1940; D. McClean 1947-60
140	Wm Miller, pastry baker c. 1875, Mrs Miller, temperance rest. 1886-1904
155	R. Bannerman to 1889; Wm McKenzie 1889-92; G. M. Frame, Coffee Rooms to c. 1960

RENFIELD STREET

12	Geo. Young's Coffee Bars c. 1960 (now China Sea Rest.)
13	Cranston's Tea Rooms Ltd 1897; rebuilt as 13-17 in 1916, inc. 13 Cranston's Confections (later R. S. McColl); 15 Cranston's de Luxe Picture House (the Classic from c. 1950); 17 Cranston's Tea Rooms to 1951; then R. S. McColl, The Classic Cafeteria, 1952-75; Trust House Forte Classic Cafeteria c. 1977 (redeveloped 1991)
19	Wm Clark 1878; John Smith, Smith (Glasgow) Ltd c. 1915
19a	Miss Buick's Tea Rooms, later Restaurant (1st floor) 1925-59; The Excelsior Chinese Restaurant from 1960; then the Diamond (fire; redeveloped 1991)
20	Kirkland's Tea Rooms 1888
21	Lockhart's Tea Rooms c. 1908-15
43	Mecca Coffee Room 1955-65
61	John MacLachlan's Palace Restaurant 1897; Whitehall Restaurant, D. Clark 1931-84 (inc. 51 W. Regent St); now The Maltman Bar Bistro
62	M. McCarthy c. 1878; P. Mullan 1890; United Coop Tea Rooms c. 1893-4
72	Regent Cinema
83	Renfield Café 1936-50; then Mecca Coffee Room
85	Ross's Dairies to c. 1965
94	Thos Jenkins, Great Western Dining Rooms (one of many branches) c. 1900; Eldon Café c. 1929-36; Quality Inn c. 1975
98	Jas Boyd c. 1870-6, Mrs Boyd c. 1885 (lic. rest.)
99	Ceylon Tea Rooms, Seaton Turner & Co. 1901, later Ceylon Café Ltd; Fred Malcolm Tea Rooms (Stakis) 1947, then Stakis, Prince's Restaurant 1949 (fire; rebuilt; demolished; now British Home Stores)
121	Miss Carswell Tea Rooms c. 1892; Mrs Kidd 1893-8
128	Green's Playhouse Cinema

ST ENOCH SQUARE

4	St Enoch Refreshment Rooms c. 1880; Jas Gillespie c. 1888
10	His Lordship's Larder (long-established lic. rest.); from 1920s listed at 2-4 St Enoch Place
20	St Enoch Luncheon & Tea Rooms c. 1903
30	Wm Skinner, baker, tea rooms 1925-77
38	R. S. McColl, Melody Restaurant c. 1960
44	Stuart Cranston's first premises as a tea retailer, 1871-5; rebuilt 1876; later James Craig's 1934-60; Peacock's Tea Rooms to 1968; then CB Light Bite and Coffee House

ST VINCENT STREET

9	St Vincent Place, St Vincent Tea Rooms, Mrs J. Wright 1889; O. A. Walker 1904-14
14a	St Vincent Place, City Café c. 1933
63	Flint's Tea Rooms 1895-9; Exchange Tea Rooms from 1900
75	Lacey's Tea Rooms c. 1907-25
78	A. T. Assafrey Luncheon and Tea Rooms 1887
79, 83	Daniel Brown (est. 1846; also 60 Queen St) c. 1875-1977 (now Caskie's Wine Bar)
105½	Cabin Tea Rooms 1890; Hydro Tea Rooms 1906; Carlton Tea Rooms, Wm & R. S. Kerr 1906-11; removed to 111
111	Carlton Restaurant, Wm & R. S. Kerr 1912-30; Cooper's, The St Vincent, 1931-41; Stakis, Ivy Restaurant 1951-65, then Alfa Restaurant 1970s
122	Rathie's Luncheon & Tea Rooms 1893; Hydro Tea Rooms 1902; Cameron's Tea Rooms, later Restaurant 1906-17
132	The Arcadian Gallery, renamed the Arcadian Food Reform Café 1907-12
142	James Craig c. 1929-60
142a	Miss Schofield, An Old Oak Tea Room, 1902-17
175	Cabin Tea Rooms 1897-1900-
272	Gainsborough Halls, Wm Kerr & Son from 1932
292	Miss Cranston's Bakery; John Smith c. 1939

SALTMARKET

20	Victoria Lunch and Tea Rooms, Wm Fullerton 1903, H. Farrell 1920
91	Jeanie Lindsay tea rooms c. 1931-52

SAUCHIEHALL STREET

10	F. F. Ferrari, Adelphi Restaurant from 1901, then Pavilion; Restaurant Ferrari 1919-75
37	D. G. Bain, then Mrs Bain 1883; Miss Paterson 1891; John Mackay 1893; Pianta & Zanetti 1894 (then at 47)
40	Empire Café 1929-51
42	The Gaiety Restaurant, A. Cross then Mrs Cross 1877; Miss Loudon 1884-95; Peacock's Tea Rooms c. 1970
47	Criterion Café Restaurant, Annovazzi 1898; Tempini c. 1921
51	Margaret Kington c. 1886
60	J. C. Galloway c. 1888; Zanetti 1895-1916
62	R. S. McColl, Lyric Restaurant c. 1963
76-8	Lauder's Bar c. 1870 to present
83-97	Alexander Henderson (store) from 1889, tea room from 1939
92	Mac's Restaurant c. 1897; Thos Berry Restaurant c. 1900; Picture Salon, with tea room c. 1914-26; Picadilly Club 1927-65; Lucky Star Restaurant (lic. Chinese) 1970s; now Victoria's night club complex
96	Lockhart's Cocoa Rooms c. 1894-1927
100	Continental Snack Rooms c. 1904; then Ferrari; The Orchid, John Marshall 1933-47
108,10	The Globe, Godenzi, then F. Ferrari, then Ferrari Bros 1890-1925-
123	James Craig 1918, rebuilt as The Rhul 1927, closed 1957 (now gutted).
128-52	Savoy Cinema
140	Picture House

145	Wellesley Tea and Luncheon Rooms 1905; Cranston's Tea Rooms Ltd 1907-27
155	La Scala Cinema 1912
165,7	Copland & Lye, Caledonia House (est. 1873) 1878-1971 (demolished)
171	A. T. Assafrey 1871-1907, absorbed by Pettigrew & Stephens
191	Pettigrew & Stephens from 1888; Manchester House 171-93 opened 1901; further expansion absorbed Fine Art Institute Building; demolished 1973
172	Washington Temperance Hotel, Mary Cranston Mason, 1872; renamed Waverley Temperance Hotel 1885-1934; then Marks & Spencer (rebuilt)
184	Madame Bain, Tea Rooms 1901-2
198	Iona Tea Rooms c. 1896
199	Daly & Co. 1897, expanded to absorb the Willow Tea Rooms 1927 (sold 1978, redeveloped)
200	Thos Muirhead's (est. 1834) taken over by House of Fraser 1936
206	Ferrari Bros Swiss Café c. 1900
213	A. T. Assafrey c. 1875
217	Miss Cranston's Willow Tea Rooms 1903; became The Kensington, Smith (Glasgow) Ltd 1918-27; then absorbed by Daly's; restored from 1978, Room de Luxe reopened as a tea room 1983
236	Central Café, Arcari c. 1940-70s
243	Wendy's Tea Rooms, Misses H. Lyle & E. J. Clink (also at 104 W. George St) 1931-64; Stakis, Blenheim steak house and cafeteria 1970s (now offices)
245	Bradford's, baker, confect. and coffee shop, opened 1989
252	Arch. Hoy 1883; R. Calderwood, pastry baker, rest. 1896; Jas Wright 1905; Wm Ward 1907
254-90	Tréron & Cie, later Tréron's, department store, including Corporation Art Galleries; tea rooms listed from 1904 to late 1970s (fire, refurbished as shops and restored McClellan Gallery)
255	J. & A. Carrs, confect. and cooks, est. by 1870; tea room listed 1904-27
274	Meng & Boullet, tea rooms c. 1894
277-9	M. & A. Brown 1879-1920s, then Lacey Ltd confect. c. 1932
283-5	M. & A. Brown's Tea Rooms 1926-89; Pars Delta Restaurant and Tea Rooms 1989-91 (closed, under redevelopment as licensed rest. 1991)
294	Jules Boullet & Bros Tea Rooms 1911-14; 292-4 Ross's Dairies 1933-62 (demolished, now Cannon cinema)
297	A. Ferguson's, confect., tea rooms 1905
303	Jean's Tea Rooms 1933-70 (upstairs; now Far East Chinese restaurant)
304-6	Wimpy c. 1962-present
326	Panorama, with ladies' café 1888-97; then used as ice-skating rink; Hengler's Circus c. 1908-22, then Waldorf Dance Hall, then Regal Cinema (now Cannon)
345	Wm Brownlie, pastry baker, lic. rest. 1860s; Jane Murdoch, University Restaurant 1877; John Black 1898
350	(Greek Thomson Grecian Buildings) Kunzle Bros, Prince of Wales Halls 1904-47; then Masco Ltd, confect. (now Third Eye Centre)
385	The Green Twig, Mrs Muriel Morrison 1933-53; then Café Continental 1960s
411	Plato's Rest 1943; Restaurant Rendezvous 1949
421	Tajmahal Indian & Chinese Restaurant 1940
451,3	James Craig 1917-62; Peacock's Tea Rooms 1963-67; The Elgin Lounge 1970s
477	Wm Skinner & Son (est. 1835; prev. at 307-9) from 1875, tea rooms 1894 or before, closed c. 1961 (demolished)

490 Charing Cross Halls, John McKay 1897-1920; Gainsborough Rest, Kerr (Caterers) Ltd 1933; then New Astoria Ballroom to c. 1962
506 New Locarno Dance Hall (later Tiffany's, then Zanzibar, now casino)
509 Marlex Tea Rooms c. 1940
516 Locarno Club (became amusement arcade)
560 Grand Hotel 1878-1968 (demolished 1969)
     Charing Cross Mansions, Jules Boullet Tea Rooms 1894-1914

TRONGATE

7 H. Farrell, Tea Rooms 1921-6 (then 17 Hope St)
24 Tontine Refreshment & Recreation Rooms 1908-11
77 Tron Tea Rooms 1907-13
121 Lockhart's Cocoa Rooms c. 1895-1909
122 Swanson's Tea Rooms 1902-20
147 Peacock's Tea Rooms c. 1931, rebuilt 1936-68; CB Light Bite from 1970s
151 Glasgow A.B.C. Tea Rooms 1907, Tron Café 1909; Lockhart's Tea Rooms, then Café c. 1915-32

UNION STREET

6 Geo. Doogan Argyle Temperance Hotel & Restaurant 1893-1921
27 Trees Tea Rooms, Miss Gibson 1933; then Mrs Miller; Angelo Lamarra 1963 to present
28 R. A. Peacock (est. 1857) from c. 1908, 28-40 rebuilt as Peacock's Georgic, 1931-55 (now Virgin Superstore)
43 James Brown, Temperance Restaurant c. 1891
51-53 James Craig's Tea Rooms 1909-55 (became Hepworth's, now Next)
54, 60 City Commercial Restaurant, long-running temperance business, Matthew Waddell c. 1870-1913; then City Picture House
101 McDougall, confect., rest. c. 1865; John Craig 1870; Jas McIntosh 1889; Union Café (lic.), Wm Hunter 1892
130-32 Victoria Restaurant, Mrs McCall 1897-1908; whole building, 122-132, redeveloped by City Bakeries as the Ca'doro Tea Rooms, opened 1921; run by Scottish Coop Wholesale Soc. from c. 1945, closed 1958; sublet in 1960s, housing Stakis restaurants El Guero, Brasserie, Tropicana (burnt 1987, gutted refurbished, now Waterstone's Booksellers and offices)

VIRGINIA STREET

17 William Logan, temperance dining rooms c. 1884
88, 94 = 87-9 Glassford St, Trades House Restaurant
117 Mrs Jane Gray c. 1867; Mrs Semple (lic.) 1870; The Victoria, Otto Bergner 1888; Thos Cuddeford 1891; Alex. Hinshaw 1905; D. Gillespie 1920; J. McDougall 1923; Griffins (Glasgow) Ltd 1926

WELLINGTON STREET

150 Mrs Hay, Tea Rooms 1940; Mrs J. Robertson 1948

WEST CAMPBELL STREET

137 Wm T. Russell (prev. 189 W. George St) 1888; Mrs Schiller Tea Rooms 1896-1916

WEST GEORGE STREET

6	C. Valente, Tea Rooms 1935; Humbert Kunz 1941; Greenham c. 1960
30, 32	Alston & Lamb, Tea and Coffee Rooms 1892, then Jas Lamb Tea Rooms; D. Campbell 1916; W. A. Parkhouse 1916; Miss Peden 1925; J. Baird Tea Rooms 1931
83-9	Lang's Luncheon Rooms (prev. 111-13) 1923-70 (now Pizza Hut)
91-5	Watson & Blane rest. 1875-1908
97	Unique, Manuel & Webster tea rooms 1920s
104	Wendy's Tea Rooms (1st floor; also at 243 Sauchiehall St) 1933-72 (demolished)
106	Nisbett & Co. Tea Rooms 1898; Flint's Tea Rooms 1900; The Kettledrum, Miss Pauline Barker 1906; Linby 1910-15
111-13	Lang's Luncheon Rooms 1897 (then at 83-9)
121	Miss Agnes Clark to 1900; G. Todd 1900-22
147	Miss Buick's Tea Rooms, later Miss Buick's Restaurants (1960) Ltd (also at 19a Renfield St) 1912-69
159	Bank Café & Tea Rooms, Braid & Co. 1892; J. McWilliam 1894; Rathie's 1897, Hydro Tea Rooms 1902-6
189	Wm T. Russell 1882 (then 137 W. Campbell St) ; Mrs Spence 1885; A. Ancell 1888; John Armour c. 1897

WEST NILE STREET

10, 14	(later 10-22) Royal Restaurant, proprietors inc. Chas Wilson c. 1865; George Mackenzie 1882; G. Brunfaut c. 1894; J. & W. McKillop 1897-02; J. Grant 1935-74 (demolished 1975)
24	The Mercantile Tea Rooms, Thos Robertson 1905-14
41	The Gresham (lic.), John Hunter c. 1898; The Grill, Robert Weir 1907; City Café 1912-27
92	Isabella McCall c. 1875
102-4	Union Tea Rooms, United Coop. Baking Soc. 1899-1915
113	Miss C. Zaccharini, tea rooms c. 1947
115	J. C. Galloway, rest. c. 1875-95
116-18	R. McDonald to 1901; Wm Young 1901; Misses McDowall & Findlay 1903
136	Monico Restaurant, Negrini, then Tempini, then Selebam, c. 1935
174-6	A. & F. Sautermeister, Vienna & foreign bakers & confect. 1896; Ferrari's Globe 1901-60

WEST REGENT STREET

51	Regent Tea Rooms 1902; The New Regent, Wm & R. S. Kerr 1912; from 1937 part of Whitehall Restaurant (= 61 Renfield)
88	The Oak Tea Rooms c. 1947
98	Miss Buick's Tea Rooms 1910-12 (then 147 W. George St)

Appendix of major tea rooms away from city centre

BANK STREET

52, 54	Greengates Tea Rooms, Miss N. Mackenzie, 1941; later an Indian Restaurant

BYRES ROAD

172 (Betty) Barclay's Restaurant, closed c. 1969
205 (Betty) Barclay's Tea & Coffee Rooms, closed c. 1969
225 Alex Colquhoun (est. 1860) baker, rest. from 1900s; CB Talisman 1970s; now Wimpy
267 James Craig 1936 (prev. at 19 Grosvenor Place, Byres Rd from 1906)

DUMBARTON ROAD

410 John McNeil, rest. c. 1908; James Craig 1915-34
494 Walter Hubbard's (est. 1848) c. 1908, rebuilt 1936; later CB Tea Rooms
572 Ross's Dairies Ltd HQ c. 1931

GREAT WESTERN ROAD

508 Walter Hubbard's (est. 1848) 1931, latterly owned by City Bakeries, closed 1970 (became Cleopatra's disco, now l'Academie)
653 Jas Craig 1907-13 then at 713, 1913-63

PAISLEY ROAD

263 Wheatsheaf Tea Rooms, later Restaurant, 1898-1960s
459 Ed. Lipsett, Coffee Rooms, later Tea Rooms 1898-1915
464 Pavilion Restaurant 1885-1920
1851 James Craig 1934, later CB

VICTORIA ROAD

441-3 David Turner, Tea Rooms & Restaurant, c. 1894; Queen's Park Rooms, Wm & R. S. Kerr 1912; A. F. Reid & Sons 1930 (now La Bussola)

Index